Statements on Management Accounting

The National Association
of Accountants
Montvale,
New Jersey 07645

PRENTICE HALL
Englewood Cliffs, New Jersey 07632

Prentice-Hall International (UK) Limited, *London*
Prentice-Hall of Australia Pty. Limited, *Sydney*
Prentice-Hall Canada, Inc., *Toronto*
Prentice-Hall Hispanoamericana, S.A., *Mexico*
Prentice-Hall of India Private Limited, *New Delhi*
Prentice-Hall of Japan, Inc., *Tokyo*
Simon & Schuster Asia Pte. Ltd., *Singapore*
Editora Prentice-Hall do Brasil, Ltda., *Rio de Janeiro*

10 9 8 7 6 5 4 3 2

ISBN 0-13-611567-5

PRENTICE HALL
BUSINESS & PROFESSIONAL DIVISION
A division of Simon & Schuster
Englewood Cliffs, New Jersey 07632

Printed in the United States of America

CONTENTS

PREFACE

The National Association of Accountants is pleased to make available this set of Statements on Management Accounting. This volume is a compilation of the 18 SMAs issued to date by the NAA. As discussed in the Statement of Purpose and Operation, SMAs are issued by the NAA when approved by its senior technical committee, the Management Accounting Practices Committee. The MAP Committee considers for SMA status draft documents developed under the guidance of its Subcommittee on SMA Promulgation.

When they are approved for publication by the MAP Committee, SMAs reflect official positions of the NAA regarding issues perceived as being of pervasive interest to the management accounting profession. They are "official" positions because, according to its charter, the MAP Committee is designated as the mechanism by which the NAA expresses its opinions on matters affecting the quality of managerial accounting and financial reporting. The NAA recognizes that unlike financial reporting *standards*, which require certain accounting or disclosure practices, SMAs are more appropriately characterized as authoritative *guidelines*. Both the MAP Committee and its Promulgation Subcommittee comprise recognized leaders in industry, public accounting, and academe. The talents of these people combined with the rigor of the developmental and exposure processes ensure widespread support for and application of these guidelines.

Development of SMAs is a continuing process, and as new ones are completed, they will be made available individually. Consideration will be given to publishing another bound volume at some time in the future after publication of additional SMAs.

The NAA appreciates the opportunity to collaborate with Prentice-Hall in the publication of this volume. We believe it represents a major contribution to authoritative accounting literature, and will be useful to practitioners, academicians, and students.

Louis Bisgay
Director, Management Accounting Practices
National Association of Accountants

Statements on Management Accounting

Statement of Purpose and Operation

In accordance with the charge to the Management Accounting Practices (MAP) Committee to issue statements on management accounting principles and practices, Statements on Management Accounting are promulgated to reflect official positions of the National Association of Accountants (NAA). The work of the MAP Committee is based on a framework for management accounting, whose principal categories are:

1. Objectives
2. Terminology
3. Concepts
4. Practices and Techniques
5. Management of Accounting Activities

Statements on Management Accounting

Statement of Purpose and Operation

National Association of Accountants

Preface

Statements on Management Accounting: Statement of Purpose and Operation was approved for publication by the Management Accounting Practices Committee of the National Association of Accountants (NAA) at its meeting on March 25, 1986. The Statement is issued with the expectation that it will clarify the purpose of Statements on Management Accounting (SMAs), their scope, and the process by which they are developed. The NAA publishes SMAs to enhance the professionalism of management accountants and the education of students of accounting.

Louis Bisgay
Director
Management Accounting Practices

Background

1. Since its founding (as the National Association of Cost Accountants) in 1919, the National Association of Accountants (NAA) has been a pioneer in the evolution of cost accounting and the broader scope of management accounting. The NAA has provided diverse educational offerings and has sponsored an extensive research program resulting in publications that supply information for the management accounting profession.

2. In 1969, the NAA created the Management Accounting Practices (MAP) Committee, its senior technical committee, which was given two charges:

   - To express the official position of the NAA on accounting and financial reporting issues raised by standard-setting groups such as the Financial Accounting Standards Board, the Governmental Accounting Standards Board, the Securities & Exchange Commission, and the International Accounting Standards Committee.
   - To provide authoritative guidance to the membership of the NAA and to the broader business community on management accounting concepts, policies, and practices.

3. Statements on Management Accounting (SMAs) are the outgrowth of the MAP Committee's objective of furnishing guidance on management accounting issues.

Statements on Management Accounting

4. The NAA has defined management accounting as "the process of identification, measurement, accumulation, analysis, preparation, interpretation, and communication of financial information used by management to plan, evaluate, and control within an organization and to assure appropriate use of and accountability for its resources. Management accounting also comprises the preparation of financial reports for nonmanagement groups such as shareholders, creditors, regulatory agencies, and tax authorities" (SMA 1A). The responsibilities assumed by management accountants in conjunction with the activities in which they are engaged are significant and vary widely, given that management accountants are not only providers of information but also full participants in the management process. The

body of knowledge for management accountants does not remain static, and management accountants frequently confront new challenges in their roles as managers and reporters.

5. Recognizing those challenges, the NAA decided that a need exists for authoritative guidelines that would help the management accountant fulfill his or her responsibilities. The guidance would take the form of (a) a recommended approach to dealing with an issue, (b) suggested alternative approaches to solving a problem, or (c) useful reference material.

Scope and Application of SMAs

6. Responsibility for identifying appropriate topics and supervising the development of SMAs lies with the MAP Committee's Subcommittee on MAP Statement Promulgation. One of the Subcommittee's first acts was the development of a Framework for Management Accounting on which to base the scope of the Subcommittee's work program. The Framework for Management Accounting comprises:

   1. Objectives
   2. Terminology
   3. Concepts
   4. Practices and Techniques
   5. Management of Accounting Activities

7. As implied by the term "guideline," Statements on Management Accounting are nonbinding. But although no one is obliged to adhere to their recommendations, a wide degree of support is expected. To a large extent, this expectation is based on the authority attributable to the quality of membership on both the MAP Committee and its Promulgation Subcommittee — members are recognized leaders in industry, public accounting, and academe, with the majority from industry. Support for the Statements also will stem from the rigor of the developmental and exposure processes.

Developmental Process

8. As noted in the foregoing section, the Subcommittee identifies appropriate topics and monitors development of SMAs. Suggestions for new projects come from various sources in

addition to Subcommittee members, including NAA staff. Projects placed on the Subcommittee's agenda must be approved first by two-thirds of the members of both the Subcommittee and the MAP Committee.

9. A member of the Subcommittee accepts the responsibility of monitoring the progress of each Statement, the drafting of which generally is done by an external consultant or by NAA staff. The person who drafts a Statement makes use of research performed specifically for the project or research results that are available already. Progress toward completion is carefully scrutinized by the Subcommittee monitor. A draft Statement is brought before the Subcommittee only on the recommendation of the monitor.

Exposure Process

10. When a majority of the Subcommittee members present at a meeting believe that a draft is ready for exposure to others, the draft is transmitted to members of two advisory panels. One panel is composed of a representative sample of NAA chapter presidents or other chapter representatives. The constituency is rotated annually. The other panel consists of nominees of other organizations having an interest in accounting, such as the American Institute of Certified Public Accountants, Financial Executives Institute, American Accounting Association, and the Society of Management Accountants of Canada. Members of this panel are changed at the option of the sponsoring organization.

11. The Subcommittee reviews all comments received from panelists and makes whatever modifications seem appropriate. The draft SMA, as modified, then is submitted to the MAP Committee for its approval. The MAP Committee will (a) approve issuance unchanged, (b) approve issuance after modification, or (c) return the draft to the Subcommittee for further development. When the MAP Committee does approve issuance of a Statement by at least a two-thirds majority, the Statement is published by the NAA within the series of Statements on Management Accounting and is reprinted in the NAA's official journal, *Management Accounting*.

•   •   •   •

12. The NAA makes SMAs available based on the belief that they will represent positive contributions to advancing the profession of management accounting. The Association is interested in enhancing the usefulness of the series and therefore solicits comments about Statements issued and suggestions for new topics from members and others. Correspondence related to Statements on Management Accounting should be sent to:

Director, Management Accounting Practices
National Association of Accountants
10 Paragon Drive
P.O. Box 433
Montvale, N.J. 07645

NATIONAL ASSOCIATION OF ACCOUNTANTS
MANAGEMENT ACCOUNTING PRACTICES COMMITTEE
1985-86

Chairman
Bernard R. Doyle
Manager-Corporate Accounting Services
General Electric Company
Fairfield, Conn.

Raymond H. Alleman
Vice President & Comptroller
ITT Corporation
New York, N.Y.

Robert N. Anthony
Professor Emeritus
Harvard Business School
Boston, Mass.

Patricia P. Douglas
Professor of Accounting and Finance
University of Montana
Missoula, Mont.

William J. Ihlanfeldt
Assistant Controller
Shell Oil Company
Houston, Tex.

Eugene H. Irminger
Senior Vice President of Finance
Centel Corporation
Chicago, Ill.

James J. Latchford
*Assistant Vice President &
Assistant Controller*
W. R. Grace & Company
New York, N.Y.

Arthur D. Lyons
Vice President-Controller
FMC Corporation
Chicago, Ill.

Allen H. Seed, III
Senior Consultant
Arthur D. Little, Inc.
Cambridge, Mass.

Norman N. Strauss
Partner
Ernst & Whinney
New York, N.Y.

Edward W. Trott
Partner
Peat, Marwick, Mitchell & Co.
Tampa, Fla.

Robert G. Weiss
Vice President & Controller
Schering-Plough Corporation
Madison, N.J.

NAA STAFF

Louis Bisgay, *Director,* Management Accounting Practices
Jonathan B. Schiff, *Manager,* Management Accounting Practices

Statements on Management Accounting

Statement Number 1A
March 19, 1981

OBJECTIVES

Definition of Management Accounting

In accordance with the charge to the Management Accounting Practices (MAP) Committee to issue statements on management accounting principles and practices, Statements on Management Accounting are promulgated to reflect official positions of the National Association of Accountants (NAA). The work of the MAP Committee is based on a framework for management accounting, whose principal categories are:

1. Objectives
2. Terminology
3. Concepts
4. Practices and Techniques
5. Management of Accounting Activities

Statement Number 1A
March 19, 1981

Objectives:
Definition of Management Accounting

National Association of Accountants

Preface

The "Definition of Management Accounting" contained in this publication represents the first of a new series of *Statements on Management Accounting* which are responsive to the Management Accounting Practices (MAP) Committee's charge to develop guidelines on management accounting concepts, policies, and practices.

Methodology

Principal responsibility for development of *Statements on Management Accounting* is assumed by the MAP Committee's Subcommittee on MAP Statement Promulgation (Subcommittee). The Subcommittee will identify the subjects to be explored and oversee the progress on each project from inception to completion. When the Subcommittee deems it appropriate, a project report will be recommended to the MAP Committee for approval.

The MAP Committee and Subcommittee hope to utilize the expertise of the broad-based Association membership. To that end, an early announcement of a project's existence will be made in *Management Accounting*; readers will be encouraged to comment at that time. Upon consideration of these comments and the completion of the research, the Subcommittee will prepare a draft statement for circulation to two groups of about 20 persons each:

1. A panel selected by the Subcommittee on the basis of background and expertise in the business and financial community
2. A panel chosen from the NAA membership-at-large on a stratified random sampling basis

When the comments from the members of the panels have been received and evaluated, the Subcommittee will consider modifications to its draft and recommend that the MAP Committee promulgate the revised version as a *Statement on Management Accounting*. The MAP Committee will review the proposed Statement and, if approved, will arrange for its distribution to the membership and the financial community.

Framework for Management Accounting

The MAP Committee concurred with the Subcommittee's conclusion that structuring a framework would be useful in comprehending the scope of management accounting and in determining specific subjects to be investigated. As envisioned, the framework will comprise principal categories, subcategories, and specific projects. At this time, only the principal categories have been resolved, and they are:

1. Objectives
2. Terminology
3. Concepts
4. Practices and Techniques
5. Management of Accounting Activities

This Statement, *Definition of Management Accounting*, is referenced to the framework as 1A—category 1 (Objectives) and subcategory A (Definition of Management Accounting).

MAP Committee Statement of Objectives

Preamble

The National Association of Accountants is an international accounting organization. Among its major purposes are:

"(a) . . . develop through research, discussion and exchange of information a better understanding of the sources, types, purposes and uses of accounting and related data as applied to all types of economic endeavor . . ."

* * *

"(e) . . . provide opportunities for members to increase their knowledge of accounting practices and methods . . ."

The Bylaws of the National Association of Accountants describe the Management Accounting Practices Committee as follows:

> "This committee shall consist of twelve members with three-year terms, with four to be appointed annually."

> "It shall be composed of members oriented toward industry, public accounting, and education, with a majority in the first category."

"It shall have the responsibility for issuing authoritative statements on accounting principles and practices by such means and in such media as it shall determine, and establish policies in this respect and submit such policies to the Executive Committee for approval."

Principal Objectives

The principal objectives of the Management Accounting Practices Committee are:

• To express the official position of NAA on relevant accounting matters to other professional groups, government bodies, the financial community, and the general public.

• To provide guidelines to the membership of the Association and business management on management accounting concepts, policies, and practices.

The impact of the Committee and, therefore, NAA as a whole will be determined by the quality of its work, the methods used to publicize such work, and the continued support of the Association and its leadership. The MAP Committee recognizes that its Statements will not carry the sanction of any outside official authority; therefore, their influence will be based solely on their intrinsic quality.

Definitions

Relevant accounting matters: For purposes of determining its scope, the Committee considers as relevant any accounting matter concerning the identification, measurement, accumulation, analysis, preparation, interpretation, and communication of historic or prospective information.

Management accounting concepts: All concepts that relate to the processes or functions included in the definition of management accounting set forth in this pronouncement.

Scope

Because "management accounting concepts" are also related to concepts useful to other users of accountancy and because "relevant accounting matters" are discussed universally, the Committee considers its purview to be very broad. Accordingly, it will be attuned to the developments occurring in all fields of accountancy. The Committee will maintain liaison with organizations throughout the world including the Financial Accounting Standards Board, the Securities and Exchange Commission, the International Accounting Standards Committee, and other appropriate agencies and committees. As part of this liaison, MAP will study their proposals and offer comments, suggestions, support, or criticism.

The Committee also is obligated to develop and promulgate statements on management accounting. These statements will be made available to NAA members and others to improve management accounting.

* * *

The work of the Committee is premised on its conclusion that accounting is an integral part of the management process. In fulfilling its objectives, the Committee welcomes the advice and counsel of the NAA membership and other interested persons.

Definition of Management Accounting

Definition

Management accounting is the process of identification, measurement, accumulation, analysis, preparation, interpretation, and communication of financial information used by management to plan, evaluate, and control within an organization and to assure appropriate use of and accountability for its resources. Management accounting also comprises the preparation of financial reports for non-management groups such as shareholders, creditors, regulatory agencies, and tax authorities.

To facilitate comprehension, the most significant terms used in the definition are defined as follows:

Management Accounting is the process of:

Identification—the recognition and evaluation of business transactions and other economic events for appropriate accounting action.

Measurement—the quantification, including estimates, of business transactions or other economic events that have occurred or may occur.

Accumulation—the disciplined and consistent approach to recording and classifying appropriate business transactions and other economic events.

Analysis—the determination of the reasons for, and the relationships of, the reported activity with other economic events and circumstances.

Preparation and Interpretation—the meaningful coordination of accounting and/or planning data to satisfy a need for information, presented in a logical format, and, if appropriate, including the conclusions drawn from those data.

Communication—the reporting of pertinent information to management and others for internal and external uses.

Management Accounting is used by management to:

Plan—to gain an understanding of expected business transactions and other economic events and their impact on the organization.

Evaluate—to judge the implications of various past and/or future events.

Control—to ensure the integrity of financial information concerning an organization's activities or its resources.

Assure accountability—to implement the system of reporting that is closely aligned to organizational responsibilities and that contributes to the effective measurement of management performance.

Many of the activities constituting the field of management accounting are interrelated and thus must be coordinated, ranked, and implemented by the management accountant in such a fashion as to meet the objectives of the organization as perceived by him or her. A major function of the management accountant is that of tailoring the application of the process to the organization so that the organization's objectives are achieved effectively.

NATIONAL ASSOCIATION OF ACCOUNTANTS
MANAGEMENT ACCOUNTING PRACTICES COMMITTEE
1980-81

Chairman
Herbert H. Seiffert
Assistant Treasurer
Johnson & Johnson
New Brunswick, N.J.

John F. Chironna
Director of Accounting—U.S. Operations
International Business Machines Corp.
Armonk, N.Y.

James Don Edwards
J.M. Tull Professor of Accounting
University of Georgia
School of Accounting
Athens, Ga.

Francis R. McAllister
Controller
ASARCO, Inc.
New York, N.Y.

Earl R. Milner
Vice President and Controller
A.O. Smith Corporation
Milwaukee, Wis.

Albert P. Roeper
Vice President—Finance and Treasurer
Thiokol Corp.
Newtown, Pa.

Hadley P. Schaefer
Director—School of Accounting
University of Florida
Gainesville, Fla.

Richard L. Snyder
Vice President and Controller
Philip Morris, Inc.
New York, N.Y.

Robert B. Sweeney
Director, School of Accountancy
University of Alabama
University, Ala.

Armin C. Tufer
Partner
Deloitte Haskins & Sells
Chicago, Ill.

Robert S. Weatherly, Jr.
President—Metals Division
Vulcan Materials Co.
Birmingham, Ala.

Charles A. Werner
Partner
Alexander Grant & Co.
Chicago, Ill.

SUBCOMMITTEE ON MAP STATEMENT PROMULGATION
1980-81

Robert B. Sweeney, Chairman

*John F. Chironna

*Hadley P. Schaefer

Herbert C. Knortz
*Executive Vice President
  and Comptroller*
International Telephone
  & Telegraph Corporation
New York, N.Y.

Donald J. Trawicki
Partner
Touche Ross & Co.
*Also member of MAP Committee   New York, N.Y.

NAA STAFF

Louis Bisgay, *Manager,* Management Accounting Practices Development

James L. Mammone, *Project Manager,* MAP Development

Statements on Management Accounting

Statement Number 1B
June 17, 1982

OBJECTIVES

Objectives of Management Accounting

In accordance with the charge to the Management Accounting Practices (MAP) Committee to issue statements on management accounting principles and practices, Statements on Management Accounting are promulgated to reflect official positions of the National Association of Accountants (NAA). The work of the MAP Committee is based on a framework for management accounting, whose principal categories are:

1. Objectives
2. Terminology
3. Concepts
4. Practices and Techniques
5. Management of Accounting Activities

Statement Number 1B
June 17, 1982

Objectives:
Objectives of Management Accounting

National Association of Accountants

Preface

The purpose of Statement No. 1B is to provide basic information about management accounting to those interested in the profession—management accountants themselves, as well as public accountants, students and teachers of accounting, and the business and financial community. The Statement also should assist management accountants in fulfilling their objectives: *providing information* and *participating actively in the management process.*

The initial phase of the Objectives project culminated in the issuance of Statement No. 1A, *Definition of Management Accounting.* The basic definition of management accounting as set forth in Statement No. 1A follows.

Definition of Management Accounting

Management accounting is the process of identification, measurement, accumulation, analysis, preparation, interpretation, and communication of financial information used by management to plan, evaluate, and control within an organization and to assure appropriate use of and accountability for its resources. Management accounting also comprises the preparation of financial reports for nonmanagement groups such as shareholders, creditors, regulatory agencies, and tax authorities.

In the context of this definition, financial information comprises broadly that information, monetary or nonmonetary, necessary to interpret the cause and effect of actual or planned business activities, economic circumstances, and asset and liability valuations.

Management accountants implement the objectives of management accounting. The term *management accountant* is used in this Statement in its broadest sense. It is intended to include persons involved in such functions as controllership, treasury, financial analysis, planning and budgeting, cost accounting, internal audit, systems, and general accounting. Management accountants thus may have titles such as chief financial officer, vice president—finance, controller, treasurer, budget analyst, cost analyst, and accountant, among many others. High-level personnel outsiae the United States often hold distinctly different titles; one that often is used is finance director.

It should be recognized that, given the wide range of management accounting activities, not all management accountants perform all the functions described in this Statement. Certain functions are usually restricted to the higher-level management accountants, who frequently also are designated as financial management.

A chart depicting the hierarchical relationships described in this Statement is appended as Exhibit A. Readers may find it helpful to examine Exhibit A before reading the text of the Statement.

Objectives

In fulfilling the objectives of management accounting, management accountants:

1. **Provide information** and
2. **Participate in the management process.**

Providing Information

Management accountants select and provide, to all levels of management, information needed for (a) planning, evaluating, and controlling operations; (b) safeguarding the organization's assets; and (c) communicating with interested parties outside the organization, such as shareholders and regulatory bodies.

Participating in the Management Process

Management accountants at appropriate levels are involved actively in the process of managing the entity. This process includes making strategic, tactical, and operating decisions and helping to coordinate the efforts of the entire organization. The management accountant participates, as part of management, in assuring that the organization operates as a unified whole in its long-run, intermediate, and short-run best interests.

Responsibilities

To fulfill the objectives, management accountants accept

certain major responsibilities. They establish and maintain the necessary practices and techniques to provide essential information to management, and they fulfill external reporting requirements. The responsibilities of management accountants, which are set forth in Statement No. 1A, are as follows:

1. *Planning*—Quantifying and interpreting the effects on the organization of planned transactions and other economic events. The planning responsibility, which includes strategic, tactical, and operating aspects, requires that the accountant provide quantitative historical and prospective information to facilitate planning. It includes participation in developing the planning system, setting obtainable goals, and choosing appropriate means of monitoring the progress toward the goals.

2. *Evaluating*—Judging implications of historical and expected events and helping to choose the optimum course of action. Evaluating includes translating data into trends and relationships. Management accountants must communicate effectively and promptly the conclusions derived from the analyses.

3. *Controlling*—Assuring the integrity of financial information concerning an organization's activities and resources; monitoring and measuring performance and inducing any corrective actions required to return the activity to its intended course. Management accountants provide information to executives operating in functional areas who can make use of it to achieve desirable performance.

4. *Assuring accountability of resources*—Implementing a system of reporting that is aligned with organizational responsibilities. This reporting system will contribute to the effective use of resources and measurement of management performance. The transmission of management's goals and objectives throughout the organization in the form of assigned responsibilities is a basis for identifying accountability. Management accountants must provide an accounting and reporting system that will accumulate and report appropriate revenues, expenses, assets, liabilities, and related quantitative infor-

mation to managers. Managers then will have better control over these elements.

5. *External reporting*—Preparing financial reports based on generally accepted accounting principles, or other appropriate bases, for nonmanagement groups such as shareholders, creditors, regulatory agencies, and tax authorities. Management accountants should participate in the process of developing the accounting principles that underlie external reporting.

Activities

Management accountants discharge their responsibilities by organizing and implementing activities in seven principal categories: reporting, interpretation, resource management, information systems development, technological implementation, verification, and administration.

Reporting

Reporting relates to both internal and external needs for information about past or future events and circumstances. Management accountants make available to managers timely reports that provide the information and perspective necessary for them to make decisions in a goal-congruent manner. The reports may concern financial, physical, and human resources and the markets and regulatory environments in which entities operate. In addition to reporting internally, management accountants make appropriate information available to shareholders, creditors, and governmental regulatory agencies and tax authorities.

Interpretation

Management accountants interpret all forms of internal and external information pertinent to the various segments of the organization and communicate the implications of the information being reviewed, including its relevance and reliability. Management accountants thus must understand both the sources and uses of the information.

Resource Management

Management accountants must establish systems which

facilitate planning and contɾɔl of the organization's resources to ensure that their use is consistent with established policies. These systems also should meet the needs of management, investors, creditors, and other interested parties. Some of these needs are:

- Custody and management of working capital, including credit and collections and inventory management
- Creating and maintaining the most appropriate debt and equity capital structure
- Developing and implementing a system to control plant, property, and equipment
- Administering a pension or similar plan
- Tax planning and compliance
- Insurance management
- Creating and operating a system of internal accounting control that can detect misuses of assets, taking into account the cost/benefit aspects of the control system

Information Systems Development

Design and development of the overall management information system implies:

- Determining the output required by users
- Specifying the data inputs needed to obtain the required output
- Developing the requirements for a processing system that converts input to output
- Managing and securing the data bases

Technological Implementation

Modern equipment and techniques should be employed to facilitate the selection, accumulation, transmission, analysis, and safeguarding of information. Management accountants therefore should be familiar with current technology relative to information processing and the accounting techniques appropriate to controlling and using the information. Some examples are:

- Computer applications
    —basic accounting functions and data-base management

—techniques in financial planning and decision making, such as models for optimizing asset utilization and resource allocation
- Network and communications systems

Verification

Management accountants assure the accuracy and reliability of information derived from the accounting system or related sources that is used throughout the organization. They also must be satisfied that actions taking place throughout the entity are consistent with policies of the organization. Both of these activities use the internal control system and are reviewed by internal audit.

Administration

Administration includes development and maintenance of an effective and efficient management accounting organization. This organization addresses and resolves issues relevant to the accounting and financial structure such as:

- Assignment of management accounting responsibilities
- Interface between accounting and other operations
- Delegation of authority and determinations relevant to centralization or decentralization
- Recruiting, training, and developing personnel in the various areas of responsibility
- Separation of duties

Other important administrative activities performed by management accountants include the development and maintenance of:

- Accounting policy and procedure manuals
- A cost-effective records management program
- Records adequate to meet the requirements of tax laws, other laws and regulatory agencies, and independent auditors

Processes

Certain operational processes are inherent throughout the

range of activities described in the preceding section. These processes are articulated in Statement No. 1A and include:

1. *Identification*—recognition and evaluation of business transactions and other economic events for appropriate accounting action.

2. *Measurement*—quantification, including estimates, of business transactions or other economic events that have occurred or forecasts of those that may occur.

3. *Accumulation*—disciplined and consistent approaches to recording and classifying appropriate business transactions and other economic events.

4. *Analysis*—determination of the reasons for the reported activity and its relationship with other economic events and circumstances.

5. *Preparation and Interpretation*—meaningful coordination of accounting and/or planning data to provide information, presented logically, and including, if appropriate, the conclusions drawn from those data.

6. *Communication*—reporting pertinent information to management and others for internal and external uses.

* * *

This Statement sets forth the objectives of management accounting recognized by the National Association of Accountants (NAA). In Statement on Management Accounting No. 1A (dated March 19, 1981), *Definition of Management Accounting,* the NAA, through its Management Accounting Practices Committee, defined the scope of the field of management accounting. The two Statements, in combination, comprise the category within the framework for management accounting that is titled *Objectives.* Other principal categories of the framework to be addressed are: *Terminology, Concepts, Practices and Techniques,* and *Management of Accounting Activities.*

Objectives of
Management Accounting

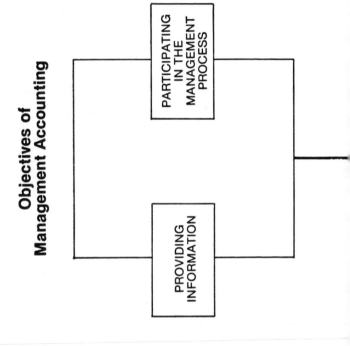

RESPONSIBILITIES

PLANNING	EVALUATING	CONTROLLING	ASSURING ACCOUNTABILITY	EXTERNAL REPORTING

PRINCIPAL ACTIVITIES

REPORTING	INTERPRETATION	RESOURCE MANAGEMENT	INFORMATION SYSTEMS DEVELOPMENT	TECHNOLOGICAL IMPLEMENTATION	VERIFI-CATION	ADMINIS-TRATION

PROCESSES

IDENTIFICATION	MEASUREMENT	ACCUMULATION	ANALYSIS	PREPARATION AND INTERPRETATION	COMMUNICATION

NATIONAL ASSOCIATION OF ACCOUNTANTS
MANAGEMENT ACCOUNTING PRACTICES COMMITTEE
1981-82

Chairman
John F. Chironna
Director of Accounting — U.S. Operations
International Business Machines Corp.
Tarrytown, N.Y.

Richard J. Bellew
Controller
Brooks Fashion Stores, Inc.
New York, N.Y.

James Don Edwards
J.M. Tull Professor of Accounting
University of Georgia
School of Accounting
Athens, Ga.

Francis R. McAllister
Controller
ASARCO, Inc.
New York, N.Y.

Earl R. Milner
Vice President and Controller
A. O. Smith Corporation
Milwaukee, Wis.

Stanley R. Pylipow
Vice President — Finance & Administration
Fisher Controls International, Inc.
St. Louis, Mo.

Albert P. Roeper
Vice President — Finance & Treasurer
Thiokol Corp.
Newtown, Pa.

Hadley P. Schaefer
Director — School of Accounting
University of Florida
Gainesville, Fla.

Howard L. Siers
Assistant Comptroller
E.I. duPont de Nemours & Co., Inc.
Wilmington, Del.

Robert B. Sweeney
Director — School of Accountancy
University of Alabama
University, Ala.

Armin C. Tufer
Partner
Deloitte Haskins & Sells
Chicago, Ill.

Charles A. Werner
Partner
Alexander Grant & Co.
Chicago, Ill.

SUBCOMMITTEE ON MAP STATEMENT PROMULGATION
1981-82

*Robert B. Sweeney, *Chairman*
*John F. Chironna
*Hadley P. Schaefer

Herbert C. Knortz
Executive Vice President & Comptroller
International Telephone
  & Telegraph Corporation
New York, N.Y.

Herbert H. Seiffert
Assistant Treasurer
Johnson & Johnson
New Brunswick, N.J.

Donald J. Trawicki
Partner
Touche Ross & Co.
New York, N.Y.

*Also member of MAP Committee

NAA STAFF

Louis Bisgay, *Director*, Management Accounting Practices
James L. Mammone, *Project Manager*, Management Accounting Practices

Statements on Management Accounting

Statement Number 1C
June 1, 1983

OBJECTIVES

Standards of Ethical Conduct for Management Accountants

In accordance with the charge to the Management Accounting Practices (MAP) Committee to issue statements on management accounting principles and practices, Statements on Management Accounting are promulgated to reflect official positions of the National Association of Accountants (NAA). The work of the MAP Committee is based on a framework for management accounting, whose principal categories are:

1. Objectives
2. Terminology
3. Concepts
4. Practices and Techniques
5. Management of Accounting Activities

Statement Number 1C
June 1, 1983

Objectives:
Standards of Ethical Conduct for Management Accountants

National Association of Accountants

Acknowledgments

We acknowledge with gratitude the work of the Ad Hoc Committee on Professional Ethics in laying the foundation for the standards being pronounced. Members of that committee were Grant U. Meyers, chairman; James J. Corboy, Donald H. Cramer, Patricia P. Douglas, Robert F. Garland, Clark H. Johnson, and Robert B. Sweeney. James Bulloch, managing director, Institute of Management Accounting, acted as secretary to the committee.

Standards of Ethical Conduct
for Management Accountants

Management accountants have an obligation to the organizations they serve, their profession, the public, and themselves to maintain the highest standards of ethical conduct. In recognition of this obligation, the National Association of Accountants has promulgated the following standards of ethical conduct for management accountants. Adherence to these standards is integral to achieving the *Objectives of Management Accounting.*[1] Management accountants shall not commit acts contrary to these standards nor shall they condone the commission of such acts by others within their organizations.

Competence

Management accountants have a responsibility to:

- Maintain an appropriate level of professional competence by ongoing development of their knowledge and skills.
- Perform their professional duties in accordance with relevant laws, regulations, and technical standards.
- Prepare complete and clear reports and recommendations after appropriate analyses of relevant and reliable information.

Confidentiality

Management accountants have a responsibility to:

- Refrain from disclosing confidential information acquired in the course of their work except when authorized, unless legally obligated to do so.

---

[1] National Association of Accountants, *Statements on Management Accounting: Objectives of Management Accounting,* Statement No. 1B, New York, N.Y., June 17, 1982.

- Inform subordinates as appropriate regarding the confidentiality of information acquired in the course of their work and monitor their activities to assure the maintenance of that confidentiality.
- Refrain from using or appearing to use confidential information acquired in the course of their work for unethical or illegal advantage either personally or through third parties.

Integrity

Management accountants have a responsibility to:

- Avoid actual or apparent conflicts of interest and advise all appropriate parties of any potential conflict.
- Refrain from engaging in any activity that would prejudice their ability to carry out their duties ethically.
- Refuse any gift, favor, or hospitality that would influence or would appear to influence their actions.
- Refrain from either actively or passively subverting the attainment of the organization's legitimate and ethical objectives.
- Recognize and communicate professional limitations or other constraints that would preclude responsible judgment or successful performance of an activity.
- Communicate unfavorable as well as favorable information and professional judgments or opinions.
- Refrain from engaging in or supporting any activity that would discredit the profession.

Objectivity

Management accountants have a responsibility to:

- Communicate information fairly and objectively.
- Disclose fully all relevant information that could reasonably be expected to influence an intended user's understanding of the reports, comments, and recommendations presented. ☐

Resolution of Ethical Conflict

In applying the standards of ethical conduct, management accountants may encounter problems in identifying unethical behavior or in resolving an ethical conflict. When faced with significant ethical issues, management accountants should follow the established policies of the organization bearing on the resolution of such conflict. If these policies do not resolve the ethical conflict, management accountants should consider the following courses of action:

- Discuss such problems with the immediate superior except when it appears that the superior is involved, in which case the problem should be presented initially to the next higher managerial level. If satisfactory resolution cannot be achieved when the problem is initially presented, submit the issues to the next higher managerial level.

  If the immediate superior is the chief executive officer, or equivalent, the acceptable reviewing authority may be a group such as the audit committee, executive committee, board of directors, board of trustees, or owners. Contact with levels above the immediate superior should be initiated only with the superior's knowledge, assuming the superior is not involved.

- Clarify relevant concepts by confidential discussion with an objective advisor to obtain an understanding of possible courses of action.

- If the ethical conflict still exists after exhausting all levels of internal review, the management accountant may have no other recourse on significant matters than to resign from the organization and to submit an informative memorandum to an appropriate representative of the organization.

Except where legally prescribed, communication of such problems to authorities or individuals not employed or engaged by the organization is not considered appropriate.

NATIONAL ASSOCIATION OF ACCOUNTANTS
MANAGEMENT ACCOUNTING PRACTICES COMMITTEE
1982-83

Chairman
John F. Chironna
Director of Accounting Practices
International Business Machines Corp.
Tarrytown, N.Y.

Dennis R. Beresford
Partner
Ernst & Whinney
Cleveland, Ohio

James Don Edwards
J.M. Tull Professor of Accounting
University of Georgia, School of
Accounting
Athens, Ga.

Penny A. Flugger
Auditor
Morgan Guaranty Trust Co.
New York, N.Y.

William J. Ihlanfeldt
Assistant Controller
Shell Oil Company
Houston, Tex.

Earl R. Milner
Vice President and Controller
A.O. Smith Corporation
Milwaukee, Wis.

Bryan H. Mitchell
Controller
A.C. Nielsen Co.
Northbrook, Ill.

Stanley R. Pylipow
*Vice-President/Finance &
Administration*
Fisher Controls International, Inc.
St. Louis, Mo.

Allen H. Seed, III
Senior Consultant
Arthur D. Little, Inc.
Cambridge, Mass.

Howard L. Siers
Assistant Comptroller
E.I. du Pont de Nemours &
Company, Inc.
Wilmington, Del.

Robert B. Sweeney
Director—School of Accountancy
University of Alabama
University, Ala.

Armin C. Tufer
Partner
Deloitte Haskins & Sells
Chicago, Ill.

SUBCOMMITTEE ON MAP STATEMENT PROMULGATION
1982-83

Robert B. Sweeney, Chairman

*John F. Chironna

*Allen H. Seed, III

*Howard L. Siers

Herbert C. Knortz
Executive Vice President & Comptroller
International Telephone & Telegraph
Corporation
New York, N.Y.

Herbert H. Seiffert
Assistant Treasurer
Johnson & Johnson
New Brunswick, N.J.

Donald J. Trawicki
Partner
Touche Ross & Co.
New York, N.Y.

NAA STAFF

Louis Bisgay, *Director,* Management Accounting Practices
Robert W. McGee, *Manager,* Management Accounting Practices
Rosemary A. Schlank, *Manager,* Management Accounting Practices

*Member of MAP Committee

Statements on Management Accounting

Statement Number 1D
June 3, 1986

OBJECTIVES

The Common Body of Knowledge for Management Accountants

In accordance with the charge to the Management Accounting Practices (MAP) Committee to issue statements on management accounting principles and practices, Statements on Management Accounting are promulgated to reflect official positions of the National Association of Accountants (NAA). The work of the MAP Committee is based on a framework for management accounting, whose principal categories are:

1. Objectives
2. Terminology
3. Concepts
4. Practices and Techniques
5. Management of Accounting Activities

Statements on Management Accounting

Statement Number 1D
June 3, 1986

Objectives:
The Common Body of Knowledge for
Management Accountants

National Association of Accountants

Preface

This Statement evolved from the National Association of Accountants' (NAA) research projects which included a profile of the management accountant, follow-up research to focus on elements of that knowledge common to management accounting, and recommendations from the Committee on Research. The Institute of Certified Management Accountants and NAA's Committee on Education supported these efforts. Based on this work, an Ad Hoc Committee appointed by NAA's president prepared this Statement on The Common Body of Knowledge for Management Accountants. The Statement received the support of the Management Accounting Practices Committee, which authorized issuance as a Statement on Management Accounting.

The Ad Hoc Committee concluded that defining and promulgating this Statement on The Common Body of Knowledge for Management Accountants would be beneficial to the management accounting profession and its associations. In preparing this Statement, the Ad Hoc Committee was guided by five objectives:

- To guide academic institutions in structuring a curriculum for management accountants
- To describe management accounting knowledge in enough detail to assist students in making career decisions
- To guide practicing management accountants in expanding or updating their professional knowledge
- To provide a basis for NAA and other professional associations to structure pertinent continuing education programs
- To establish a foundation from which the Certified Management Accountant program can continue to evolve

This Statement can be adapted to the changing environment of management accounting. While it provides overall guidance for the Association, educators, and aspiring accountants, it lacks the specificity that would soon diminish its usefulness.

Consistent with other NAA promulgations, the terms *management accounting* and *management accountants* are used in their broadest context as described in NAA Statements on Management Accounting Numbers 1A and 1B. Pertinent excerpts follow:

Management accounting is the process of identification, measurement, accumulation, analysis, preparation, interpretation, and communication of financial information used by management to plan, evaluate, and control within an organization and to assure appropriate use of and accountability for its resources. Management accounting also comprises the preparation of financial reports for nonmanagement groups such as shareholders, creditors, regulatory agencies, and tax authorities.

The term management accounting is intended to include persons involved in such functions as controllership, treasury, financial analysis, planning and budgeting, cost accounting, internal audit, systems, and general accounting. Management accountants thus may have titles such as chief financial officer, vice president-finance, controller, treasurer, budget analyst, cost analyst, and accountant, among many others.

Summary Statement

1. This Statement identifies the composite subject matter that constitutes the body of knowledge common to management accounting as practiced at the professional level of competency.
2. The Statement focuses on the professional core of management accounting knowledge. Comprehension and effective utilization of this knowledge requires a general education background, a capacity for life-long learning, an ability to assimilate ancillary knowledge, and a capability for developing leadership and interpersonal skills. Management accountants must interact positively with persons outside and inside the entity.
3. For purposes of this Statement, the common body of knowledge is categorized into three areas:
   - Information and decision processes, including management decision processes, internal reporting, and planning and performance evaluation
   - Accounting concepts and principles, including an understanding of the organization and management of the accounting function
   - Entity operations, including its operating environment, taxation, external reporting, and information systems
4. These three broad areas of knowledge are defined further in the section titled "Core of Knowledge Areas." The table on page 2 provides an overview of these areas.
5. Categorizing the common body of knowledge into areas accommodates typical approaches to education. Nonetheless, a particular area should not be considered solely as a separate topic for study, but also as part of an integrated educational program.
6. The headings are intended as generic terms rather than as definitions or course titles, and the order of discussion is not meant to imply emphasis.
7. The extent to which management accountants utilize any given area varies with the stages of their professional careers and with their areas of responsibility. At the entry level, for example, knowledge related to generating and organizing accounting data is paramount. As an accountant gains experience and added responsibilities, knowledge and attendant skills related to analyzing, interpreting, presenting, and communicating information become preeminent.

8. In executing their responsibilities, management accountants are expected to adapt to a changing profession. They maintain their competency by participating in professional activities. Professional associations should continually re-evaluate and develop suitable activities and programs.

The Common Body of Knowledge for Management Accountants
Core of Knowledge Areas

Information and Decision Processes	Accounting Principles and Functions	Entity Operations
· Management decision processes · Internal reporting · Financial planning and performance evaluation	· Organizational structure and management · Accounting concepts and principles	· Principal entity operations · Operating environment · Taxation · External reporting · Information systems

Core of Knowledge Areas

Information and Decision Processes

Management Decision Processes

At various levels within an organization, management accountants participate in decision processes which establish, implement, and revise short-term, intermediate, or long-term plans. Management accountants also help coordinate decision-making activities for an entire organization. They therefore develop and maintain reporting systems that are aligned with organizational structures and that provide decision-useful information on an organization's performance. Management decision processes fall into three categories:

- Repetitive
- Nonprogrammed
- Strategic

Repetitive. This area of decision making requires knowledge of an organization's routine operations as governed by management policies and procedures. Management accountants assist in setting policies and objectives and in monitoring their implementation.

Nonprogrammed. Some events cannot be anticipated; reports and judgments about optimum courses of action must be made as the need arises. Management accountants must be able to act quickly in applying analytical skills and reporting techniques to supply relevant information for nonprogrammed decision making. Innovation and creative approaches are often needed to provide proper perspective.

Strategic. Strategic decisions involve planning the directions and undertaking the actions needed to achieve an entity's long-range goals and objectives. Defining an entity's businesses, market share, sales and earnings growth, profitability, financial risk, and technological position provides some of the factors considered in strategic decision making. Management accountants integrate knowledge from an organization's environment, its history, and its principal operations to help management develop alternatives and to track strategic plans.

Internal Reporting

Management accountants design, implement, and maintain internal reporting systems. These systems should be designed to contribute to effective decision making and to monitor managerial policies. Once implemented, reporting systems should be reviewed continually and revised as needed to ensure that they properly reflect internal requirements. Management accountants, then, synthesize, analyze, and edit data and convey the resulting information to management in a usable form. Analytical, design, and communication skills, along with accounting skills, are critical to their performance. In addition to accounting, these skills can be delineated into the following areas:

- Generating Data
- Organizing and Analyzing Information
- Presenting and Communicating Information

Generating Data. A well-designed system enables an entity to catalogue, combine, and produce relevant and timely financial and selected nonfinancial data. Knowledge about the design and implementation of a system is important, as is an understanding of the procedures for monitoring and modifying the system to reflect changing economic and/or managerial needs.

Organizing and Analyzing Information. This skill involves deciding what data elements are significant, how they should be accumulated (and in what sequence), as well as what they reveal about an organization. Necessary to this process is an understanding of user needs and preferences. Through this understanding and through techniques of analysis, management accountants transform data into meaningful information.

Presenting and Communicating Information. An understanding of how to assemble and convey information is necessary for effective communication. Knowledge about communication techniques and the needs of users is necessary to determine the most effective medium and appropriate presentation style. Oral or written reports accompanying the information must be concise, clear, and relevant.

Financial Planning and Performance Evaluation

In the planning process, management accountants help management understand business transactions and events and measure their impact on organizations. They also help define an organization's objectives and select the best strategies to accomplish those objectives.

Knowledge about an entity's products/services and operations, and an ability to work with people in other disciplines, are important to efficient planning.

The following skills provide a foundation for planning:

- Forecasting and Budgeting
- Analysis and Evaluation

Forecasting and Budgeting. Forecasting, the projection of future actions and their implications for an organization, is a key part of planning. Management accountants incorporate expected transactions and events into an organization's plans by establishing budgets that can be compared to actual results. Management accountants discern cost and revenue patterns, assess interrelationships among various financial elements, and utilize this information in subsequent planning efforts.

Analysis and Evaluation. Reviewing and appraising actual results and projections, identifying causes of variations, and assigning responsibility to particular events and organizational units constitute analysis and evaluation.

Many different analyses are required to examine, interpret, and evaluate alternative decisions. Management accountants use general-purpose techniques such as cost-volume-profit, sensitivity, and incremental analyses, as well as statistical techniques such as correlation and regression, probability, and statistical inference tests.

Judgments concerning performance cannot be made solely from a quantitative perspective. Frequently, these judgments require a synthesis of quantitative and nonquantitative information such as the general economic environment, the perception of the marketplace, and governmental influences.

Accounting Principles and Functions

Organizational Structure and Management

An understanding of how the accounting function is organized and managed and how it relates to other organizational units is important to management accountants. Organizational relationships, processes for identifying and assigning responsibilities, and internal communication patterns are all important attributes of the accounting function's structure. Management accountants must understand the management systems and practices employed by their organizations. Establishing and evaluating accountability and control processes are critical aspects of this knowledge. The following areas contribute to management accountants' understanding of an organization's structure and management:

- Structure and Management of the Accounting Function
- Internal Control
- Internal Auditing

Structure and Management of the Accounting Function. Understanding how the accounting function fits into the overall organizational structure is important to an accountant's performance. How the function is organized and managed, how it contributes to organizational performance, and how operational details are handled on a routine basis are attributes of that understanding.

Internal Control. Management ensures the integrity of an organization's financial information through internal control. Internal control encompasses plans, methods, and measures adopted by an entity to safeguard assets, check the accuracy and reliability of accounting data, promote operational efficiency, and encourage adherence to managerial policies. Management accountants are expected to understand the purposes of internal control and develop the techniques for employing it within organizations. They participate in the process by designing internal control systems, including the control aspects of computer-based systems, by preparing and evaluating internal control reports, and by undertaking internal audits.

Internal Auditing. Internal auditing involves both financial and operational auditing. Financial auditing verifies assets and validates financial data. Measuring the efficiency, effectiveness, and performance of an entity are aspects of operational auditing. Management uses information from internal audits to improve operations. Effective internal control requires integrating knowledge of an entity's management information system, its accounting policies, and its principal business operations.

Accounting Concepts and Principles

A good grasp of the functions of accounting, of the underlying concepts that constitute accounting theory, and of the accounting standards that guide specific applications is essential to the practice of management accounting. Knowledge of the accounting information required for both internal and external uses also is paramount in applying accounting practices to particular decision processes. This area includes:

· Nature and Objectives of Accounting
· Accounting Practices

Nature and Objectives of Accounting. This area encompasses the environment in which accounting is practiced, the types and uses of accounting information, as well as measurement, recognition, and presentation issues. The contributions of various segments of the accounting profession should be examined, as well as how accounting practices vary among organizations.

Accounting Practices. Management accountants are responsible for developing an organization's accounting practices. They must understand the accumulated body of accounting and reporting principles from which accounting practices are derived. Knowledge of the processes by which accounting and reporting principles are developed will increase the management accountant's ability to recommend appropriate practices. The accounting practices selected will be those that meet the organization's needs as determined by such organizational characteristics as management style, industry, and external reporting requirements.

Entity Operations

Principal Entity Operations

In addition to a general education background and technical accounting skills, management accountants should understand basic entity functions. They should be able to participate in decisions regarding which products or services will be developed and produced; how they will be marketed, distributed, and sold; and the means by which the entire production effort will be financed.

Management accountants rely on knowledge about human and organizational forces that influence management. In addition, knowledge of principal entity operations is necessary in order to provide and interpret financial information pertinent to each area. Principal entity operations include the following management areas:

- Finance and Investments
- Engineering and Research and Development
- Production and Operations
- Sales and Marketing
- Human Resources

Finance and Investments. Evaluating alternative investments and determining their effects on an organization are important tasks within the management accounting function. Management accountants who are involved with the treasury function evaluate capital needs, identify sources of capital, and measure the risk and return associated with alternative uses of financial resources.

Engineering and Research and Development. Discovery of new knowledge about existing or proposed product/service areas and translation of that information into operational plans are critical functions for many organizations. While management accountants are not researchers or engineers, they need a working knowledge of research and development processes, particularly as they relate to other organizational activities. They should be able to evaluate this area's contribution to an organization and to furnish relevant information on research and development expenditures.

Production and Operations. An understanding of production engineering processes, cost patterns, and control techniques is important to management accountants. Management accountants design and maintain cost accounting and inventory control systems. They report on actual costs and on variances from standards and budgets to aid management in controlling current and future operations.

Sales and Marketing. Understanding the processes by which goods and services are marketed, distributed, and sold is important to supplying information for decision making. Management accountants design and maintain information systems used to report revenues and variances from projected revenues; the systems are also used to interpret changes in price, volume, product mix, and market share. Management accountants also contribute to the identification and control of distribution costs.

Human Resources. Knowledge of human resource management provides an understanding of how employees are hired, trained, motivated, and compensated. Employee relations is a key facet of this knowledge.

Operating Environment

Just as the accounting function operates within an entity's structure, each organization operates within the larger context of legal, economic, ethical, and social structures. Effective decision making within this context requires an ability to assess the implications of those structures for policy decisions. An understanding of economic theory and conditions is encompassed within this segment. National and international social objectives also are important as a foundation for evaluating and implementing strategic plans. This area includes:

- Legal Environment
- Economic Environment
- Ethical and Social Environment

Legal Environment. Statutes, customs, court precedents, and administrative agency regulations constitute aspects of the law with which accountants should be familiar. Of particular concern to management accountants are the effects of the legal environment on an entity's decision-making processes. When specific legal questions are involved, they work with legal counsel to provide information and to assist in assessing courses of action.

Economic Environment. Because accounting measures economic performance, the two fields are closely related, and accounting draws heavily on economic concepts. An understanding of monetary and fiscal theories, national employment objectives, business cycles, and government policies related to spending and economic planning enables accountants to view their own functions from a broader perspective.

Ethical and Social Environment. One distinguishing feature of a profession is that it has a code or standards of ethical conduct by which performance is judged. Accountants' professional standards constitute a facet of the environment in which accountants perform their duties. Social mores also help shape the accounting environment. Management accountants are expected to assess the financial impact of social policies on strategic plans. Of particular importance to accounting are the differences among countries.

Taxation

Some taxes levied by national, state, and local governments are based on accounting concepts; others are based on value added or asset transfers. They are used as sources of revenue and as incentives or disincentives to accomplish political or economic goals. Because taxation influences corporate decisions and because accountants often prepare tax returns, they should be knowledgeable about the impact of taxation, both domestic and international, on financial planning and resource allocation decisions. The following topics characterize this knowledge area:

- Taxation Policies
- Structure and Types of Taxes
- Tax Planning

Taxation Policies. Central to this area is an understanding of the justification for taxation and the system employed to levy taxes. Management accountants must analyze the impact of taxation on an organization's investment, production, and marketing decisions. How particular assets, income, or transfers are defined for tax purposes is critical to an understanding of taxation and its effect on decision making.

Structure and Type of Taxes. Knowledge of principal types of taxes, such as income, property ownership and transfer, sales, and value added, is critical to assessing the impact of taxation on organizational decisions. Although management accountants may not be directly involved in tax law research, tax administration practices, or compliance regulations, they need a general understanding of them to fulfill their responsibilities.

Tax Planning. Because most decisions have tax implications, examining tax alternatives can be a major aspect of decision analysis. Together with tax specialists, management accountants analyze the business alternatives available to an entity and identify courses of action that will minimize the tax burden.

External Reporting

Many management accounting reports are designed for internal use; others are prepared for external users such as shareholders, creditors, financial analysts, and regulatory agencies. Reports issued to shareholders and creditors usually take the form of an annual or quarterly report. Information to other external user groups may have prescribed formats and content that differ markedly from both internal reports and general-purpose financial reports. Management accountants assess the information needs of each group, participate in due process procedures that establish these requirements, and examine any legal and regulatory requirements, particularly those that differ from general reporting practices. The necessary skills can be described under these headings:

- Reporting Standards
- Information Needs of User Groups

Reporting Standards. Understanding the evolution of private-sector standard setting in the United States helps management accountants apply particular standards to reports prepared for internal or external users. The U.S. standard-setting process generally has resulted in broad accounting standards, so management accountants must make extensive use of professional judgment.

For multinational operations, knowledge about national and international standards and the processes by which they are established is essential.

A hierarchy of sources of accounting principles exists, ranging from the authoritative statements and interpretations of the Financial Accounting Standards Board to nonauthoritative sources such as textbooks and articles on accounting matters. Management accountants select the principles used in developing an entity's financial statements; therefore, an understanding of accounting standards, the standards-setting process, and the legislative background is critical. Because management accountants are responsible for the principles, they also should participate in the standards-setting process.

Information Needs of User Groups. A clear distinction exists between the information needs of management and those of various external groups. External users typically are interested in the aggregate performance of the entity, while internal users additionally want to measure the contribution of any number of cost, profit, and other responsibility centers within the entity. Each performance measurement may require different benchmarks for evaluation. Other differences among user groups may result from accounting standards or regulations that mandate reporting requirements. Management accountants must understand these differences in order to discharge their duties effectively.

Information Systems

All segments of the accounting function have been affected by computer technology, so information systems literacy is a significant part of a management accountant's knowledge. A familiarity with the concepts, processes, and security aspects of information and communication systems is important for practicing management accountants. These aspects include:

- Systems Analysis and Design
- Database Management
- Software Applications
- Technological Literacy
- Systems Evaluation

Systems Analysis and Design. An important part of a management accountant's knowledge is a familiarity with how systems are designed. This would include concepts and techniques relating to a system's life cycle: design, implementation, installation, operation, modification, and evaluation. A particular expertise which a management accountant can contribute to the analysis and design of information systems is knowledge of control techniques. This knowledge covers issues relating to security and privacy and to abuse of systems.

Database Management. Database management involves defining, creating, revising, and maintaining integrated files. Management accountants participate in the analysis, design, administration, and management of databases. Knowledge about inputting and accessing transactions on a timely basis, updating data files, and providing protection against unauthorized access is important to effective management of a database.

Software Applications. Rapid technological change has expanded the ways in which computers can be employed in the accounting function. Software can be used to speed up routine aspects of planning, budgeting, and forecasting. Other software is designed to enhance management accountants' analytical, interpretive, and communication skills. Familiarity with generalized software such as spreadsheets, graphics, and statistical packages is an important part of a management accountant's knowledge. Specialized application packages, such as linear programming and materials resource planning, are important decision-support tools for a management accountant.

Technological Literacy. Management accountants should be conversant with the principles and levels of programming languages, without which they cannot communicate effectively with computer analysts or professional programmers. As important users of computer systems, they should be aware of the latest developments in computer technology.

System Evaluation. Organizations establish information systems to provide information for decision making and to ensure adherence to organizational objectives and operational plans. Management accountants test the efficacy of these systems, assessing how well they help an entity meet its objectives. Management accountants also participate in decisions leading to system modification; for example, they evaluate whether an information system provides timely feedback about those factors critical to the successful operation of an organization.

Concluding Observations

The areas of knowledge discussed in this Statement are vital to practicing management accountants. They provide an understanding of the nature and role of management accounting so that contemporary issues and concerns can be evaluated and integrated appropriately to provide comprehensive training.

As is evident from the broad coverage in this Statement, management accounting requires not only procedural and technical skills, but also skill in judgment, in oral and written communications and interpersonal relations, in integrating knowledge from different areas, in identifying important issues, and in developing a thorough understanding of the environment in which entities operate.

This Statement is intended as a foundation on which academic institutions, business and nonbusiness entities, professional associations, and groups internal to NAA can build identifiable programs to serve the practicing and aspiring management accountant.

AD HOC COMMITTEE
ON THE
COMMON BODY OF KNOWLEDGE
FOR
MANAGEMENT ACCOUNTANTS

Chairman
Grant U. Meyers
Chairman & President
The Grandor Corporation
Corsicana, Tex.

Jerry L. Dodson
Senior Vice President-
Corporate Development
Ken's Restaurant Systems Inc.
Tulsa, Okla.

Patricia P. Douglas
Professor of Accounting
and Finance
University of Montana
Missoula, Mont.

James R. Hebdon
Controller
Delco-Remy Division
General Motors Corporation
Anderson, Ind.

Donald T. Hughes
Controller, Corporate Research
and Development Staff
Monsanto Company
St. Louis, Mo.

William J. Ihlanfeldt
Assistant Controller
Shell Oil Company
Houston, Tex.

Thomas E. Martin
Executive Vice President,
Finance and Administration
Ramada Inns, Inc.
Phoenix, Ariz.

Thomas J. Reardon
Vice President-Finance and
Administration
A.J. Ross Logistics, Inc.
Keasbey, N.J.

William G. Shenkir
William Stamps Farrish Professor
University of Virginia
Charlottesville, Va.

George Smith
J.M. Tull Foundation
Atlanta, Ga.

Robert B. Sweeney
Chairman of Accountancy
College of Business Administration
Memphis State University
Memphis, Tenn.

Charles A. Werner
Professor
School of Business Administration
Loyola University-Chicago
Chicago, Ill.

Derrick Willingham
Senior Vice President,
Finance and Administration
Vulcan Industrial
Berkeley Square, London

James Bulloch, *Secretary*
Managing Director
Institute of Certified Management Accountants
National Association of Accountants
Montvale, N.J.

NATIONAL ASSOCIATION OF ACCOUNTANTS
MANAGEMENT ACCOUNTING PRACTICES COMMITTEE
1985-86

Chairman
Bernard R. Doyle
Manager-Corporate Accounting Services
General Electric Company
Fairfield, Conn.

Raymond H. Alleman
Vice President & Comptroller
ITT Corporation
New York, N.Y.

Robert N. Anthony
Professor Emeritus
Harvard Business School
Boston, Mass.

Patricia P. Douglas
Professor of Accounting and Finance
University of Montana
Missoula, Mont.

William J. Ihlanfeldt
Assistant Controller
Shell Oil Company
Houston, Tex.

Eugene H. Irminger
Senior Vice President of Finance
Centel Corporation
Chicago, Ill.

James J. Latchford
*Assistant Vice President &
Assistant Controller*
W. R. Grace & Company
New York, N.Y.

Arthur D. Lyons
Vice President-Controller
FMC Corporation
Chicago, Ill.

Allen H. Seed, III
Senior Consultant
Arthur D. Little, Inc.
Cambridge, Mass.

Norman N. Strauss
Partner
Ernst & Whinney
New York, N.Y.

Edward W. Trott
Partner
Peat, Marwick, Mitchell & Co.
Tampa, Fla.

Robert G. Weiss
Vice President & Controller
Schering-Plough Corporation
Madison, N.J.

NAA STAFF

Louis Bisgay, *Director,* Management Accounting Practices
Jonathan B. Schiff, *Manager,* Management Accounting Practices

Statements on Management Accounting

Statement Number 1E
November 17, 1987

OBJECTIVES

Education for Careers in Management Accounting

In accordance with the charge to the Management Accounting Practices (MAP) Committee to issue statements on management accounting principles and practices, Statements on Management Accounting (SMA) are promulgated to reflect official positions of the National Association of Accountants (NAA). The work of the MAP Committee is based on a framework for management accounting, whose principal categories are:

1. Objectives
2. Terminology
3. Concepts
4. Practices and Techniques
5. Management of Accounting Activities

Statement 1E, *Education for Careers in Management Accounting,* is the fifth Statement issued within the category of *Objectives.*

Statements on Management Accounting

Statement Number 1E
November 17, 1987

Objectives:
Education for Careers in
Management Accounting

National Association of Accountants

Acknowledgments

The National Association of Accountants acknowledges with gratitude the contributions made by the members of the Committee on Education chaired by Donald W. Baker and its Subcommittee on Management Accounting Curriculum in the development of what ultimately was to be published as SMA No. 1E, *Education for Careers in Management Accounting.*

Special thanks are extended to Subcommittee Chairman Grover L. Porter and other members of the Subcommittee: Robert E. Gove, Paul Krause, Lawrence J. Pacl, and Bradley M. Roof.

In addition, appreciation is extended to Donald T. Hughes and Douglas Sharp for their advice regarding the consonance of the management accounting curricula with accreditation guidelines.

Introduction

In 1986, the National Association of Accountants (NAA) published Statement on Management Accounting (SMA) No. 1D, *The Common Body of Knowledge for Management Accountants* (CBOK). The CBOK "identifies the composite subject matter that constitutes the body of knowledge common to management accounting as practiced at the professional level of competency." Among its uses is the provision of overall guidance for structuring a curriculum appropriate for students of management accounting. The suggested curricula contained herein, amplified by the course descriptions that follow, build on the CBOK by giving detailed guidance for educational organizations in developing curricula that will advance the professionalism of management accountants.

History

In 1984, when the president of the NAA first appointed an ad hoc committee for the purpose of developing a common body of knowledge for management accountants, NAA's Committee on Education established a subcommittee to determine whether a need for a management accounting curriculum exists and, if so, to recommend an appropriate curriculum. The subcommittee conducted research and discussed many issues concurrent with the development of the CBOK but deferred proceeding into the final phase of its work until the CBOK was issued by the NAA.

Based on the conclusions and contents of the completed CBOK and the results of its own research, the subcommittee recommended to the Committee on Education that the NAA endorse the subcommittee's suggested curricula for management accountants. The Committee on Education agreed, as did NAA's Executive Committee. Upon review and approval by the Management Accounting Practices (MAP) Committee and its Subcommittee on SMA Promulgation, the suggested curricula and related papers are herein issued by the NAA as SMA No. 1E, *Education for Careers in Management Accounting.*

Significance

Consistent with other NAA publications, the terms *management accounting* and *management accountant* are used in the broad contexts described in SMAs Nos. 1A and 1B. NAA believes the suggested curricula recommended in this publication represent a preferred approach to establishing an educational program designed to prepare graduates for entry into the management accounting profession. As implied by the title, the curricula for management accountants are NAA's recommendation, carefully constructed to be in harmony with the CBOK. NAA offers the curricula with the expectation that they will assist colleges and universities in the development of educational programs and, thereby, strengthen the management accounting profession.

Management Accounting Curricula

The CBOK provides overall guidance for structuring a curriculum for management accountants. With the CBOK as the foundation, the suggested curricula for management accountants recommended in this publication provide guidance for a more specific educational program for aspiring management accountants. Exhibit I provides an overview of the suggested curricula, while course descriptions are presented on the following pages. The course descriptions are designed to provide further insight into the intent of the curricula derived from the CBOK that NAA recommends for undergraduate and graduate accounting education.

General Education

GE1. Communications
> A study of the principles of grammar and their usage in written composition and oral presentations; analysis of written works for logical arrangement, clarity, and interest; development of research techniques and effective library skills.

GE2. Behavioral Sciences
> A study of individual or aggregate human behavior through psychology, sociology, or both.

GE3. Mathematics and Statistics
> A study of mathematics and its relationship to business

EXHIBIT I

MANAGEMENT ACCOUNTING CURRICULA

TOPICS	120 S.H. PROGRAM	150 S.H. PROGRAM
GENERAL EDUCATION[1]		
Communications (GE 1)	9	9
Behavioral Sciences (GE 2)	6	6
Mathematics and Statistics (GE 3)	9	9
Principles of Economics (GE 4)	6	6
Introduction to Information Systems (GE 5)	3	3
Introduction to Accounting (GE 6)	6	6
Other General Education (GE 7)	21	21
	60	60
BUSINESS EDUCATION[1][2]		
The Legal Environment (BE 1)	3	3
The Ethical and Social Environment (BE 2)	3	3
The Global Economic Environment (BE 3)	3	3
Financial Planning and Evaluation (BE 4)	6	6
Technology Management (BE 5)	3	3
Production and Operations Management (BE 6)	3	3
Marketing and Distribution Management (BE 7)	3	3
Human Resources and Behavior (BE 8)	3	3
Quantitative Applications (BE 9)	3	3
Business Communications (BE 10)	3	3
Business Policy (BE 11)	3	3
Other Business Education (BE 12)		0-15
	36	36-51
ACCOUNTING EDUCATION[1][2][3]		
Information Systems (AE 1)	3	6
Managerial/Cost Accounting (AE 2)	6	9
Financial Accounting (AE 3)	6	9
Tax Policies and Planning (AE 4)	3	3
Auditing Concepts and Standards (AE 5)	3	3
Contemporary Accounting Issues (AE 6)[4]	3	3
Internal and Operational Auditing (AE 7)		3
Contemporary Management Accounting Issues (AE 8)[4]		3
Other Accounting Education (AE 9)		15-0
	24	54-39
Total semester hours required for bachelor's degree and master's degree[5]	120	150

[1]Throughout the curricula and especially in "The Global Economic Environment" course, the program focuses on developing a thorough understanding of the domestic and international environment in which entities operate.

[2]The program is flexible enough to allow the completion of either a Master of Accountancy or a Master of Business Administration degree within the framework of the 150-hour curriculum.

[3]The program includes accounting for both profit-oriented and not-for-profit entities.

[4]A student in the 120-hour program may select "Contemporary Management Accounting Issues" instead of the "Contemporary Accounting Issues" course.

[5]NAA recognizes that the importance of ethical considerations and communication skills should be stressed throughout the curricula.

problems and opportunities. Topics addressed include calculus and statistics.

GE4. Principles of Economics

A study of the organization and functioning of national economic systems, including national income, employment, banking systems, and economic policy; also, the study of supply and demand, consumer choice, firm and industrial economics, economics of production and distribution, and international trade.

GE5. Introduction to Information Systems

A study of the principles of management information systems design and operation; emphasis on planning, development, implementation, and control of information systems and integration of computer resources into organization information and decision-support systems.

GE6. Introduction to Accounting

A survey of accounting principles, practices, and decision making in organizations. Topics addressed include managerial, financial, not-for-profit, taxation, international accounting, and development of analytic accounting skills and techniques and their application to decision making.

GE7. Other General Education

A study of liberal arts not addressed elsewhere in the curricula. Disciplines addressed may include but are not restricted to fine arts, humanities, languages, natural sciences, and social sciences. These elective courses are intended to allow students to acquire a broad knowledge of arts and sciences.

Business Education

BE1. The Legal Environment

A study of the American and international legal systems from the standpoint of their sources and philosophies, with special emphasis on relations between businesses and governments' effect upon them.

BE2. The Ethical and Social Environment

A study of business and its relationships with various constituencies; emphasis on: (1) the importance of contemporary ethical issues and problems throughout industry and the business professions and (2) the consideration of ethical issues in domestic and international decision making.

BE3. The Global Economic Environment

A study of aggregate economics: effect of key domestic and international economic variables on employment, production, consumption, investment, saving, monetary supply, foreign exchange, government expenditures, and price levels.

BE4. Financial Planning and Evaluation

A study of theoretical concepts and analytic techniques to aid management decisions on domestic and international financial problems such as working capital and fixed asset management, capital development and maintenance, and profit management; emphasis on solving practical problems through integrated business analysis of the firm and its environment, including financial markets.

BE5. Technology Management

A survey of the domestic and international technological environment of business; emphasis on the role of engineering and management in research and development, capital projects, international technology transfer, and the production and marketing processes.

BE6. Production and Operations Management

A study of production and operations management including planning, organizing, and controlling production processes. Topics include facility location, plant and production-line design, production scheduling, job analysis and design, quality control, inventory management, and project management.

BE7. Marketing and Distribution Management

A survey of the principles involved in domestic and international marketing of goods and services; emphasis on the channels, strategies, and techniques of effective product distribution.

BE8. Human Resources and Behavior

A study of human behavior and motivation in the business organization; behavioral research and literature are analyzed in relation to practical domestic and international organizational management.

BE9. Quantitative Applications

The application of quantitative methods to practical decision making in the business organization; emphasis on decision theory, linear programming, forecasting, queuing, and business simulation.

BE10. Business Communications
The study and application of written and oral business communications including report writing, commercial correspondence, legal agreements and documents, and presentational speaking.

BE11. Business Policy
The study of business strategy and policy and their formulation and implementation; the effect of strategic decisions on the organization and the firm's environment; emphasis on the integration of business disciplines to solve complex domestic and international problems.

BE12. Other Business Education
A study of business topics not addressed elsewhere in the curricula. Disciplines addressed may include but are not restricted to administrative processes, finance, industrial engineering, international business practices, and production. These elective courses are intended to allow students to acquire a broad knowledge of business.

Accounting Education

AE1. Information Systems
The development, use, and evaluation of computer-based information systems to collect, process, analyze, and report information about organizational plans and performance. A study of modern information systems concepts as related to accounting systems design for organizations of differing character and complexity; emphasis on the integration of accounting systems with organizational decision-support systems and other information systems.

AE2. Managerial/Cost Accounting
A study of managerial and cost accounting concepts and their application to the planning and control of the firm; topics include accounting for the production process and supporting activities, performance and productivity measurement, and revenue and cost analysis for decision making. Furthermore, the investigation of modern managerial accounting decision and analytical techniques, integration of managerial accounting and technological innovation, and the effective use of cost accounting information in decision making.

AE3. Financial Accounting

A study of theory, concepts, and financial accounting standards and their application to decision making, including such topics as financial statements, the accounting model, assets, liabilities, stockholders' equity, and other financial accounting issues. A study of the relationships between required financial disclosures and the firm's decision-making processes; emphasis on the effects of accounting principles on decision making, the external disclosure consequences of corporate decisions, and the impact of private sector influence on the regulatory and standard-setting environment.

AE4. Tax Policies and Planning

A survey of domestic and international taxation, philosophy, concepts, legislation, and practices; emphasis on both corporate and individual issues and topics. A study of the influence of federal taxation on the planning, operations, and structure of business enterprise; emphasis on the effects of tax on profit, cash flow, and financial position arising from business decisions and changes in taxation legislation.

AE5. Auditing Concepts and Standards

A survey of financial and operational auditing philosophy and techniques; topics include auditing standards, internal control design and evaluation, statistical applications in auditing, evidence, report writing, governmental role in auditing, legal and ethical issues, and the role of auditing as an agent of organizational change and evolution.

AE6. Contemporary Accounting Issues

A seminar course addressing the most current issues in accounting; emphasis on an in-depth understanding of recent pronouncements and actions of the Financial Accounting Standards Board, Governmental Accounting Standards Board, Internal Revenue Service, Securities & Exchange Commission, National Association of Accountants and other professional associations and the implications of these pronouncements and actions for decision making; preparation and presentation of reports by students.

AE7. Internal and Operational Auditing

A study of the methodology of internal and operational auditing and the utilization of the results of the audit by management in decision making.

AE8. Contemporary Management Accounting Issues

A seminar course addressing the most current issues in management accounting; emphasis on an in-depth understanding of recent Statements by NAA's Management Accounting Practices Committee and other professional organizations and their implications for decision making; preparation and presentation of reports by students.

AE9. Other Accounting Education

A study of accounting topics not addressed elsewhere in the curricula. Disciplines addressed may include but are not restricted to accounting theory, auditing, information systems, international accounting, and taxation. These elective courses are intended to allow students to acquire an in-depth knowledge of accounting.

Concluding Observations

The Certified Management Accountant (CMA) designation is the official recognition of professional competence in management accounting. For those who aspire to attain the CMA certificate and leadership positions in management accounting, NAA encourages completion of the 150-hour model program leading to a master's degree.

The continuing expansion of the scope of management accounting practice and the increasing development of new information concepts remain a dynamic process. NAA believes that, while the prevailing educational standard for collegiate education of accountants is a 120-hour program leading to a baccalaureate, and while many students today find it necessary to enter the employment market after obtaining the bachelor's degree, accounting students of the future will find the 150-hour model program increasingly necessary preparation for a professional career in management accounting.

The curricula outlined in this publication therefore include both 120-hour and 150-hour programs. Irrespective of the quality and the extent of education acquired by students during their collegiate years, those who aspire to leadership positions in management accounting must realize that learning is a lifelong process.

Bibliography

Articles

Deakin, E. and E. Summers, "A Survey of Curriculum Topics Relevant to Management Accounting," *The Accounting Review*, April 1975.

Elnicki, R. A., "The Genesis of Management Accounting," *Management Accounting*, April 1971.

Flesher, D. L. and F. M. McNair, "How Valuable Is the CMA?" *Management Accounting*, November 1985.

Jayson, S. and K. Williams, "CMA: Progress and Prospects," *Management Accounting*, November 1985.

Porter, G. L. and M. D. Akers, "In Defense of Management Accounting," *Management Accounting*, November 1987.

Van Zante, N.R., "Educating Management Accountants: What Do CMAs Think? " *Management Accounting*, August 1980.

Statements

National Association of Accountants, *Statement on Management Accounting No. 1A: Definition of Management Accounting*, NAA, March 19, 1981.

National Association of Accountants, *Statement on Management Accounting No. 1B: Objectives of Management Accounting*, NAA, June 17, 1982.

National Association of Accountants, *Statement on Management Accounting No. 1D: The Common Body of Knowledge for Management Accountants*, NAA, June 3, 1986.

NATIONAL ASSOCIATION OF ACCOUNTANTS
MANAGEMENT ACCOUNTING PRACTICES COMMITTEE
1987-88

Chairman
William J. Ihlanfeldt
Assistant Controller
Shell Oil Co.
Houston, Tex.

Robert N. Anthony
Professor Emeritus
Harvard Business School
Boston, Mass.

Terry M. Ashwill
Vice President & Controller
Ryder System, Inc.
Miami, Fla.

F. Gordon Bitter
Senior Vice President &
Chief Financial Officer
The Singer Co.
Montvale, N.J.

James P. Colford
Director of Accounting Practices
IBM Corp.
Tarrytown, N.Y.

Bernard R. Doyle
Manager—Corporate Accounting
Services
General Electric Co.
Fairfield, Conn.

Robert A. Howell
Clinical Professor of
Management and Accounting
New York University
New York, N.Y.

James J. Latchford
Controller
Chemical Bank
New York, N.Y.

Arthur D. Lyons
Vice President—Finance
FMC Corp.
Chicago, Ill.

Frank C. Minter
Vice President and CFO (Ret.)
AT & T International
Basking Ridge, N.J.

Timothy P. Murphy
Vice President/
Finance—Administration
GTE, Inc.
Stamford, Conn.

John J. Perrell, III
Vice President, Corporate
Accounting & Reporting
American Express Co.
New York, N.Y.

Stanley A. Ratzlaff
Vice President & Controller
Pacific Lighting Corp.
Los Angeles, Calif.

Bruce J. Ryan
Vice President & Controller
Digital Equipment Corp.
Maynard, Mass.

John E. Stewart
Partner
Arthur Andersen & Co.
Chicago, Ill.

Norman N. Strauss
Partner
Ernst & Whinney
New York, N.Y.

Edward W. Trott
Partner
Peat Marwick Main & Co.
Tampa, Fla.

Robert G. Weiss
Vice President & Controller
Schering-Plough Corp.
Madison, N.J.

NAA STAFF

Louis Bisgay, *Director,* Management Accounting Practices
John F. Towey, *Manager,* Management Accounting Practices

Statements on Management Accounting

Statement Number 2
June 1, 1983

Management Accounting Terminology

In accordance with the charge to the Management Accounting Practices (MAP) Committee to issue statements on management accounting principles and practices, Statements on Management Accounting are promulgated to reflect official positions of the National Association of Accountants (NAA). The work of the MAP Committee is based on a framework for management accounting, whose principal categories are:

1. Objectives
2. Terminology
3. Concepts
4. Practices and Techniques
5. Management of Accounting Activities

Statement Number 2
June 1, 1983

Management Accounting Terminology

National Association of Accountants

Preface

This glossary is intended to be a practical guide for understanding terms used in the practice of management accounting. It is designed primarily for management accountants, nonfinancial managers, and students of accounting, all of whom may benefit from succinct explanations of terms often employed. The glossary is not encyclo-pedic in scope but, rather, comprises those terms considered most relevant to management accounting. Some terms have multiple meanings, but only those pertinent to the field of management accounting are included.

Definitions of certain terms relating to external financial reporting are derived from pronouncements recognized as bases of generally accepted accounting principles. Because this glossary is not intended to provide comprehensive guidance in the application of generally accepted accounting principles, readers should refer to complete texts appearing in the authoritative literature, where applicable.

The National Association of Accountants maintains a continuing interest in effective communications and hopes that its glossary contributes to this end. The Management Accounting Practices Committee plans to review the glossary periodically and to make revisions necessary to reflect current practice.

Comments from users are welcomed.

Acknowledgments

Many definitions in the glossary first appeared, in whole or in part, in a series of NAA Statements on Management Accounting Practices issued between 1971 and 1978. Other definitions were obtained from various sources within the literature of accounting, such as Statements of Financial Accounting Concepts and Statements of Financial Accounting Standards issued by the Financial Accounting Standards Board, Accounting Principles Board Opinions and Accounting Research Bulletins (issued by previous constituent groups of the American Institute of Certified Public Accountants), and accounting textbooks.

Because of the extensive interface between management accounting and management information systems, the glossary includes a representative group of terms primarily used in data processing. Many of the definitions are reprinted from publications of International Business Machines Corporation, the Computer and Business Equipment Manufacturers Association, the American National Standards Institute, and the International Organization for Standardization. Permission to reprint is appreciated.

The National Association of Accountants is grateful to the many persons and groups whose past efforts or current cooperation contributed significantly to the publication of the glossary. We are especially grateful to Dr. Norton M. Bedford, Arthur Young Distinguished Professor of Accounting at the University of Illinois, who chaired the subcommittee responsible for the earlier NAA Statements on Management Accounting Terminology.

Management Accounting Terminology

Abandonment Value

The amount that can be realized by liquidating an asset or project before its economic life has ended. See *liquidation value.*

Absorbed Overhead

That portion of factory indirect costs which has been allocated to a specific product or salable service. The allocation process is usually carried out by the application of an appropriate overhead rate to specific units of production.

Absorption Costing

See *full absorption costing.*

Accelerated Cost Recovery System (ACRS)

A method of depreciation, established by the Economic Recovery Act of 1981, that allows for depreciation over periods of 3, 5, 10, and 15 years. These periods are not intended to represent the useful lives of the assets involved, and in most cases will be much shorter than the actual useful lives. Under this system, the concept of salvage value is eliminated in the calculation of depreciation.

Accelerated Depreciation

Any pattern of depreciation that systematically writes off depreciable costs so that progressively smaller amounts are allocated each year.

Access Time*

The time interval between the instant at which an instruction control unit initiates a call for data and the instant at which

All entries marked by an asterisk (*) are quoted from the American National Dictionary for Information Processing.

delivery of the data is completed. Access time equals latency plus transfer time.

Accounting Concepts

Those observations about the economic environment that are pertinent to the development of accounting standards and that explain and guide the preparer's actions in identifying, measuring, and communicating economic information.

Accounting Control

The methods and measures adopted within a business to safeguard its assets and check the accuracy and reliability of its accounting data and financial records. It includes such controls as the system of authorization and approval, physical control over assets, and internal auditing. It also includes controls for separating duties concerned with record keeping and accounting reports from those concerned with operations or asset custody.

Accounting Cycle

The steps involved in recording the effect of transactions and events completed during an accounting period, beginning with the entries in the books of original entry and ending with the reversing entries.

Accounting Manual

A handbook of accounting policies, standards, and practices governing the accounts of a business enterprise; it sometimes includes the classification of accounts.

Accounting Objectives

A set of goals to be achieved through the accounting practices and procedures implemented in a particular organization.

Accounting Policies

"The specific accounting principles and the methods of applying those principles that are judged by the management of the enterprise to be the most appropriate in the circumstances."[1]

---

[1] Accounting Principles Board Opinion No. 22, p. 6, AICPA, New York, N.Y.

Accounting Practices

Practices that are acceptable for implementing accounting standards and that provide for consistent accounting methods for similar activities within the enterprise. Over a period of time a particular accounting practice may come to be recognized as the only appropriate way to deal with a particular situation.

Accounting Principles

See *accounting standards.*

Accounting Principles Board (APB)

Predecessor body to the Financial Accounting Standards Board (FASB) in establishing accounting standards. It was a committee of the American Institute of Certified Public Accountants that was discontinued in 1973.

Accounting Series Release (ASR)

A release issued by the Securities and Exchange Commission setting financial accounting and reporting disclosure requirements for registered companies. The series has been discontinued and replaced by Financial Reporting Releases (FRR).

Accounting Standards

Those rules and conventions that give guidance to the measurement, classification and interpretation of economic information and to the communication of this information through financial statements and reporting. Synonymous with accounting principles.

Accrual Basis

A process whereby revenue is recognized as services are performed and expenses are recognized as efforts are expended or services used, regardless of when cash is received or disbursed.

Accumulated Earnings Tax

A tax imposed by the federal government designed to prevent a taxpayer from using the corporate form of organization to avoid personal income tax. The accumulated earnings tax is assessed on earnings retained (not paid out in dividends) in the business "beyond reasonable needs."[2]

---

[2] Internal Revenue Code, Sec. 533(a).

Acid Test

See *ratios.*

Acoustic Coupler

A type of data communication equipment that permits use of a telephone handset as a connection to a telephone network for data transmission by means of sound transducers.

Acquisition Cost

The cash or cash equivalent value exchanged on the acquisition date to acquire goods or services and have them available for use.

ACRS

See *accelerated cost recovery system.*

Actuarial Gain or Loss

The effects of (a) deviations in the current period between actual experience and the actuarial assumptions used and (b) changes in actuarial assumptions about the future. Actuarial assumptions that may result in actuarial gains and losses include mortality, turnover, early retirement, return on invested assets, and salary increases.

ADR

See *asset depreciation range.*

Algorithm*

(ISO)[3] A set of well-defined rules for the solution of a problem in a finite number of steps, for example, a full statement of an arithmetic procedure for evaluating sin x to a stated precision.

All-Inclusive Income Statement

The notion that all items of revenues, expenses, gains, and losses are included in the income statement rather than charged or credited to retained earnings.

Allocation

The assignment of cost or revenue to one or more segments of

---

[3]All entries with the designation ISO are reprinted by permission of the International Organization for Standardization.

an organization according to expected benefits received, or assigned on some other basis.

Alphanumeric*

Pertaining to a character set that contains letters, digits, and usually other characters, such as punctuation marks. Synonymous with alphameric.

Alternative Cost

The cash or cash equivalent associated with a method of operation that differs from the usual approach. It may refer to a change in the production function, the materials to be processed, or to any change in the operating process.

Amortization

The gradual extinguishment of a deferred charge or a deferred credit by charges or credits to the income statement over two or more periods.

Analog Computer

A computer that solves problems by translating the physical conditions into electrical quantities. It measures continuous electrical or physical magnitudes rather than operating on digits. Contrast with digital computer.

Analytical Review

A review of financial statement ratios, changes in balances from one period to the next, and trends in financial data to obtain a broad understanding of financial position and results of operations and to identify unusual fluctuations and questionable items for further investigation.

Annuity

An agreement providing for a series of economic benefits or cash flows of an amount payable at fixed intervals and normally resulting from an investment in tangible or intangible assets.

Annuity Method of Depreciation

A method of recording depreciation that provides for an imputed interest return on the amount invested in an asset.

APB

See *Accounting Principles Board.*

APL (A programming language)

(SC1)[4] A programming language with an unusual syntax and character set, primarily designed for mathematical applications, particularly those involving numeric or literal arrays.

Application Controls

Controls that relate to a specific data processing activity such as payroll. They are adopted to safeguard the applications' records and to check the accuracy and reliability of the information generated. Their purpose is to provide reasonable assurance that data are properly processed, recorded, and reported. Application controls often are categorized as "input controls," "output controls," and "processing controls."

Applied Research

Research directed at the near-term resolution of practical problems.

Apportionment

The process of spreading revenues and costs among several time periods, functions, products, or other units.

Appraisal

An estimate of the economic value (usually reflecting the expected market price) of a resource, liability, equity, or entity made by an expert after appropriate physical examination, comparative pricing, and engineering review.

Appreciation

An increase in value due to physical changes, aging, or other factors.

Appropriation

An expenditure authorization for the acquisition of assets to meet a present or anticipated need or objective. In government, the

---

[4]All entries designated SC1 are reprinted from a working document of ISO Technical Committee 97/Subcommittee.

legislative authority that obligates government funds to be used for a specific purpose and in a limited amount. In industry, the authorization for specific future capital expenditures.

Asset Depreciation Range (ADR)

Upper and lower limits set by the Internal Revenue Service for asset lives; an asset may be depreciated, for federal income tax purposes, over a useful life selected from within this range, without further justification.

Assets

"[P]robable future economic benefits obtained or controlled by a particular entity as a result of past transactions or events."[5]

ASR

See *Accounting Series Release.*

Attestation Function

The function of certifying or confirming the validity of an assertion or representation of actions and events. An audit normally provides the evidential base for an attestation.

Audit

The systematic examination by analyses, confirmation, and tests of accounting records to confirm with a high degree of confidence that the records adequately reflect economic status and operations. It may be conducted by an internal or external auditor.

Audit Committee

A committee of the board of directors that may have various responsibilities, often including overseeing the financial reporting function, nominating or selecting outside auditors, approving the overall audit scope, reviewing the results of the audit, and reviewing the company's internal controls, including the activities of the internal audit staff.

Audit Evidence

Information acceptable to an auditor that is sufficient (a measure

---

[5]Statement of Financial Accounting Concepts No. 3, "Elements of Financial Statements of Business Enterprises," Financial Accounting Standards Board, Stamford, Conn.

of quantity) and competent (a measure of quality) for an auditor to infer the relative validity of assertions. Audit evidence is sometimes classified into three types: (a) real evidence, for examination of the thing itself; (b) testimonial evidence, for assertions of human beings; and (c) indirect evidence, for all other facts.

Auditing

A systematic and objective process of obtaining and evaluating evidence regarding assertions about economic actions and events. It normally is employed in four types of activities: (1) the attest function, (2) the compliance audit, (3) the internal audit, and (4) the operational audit.

Auditing Procedures

The acts and methods of applying auditing techniques to particular aspects of activities and conditions.

Auditing Standards

Criteria or measures of performance to be observed by auditors throughout the audit process for the attainment of the audit objectives. They serve as the benchmark against which the quality of an auditor's performance can be measured.

Auditor's Opinion

That portion of the auditor's report in which the auditor expresses his conclusions, based upon his professional judgment, regarding the financial statements that were examined.

Auditor's Report

A signed communication between the auditor and addressee that defines the scope of the auditor's examination, including the name of the company, the specific financial statements covered, the period that each financial statement covers, and the nature of the auditor's examination. The report also presents the auditor's opinion regarding those financial statements.

Audit Program

A detailed outline of the verification steps to be performed, specifying the procedures to be followed to verify each item in the financial statements and other records. This program gives the estimated time required, number of persons required, and relative proportions of senior and staff assistant hours.

Audit Trail

A record of documentary evidence of data inputs, ordinarily in large volume, to support the outputs, ordinarily in summary form, of the accounting system. For example, linking a large volume of documents representing individual transactions to summary figures would represent an audit trail.

Audit Work Papers

The papers on which the auditor records information about the work done, methods and procedures followed, and conclusions developed. In the work papers, which assume a wide variety of forms and arrangements, the auditor collects the basis for his[6] report, evidence of the extent of his examination, and documentation of the due audit care exercised in his investigation.

Automatic Check

See *hardware check*.

Avoidable Cost

An ongoing cost that may be eliminated by ceasing to perform some economic activity or segment thereof or by improving the efficiency by which such activity is accomplished.

Backlog

The orders on hand that have not been shipped or otherwise converted to revenue.

Bad Debts

Accounts or notes receivable that management determines to be uncollectible after a reasonable effort to collect has been attempted without success. When such determination has been made, the receivable is credited. If the company is on the reserve method, the allowance account is debited. For companies on the direct write-off (charge-off) method, the debit is to profit and loss.

Balance Sheet

The statement of financial position that discloses the assets, liabilities, and owners' equity accounts of an entity as of one particular date.

---

[6]To enhance readability of the definitions, the pronouns "he" and "his" are used rather than "he/she" or "his/her". The reader has, of course, the option to substitute "she" or "her" as appropriate.

BASIC (Beginner's All-Purpose Symbolic Instruction Code)

(SC1) A programming language with a small repertoire of commands and a simple syntax, primarily designed for numerical applications.

Basic Research

Research that is intended to contribute to fundamental knowledge.

Basic Standard Cost

A standard cost used as a reference point for comparison with new standard costs developed to accommodate changing price or business conditions.

Basket or Lump Sum Purchase

The purchase at a single price of a group of distinguishable assets without any specific designation of the acquisition cost of each asset.

Batch Processing*

(1) (ISO) The processing of data or the accomplishment of jobs accumulated in advance in such a manner that each accumulation thus formed is processed or accomplished in the same run. (2) Processing of data accumulated over a period of time. (3) Loosely, the execution of computer programs serially. (4) Pertaining to the technique of executing a set of computer programs such that each is completed before the next program of the set is started. (5) Pertaining to the sequential input of computer programs or data. (6) In realtime systems, the processing of related transactions that have been grouped together.

Betterment

An expenditure that is expected to improve materially the useful life, quality or quantity of output, or operating costs of an existing fixed asset.

Bill of Materials

A list of direct materials allowed for the production of a given output. Such a listing may also reflect the standard costs applicable to the materials and an allowance for scrap or spoilage.

Binary Code*

A code that makes use of exactly two distinct characters, usually 0 and 1.

Binary Digit

See *bit*.

Bit*

(ISO) In the pure binary numeration system, either of the digits 0 and 1. Synonymous with binary digit.

Bond Indenture

The bond contract between the corporation and bondholder.

Book Value

The amount at which an asset or a liability is carried on the books of account, net of any contra account; sometimes referred to as net book value.

Breakeven Analysis

An analysis of the functional relationship of cost and revenue. It characteristically emphasizes the point in output at which there is neither profit nor loss and the influence of fixed and variable factors on the profit expectations at various levels of operation.

Breakeven Chart

A chart showing the profit or loss associated with volume when sales price per unit is constant, some expenses are fixed, and some expenses vary directly with sales. The breakeven point indicates where revenues equal expenses and profits are zero.

Budget

A quantification of planned future revenues and expenses to establish objectives for revenues, expenses, assets, liabilities, and the like. A budget provides guidelines for future operations and the appraisal of performance.

Budgetary Authority

The authority to spend the amount in a budget.

Budgetary Control

The actions necessary to ensure that budget objectives, plans, policies, and standards are attained or are revised.

Budget Calendar

A list of dates indicating when specific information useful in the preparation of a budget is to be presented by one information source to others. The calendar is so structured that information cumulates until the complete budget is issued at a specified date.

Budget Ceiling

The initial proposed allowance provided to develop a budget.

Budget Control Basis

The classification of budgeted costs or expenses as variable, semivariable, and fixed. The purpose of the classification is to establish a basis for adjusting the budgeted items and to provide a budget cost allowance for a budget center under flexible or variable budgetihg.

Budget Cost (Expense) Allowance

The amount of cost or expense that a budget center or other budgetary entity is authorized to incur during a budget period.

Budget Cycle

The recurring sequence of activities involved in the preparation of a budget for a period of time or a project.

Budgeting

The process of planning all flows of financial resources into, within, and from an entity during some specified future period. It includes providing for the detailed allocation of expected available future resources to projects, functions, responsibilities, and time period.

Budget Manual

A set of instructions for the development, preparation, and use of a budget for a specific enterprise or industry.

Budget Period

The period of time for which plans should be reduced to budget form for guidance.

Budget Revision Variance

See *variances.*

Budget Variance

See *variances.*

Buffer

A storage device used to compensate for the difference in rates of flow of data from one device to another, e.g., from an input/output device to the central processing unit.

Burden

All factory costs other than direct labor and direct material, generally referred to as factory overhead. Factory overhead typically includes indirect labor, factory supplies, supervisors' salaries, maintenance, utilities, depreciation on plant and manufacturing equipment, and the like.

Business Combinations

The bringing together of two or more business entities into a single entity.

By-product

(1) A secondary product recovered in the course of manufacturing a primary product. (2) A product whose total sales value is relatively minor in comparison with the sales value of the main product(s).

Byte

(1)* A binary character operated upon as a unit and usually shorter than a computer word. (2) The internal representation of a character.

Callable Bond

A bond redeemable at the option of the corporation.

Capacity

As used in information processing, the number of characters that can be stored in a computer memory, which is defined in terms of bytes. 1K=1,024 bytes. If the storage capacity of a computer is 16K, the capacity is 16,384 characters (1,024 x 16). See *character.*

Capacity Cost

The fixed cost of an entity resulting from the need to provide operating facilities to process material and services.

Capacity Ratio

See *ratios.*

Capacity Variance

See *variances.*

Capital

(1) The amount invested in an entity by its owners. (2) The net assets: total assets less liabilities.

Capital Addition

The physical addition of a new part of an existing resource so that the service capacity of the resource is increased. It does not include replacements of old parts with new, improved parts nor does it include increases in service capacity that do not arise from the adding of a physical part.

Capital Budget

A list, frequently ranked, of all approved long-range projects on which expenditures will be made to improve the operating capacity or efficiency of an entity. Contrast with operating budget.

Capital Budgeting

A process for evaluating proposed long-range projects or courses of future activity for an economic entity for the purpose of allocating limited resources to desirable projects.

Capital Consumption

The using up of capital through wear and tear, obsolescence, or accidental damage.

Capital Expenditure

An amount spent to acquire a long-term asset.

Capital Lease

See *lease.*

Capital Leverage

A company's ability to generate an additional return for stock-holders by borrowing, then using the borrowed funds to obtain a return greater than the interest rate; the excess thus accrues to the stockholders.

Capital Maintenance Concept

The idea that before income can emerge, revenues must be adequate to maintain the productive capacity of the entity.

Capital Rationing

A process by which the capital of the firm is divided among various projects or departments. The rationing may be done by an intuitive assignment, but in its more analytic mode the allocation is accomplished by the use of such standards as a minimum level for rate of return or net present value results. By intent, those activities which best justify their claim for support should receive the greatest relative share in the pool of limited capital.

Carryback and Carryforward

The use of losses or tax credits to reduce taxes payable in previous (carryback) or future (carryforward) periods.

CASB

See *Cost Accounting Standards Board.*

Case Study

A type of descriptive research in which the researcher analyzes in detail a person, event, or thing. Such research is often used to test a theory or provide a data base.

Cash Basis

A basis of keeping accounts, whereby revenue and expenses are reflected when they are received and paid, without consideration of the period to which they apply.

Cash Budget

A period-by-period statement of cash on hand at the start of a budget period; expected cash receipts classified by source; expected cash disbursements classified by function, responsibility, and form; and the resulting cash balance at the end of the budget period.

Cash Equivalent

(1) A monetary valuation of noncash payments or receipts measured in terms of current market cash price. (2) A readily marketable security that is convertible to cash almost instan-taneously.

Cash Flow

The stream of cash inflows and outflows of a specific entity or segment of operation. Analytically the presentation of cash flow should identify the timing, amount, and source of the related cash movements.

Catalog

(1) (ISO) A directory of locations of files and libraries. (2)* An ordered compilation of item descriptions and sufficient informa-tion to afford access to the items. (3) The collection of all data set indexes that are used by the control program to locate a volume containing a specific data set. (4) (ISO) To enter information about a file or a library into a catalog. (5) To include the volume identification of a data set in the catalog.

Central Limit Theorem

A theorem of statistical inference, it states that the distribution of means of random samples approaches a normal distribution as the sample size is increased.

Centralized Management

An organizational approach in which a supervising function maintains significant direction and authority over operations and policies relating to a number of identifiable, separate activities and operations. Centralized management allows only minimal areas for decision making at the level of the separate units.

Central Processing Unit (CPU)

(ISO) A unit of a computer that includes circuits controlling the interpretation and execution of instructions.

Certificate in Management Accounting (CMA)

A professional designation awarded by the Institute of Manage-ment Accounting to an accountant who has met the require-ments of the Institute, including satisfactory completion of a comprehensive examination in economics and business finance;

organization and behavior; public reporting standards, auditing, and taxes; periodic reporting for internal and external purposes; and decision analysis, including modeling and information systems.

Channel

(1)* (ISO) In information theory, that part of a communication system that connects the message source with the message sink. Mathematically, this part can be characterized by the set of conditional probabilities of occurrence of all the possible messages received at the message sink when a given message emanates from the message source. (2)* A path along which signals can be sent, for example, data channel, output channel. (3)* The portion of a storage medium that is accessible to a given reading or writing station, for example, track, band. (4) (SC1) In data transmission, a means of one-way transmission. (5) A device that connects the processing unit and main storage with the I/O control units.

Channel, Duplex

A channel providing simultaneous transmission in both directions.

Channel, Half Duplex

A channel capable of transmission in both directions, but only one direction at a time.

Channel, Simplex

A channel that permits transmission in one direction only.

Character*

(1) (ISO) A member of a set of elements upon which agreement has been reached and that is used for the organization, control, or representation of data. Characters may be letters, digits, punctuation marks, or other symbols, often represented in the form of a spatial arrangement of adjacent or connected strokes or in the form of other physical conditions in data media. (2) A letter, digit, or other symbol that is used as part of the organization, control, or representation of data. A character is often in the form of a spatial arrangement of adjacent or connected strokes.

Character Display Device

(ISO) A display device that gives a representation of data only in the form of characters; synonymous with read-out device.

CMA

See *Certificate in Management Accounting.*

Coefficient of Correlation

An indication of the relationship between numerals that represent dependent and independent variables.

Coefficient of Variation

A relative measure of the dispersion in a probability distribution. It is calculated as the standard deviation of the distribution divided by the arithmetic mean of the distribution.

Combined Financial Statements

Financial statements that are combined for a commonly controlled group of companies, or a group of companies under common management influence. Where the units do not have an investment interest in each other, combined financial statements are prepared on the same basis as consolidated financial statements except that an investment interest does not exist. Intercompany transactions, balances, and profit or loss should be eliminated.

Comfort Letter

A statement by certified public accountants in connection with a securities offering, given to the underwriter and legal counsel, asserting that the CPA has no information to indicate that the company's financial statements are false or misleading.

Committed Costs

Those fixed costs arising from the possession of plant and equipment and a basic organization and thus affected primarily by long-run decisions as to the desired level of capacity.

Common Cost

A cost of resources employed jointly in the production of two or more outputs; the cost cannot be directly assigned to those outputs. Customarily, assignment is made through a series of consistent allocation procedures.

Common-Size Statement

A statement that shows the separate items appearing on it in percentage form rather than in dollar form. The preparation of common-size statements is known as vertical analysis.

Common Stock Equivalent

A security that is not, in form, a common stock but that usually contains provisions to enable its holder to become a common stockholder. Because of its terms and the circumstances under which it was issued, it is in substance equivalent to a common stock. The holders of these securities can expect to participate in the appreciation of the common stock's value. This appreciation results principally from the earnings and earnings potential of the issuing corporation.

Communicating Word Processor

A standard word processing device equipped with a telecommunication facility to permit text transmission, inquiry to CPU data base, and electronic mail.

Communication Controller

A type of communication control unit whose operations are controlled by a program stored and executed in the unit.

Comparability

A characteristic of information that makes it possible to assess similarities, differences, and trends in a meaningful way.

Compile*

(1) (ISO) To translate a computer program expressed in a problem-oriented language into a computer-oriented language. (2) To prepare a machine language program from a computer program written in another programming language by making use of the overall logic structure of the program, or generating more than one computer instruction for each symbolic statement, or both, as well as performing the function of an assembler. (3) To translate a source program into a series of instructions in machine language; an object program.

Complementary Products

Those products for which changes in production or sales of one good create similar (i.e., high positive coefficient of correlation) changes in the volume of other goods within a reasonable period of time.

Completed Contract Method

A method that recognizes income or loss from long-term construction-type contracts only when the contract is completed, or substantially so. Accordingly, costs of contracts in process and current billings are accumulated, but there are no interim charges or credits to income other than provisions for losses. See *percentage of completion method.*

Compliance Audit

A systematic process of objectively obtaining and evaluating evidence regarding assertions, actions, and events to ascertain the degree of correspondence between them and established performance criteria.

Component Part

An essential, distinct part of an asset, organization unit, or operating process.

Comprehensive Budgeting

The use of a systematic and formalized approach to the budgeting process to plan, coordinate, and control all activities of an entity. It is an integrated approach for reducing to budget form all the objectives and efforts of the entity for the purpose of coordinating all activities.

Computer Architecture

The organization of a computer's registers, memory elements, and other components.

Computer Language*

(ISO) A computer-oriented language whose instructions consist only of computer instructions. Synonymous with machine language.

Conceptual Scheme

A set of concepts interrelated by hypothetical and theoretical propositions.

Condensed Financial Statements

Summary financial statements developed by aggregating customary financial accounts into broader categories.

Conditional Probability

The probability of an event given that the event possesses certain characteristics that distinguish it from some but not all possible events that might occur.

Confidence Interval

The interval of numbers within which the true or actual results should be within specified limits. For example, if one is 95% confident that the true value of the inventory is between $100,000 and $110,000, the confidence interval will be $10,000.

Configuration

In Systems Network Architecture (SNA), the group of links, nodes, machine features, devices, and programs that make up a data processing system, a network, or a communication system.

Confirmation

A written or oral statement from a third party, in response to an auditor's request, as to the accuracy of information.

Conservatism

"A prudent reaction to uncertainty to try to ensure that uncertainty and risks inherent in business situations are adequately considered."[7]

Consistency

Continued uniformity, during a period or from one period to another, in methods of accounting, mainly in valuation bases and methods of accrual, as reflected in the financial statements of the entity.

Console*

A part of a computer used for communication between the operator or maintenance engineer and the computer.

---

[7]Statement of Financial Accounting Concepts No. 2, "Qualitative Characteristics of Accounting Information," Financial Accounting Standards Board, Stamford, Conn.

Consolidated Financial Statements

Financial statements that include results of operation, changes in financial position, and financial position of a parent company and its subsidiary or subsidiaries. They are presumed to be more meaningful than separate statements, and they are intended primarily for the parent company's investors rather than for minority stockholders and subsidiary creditors. Financial statements of subsidiaries are not consolidated if the parent company's control is deemed to be temporary or if control does not lie with the parent (as in the case of bankruptcy) or if the operations of the subsidiary differ greatly from those of the parent company. Consolidated reporting emphasizes the economic entity rather than the legal entity. Currently generally accepted accounting principles prescribe methods of consolidated reporting, including:

(1) *Full consolidation*—consolidated financial statements are prepared when the parent controls the voting interest of over 50% in a subsidiary. They are prepared by combining, on a line-by-line basis, the amounts that appear in the separate financial statements of the parent and subsidiary companies. In the combining process, however, certain adjustments are made to eliminate the effects of intercompany transactions and thus to reflect the assets, liabilities and stockholders' equity from the viewpoint of a single entity.

(2) *Equity method*—referred to as a one-line consolidation, the equity method reports investment income in a single amount on one line of the investor's income statement (except when the investee has extraordinary items that require separation and disclosure) and the investment balance in a single amount on one line of the investor's balance sheet.

Constant Dollar Accounting

A method for restating various elements of financial statements in dollars of the same purchasing power; this method uses an appropriate index.

Constraint

An activity, resource, or policy that limits or bounds the attainment of an objective.

Contingent Liabilities

Potential obligations for which the resolution depends upon some future events which are uncertain or for which the amount is so uncertain that it cannot be reasonably estimated. Only those liabilities which are probable and reasonably measurable are appropriate for inclusion in financial statements:

Continuous Budget

A budget that adds a time period in the future as the time period just ended is dropped. See *multiple budget.*

Contract Costing

The measurement of the cost of the goods and services used in complying with the provisions of an agreement between a buyer and seller.

Contributed Capital

The amount paid in and left in the business by stockholders for use by the business in exchange for shares of stock. The part of stockholders' equity contributed by the shareholders plus an amount capitalized as a result of stock dividends. Thus, total stockholders' equity less retained earnings is equal to contributed (paid-in) capital. It normally would include capital stock accounts for the par or stated value of outstanding shares and paid-in capital in excess of par or stated value.

Contribution Approach

A method of preparing income statements that separates variable costs from fixed costs to emphasize the importance of cost behavior patterns for purposes of planning and control.

Contribution Margin

The excess of sales prices over variable costs. Also referred to as marginal income. It may be expressed as a total, as a ratio, or on a per unit basis.

Control Group

The group of elements among several groups tested in an experiment that has not been subjected to some type of experimental activity. The effect of the "manipulation" may be determined by noting how the control group reaction differs from the experimental group.

Controllable Cost

A cost that may be directly regulated at a given level of managerial authority, either in the short run or in the long run.

Control Total

A sum, resulting from the addition of a specified field from each record in a group of records, that is used for checking machine, program, and data reliability. Synonymous with hash total.

Conversational

Pertaining to a program or a system that carries on a dialog with a terminal user, alternately accepting input and then responding to the input quickly enough for the user to maintain his train of thought. See *interactive*.

Conversational Mode

(ISO) A mode of operation of a data processing system in which a sequence of alternating entries and responses between a user and the system takes place in a manner similar to a dialog between two persons. Synonymous with interactive mode.

Conversion

(1) "The exchange of one currency for another."[8] (2) The process of changing from one method of data processing to another or from one data processing system to another. (3) The process of changing from one form of representation to another, e.g., to change from decimal representation to binary representation. (4) The process of transforming raw materials and purchased parts into a salable finished product.

Conversion Cost

The sum of direct labor, indirect materials, and factory overhead which is directly or indirectly necessary for transforming raw materials and purchased parts into a salable finished product.

Convertible Bonds

Bonds that, under the terms of the bond indenture, may be exchanged, at the option of the holder and subject to specified limitations of time, rate of exchange, and other conditions, for common stock or another security of the issuer.

Copy*

(ISO) To read data from a source, leaving the source data

---

[8]Statement of Financial Accounting Standards No. 52, "Foreign Currency Translation," Financial Accounting Standards Board, Stamford, Conn.

unchanged, and to write the same data elsewhere in a physical form that may differ from that of the source.

Cost

The cash or cash equivalent value required to attain an objective such as acquiring the goods and services used, complying with a contract, performing a function, or producing and distributing a product.

Cost Accounting

A technique or method for determining the cost of a project, process, or thing used by the majority of the legal entities in a society, or specifically prescribed by an authoritative accounting group.·This cost is determined by direct measurement, arbitrary assignment, or systematic and rational allocation.

Cost Accounting Standard

A guideline or principle that indicates how a specific cost should be determined or assigned to cost objectives for a specific purpose. Such a standard seeks to assure that the cost of a product or activity is determined or estimated on an accurate, verifiable, comparable and uniform basis. The goal is an equitable and reasonable determination or estimate of cost.

Cost Accounting Standards Board (CASB)

Government regulatory agency once responsible for setting cost accounting standards which must be followed by companies involved in certain government contracts; the agency has been defunct since 1980.

Cost Allocation

A process of classifying costs into categories at the time of acquisition and into their subsequent reclassification as costs of activities, products, responsibilities or other cost objectives.

Cost-Benefit Analysis

A tool for planning and reporting that involves the identification and measurement of all costs and benefits attributed to an activity.

Cost Center

A grouping of operating costs having some common characteristics for measuring performance and assigning responsibility.

Cost Measurement

An assignment and accumulation of monetary amounts in accordance with cost accounting standards for the recognition, classification, and assignment to goods and services acquired or used in complying with the requirements of a reporting objective. This measurement may be based on physical observation or careful estimation.

Cost Objective

A function, organizational subdivision, contract, product, or other unit for which arrangement is made to accumulate and measure cost. It includes any specified act or group of acts planned, in process, or completed for which costs are to be measured.

Cost of Capital

The overall cost of capital of the firm; it is composed of the costs of the various components of financing which, for a particular firm, might be:

(1) *Cost of equity capital:* the minimum rate of return that a company must earn on the equity-financed portion of its investments in order to leave unchanged the market price of its stock and to compensate investors for the risk of their investment.

(2) *Cost of debt:* the interest rate investors require on debt issues, adjusted for the reduction of income taxes payable because interest expense is deductible in the computation of taxable income.

(3) *Cost of lease financing:* a form of financing due to the contractual nature of lease obligations. It is used in place of other methods of financing to acquire the use of an asset. An alternative method of financing might be to purchase the asset and finance its acquisition with debt. In analyzing the alternatives, a comparison should be made of the present value of future cash outflows for each financing method.

Cost of Money

The payment necessary to induce a supplier of funds to provide cash. When paid for on a periodic basis according to agreement, the cost of money is referred to as interest.

Cost Pool

An aggregation of indirect costs for the purpose of identification with or allocation to segments, cost centers, processes, or products. Cost pools often are established to facilitate the use of a particular cost allocation method by grouping items having a common basis.

Cost to Buy

All past, present, and future direct and indirect costs, measured in terms of cash or cash equivalents, needed to purchase the ownership interest in a resource capacity and have it available for operations. This term often is used in make-or-buy and buy-or-lease analysis.

Cost to Lease

The cost required under a lease to acquire the right to use a resource capacity and have it available for operations. This term often is used in buy-or-lease analysis.

Cost to Make

The amount of resources sacrificed, measured according to cost accounting standards on the date used, in the manufacture of product or performance of service. The costs of all direct and indirect services used in developing the resource to the point where it is available for use are a part of the cost to make. This term often is used in make-or-buy analysis.

Cost-Volume-Profit Analysis

The study of the effects on profits of changes in fixed costs, variable costs, sales quantities, sales prices, and sales mix.

Coupon Bond

A bond to which interest coupons are attached; the coupons may be clipped and presented by the bearer for payment when due.

CPU*

Central processing unit.

Cross-Sectional Analysis

An analysis of all of a particular situation or state of affairs of a composite group of things at one moment in time in order to obtain a detailed description of conditions at that moment.

CRT Display*

Cathode ray tube display.

Current Assets

Cash and other assets that are expected to be sold, converted into cash, or otherwise consumed during the normal operating cycle of a business or within one year, whichever is longer.

Current Cost Accounting

(1) "A method of measuring and reporting assets, and expenses associated with the use or sale of assets, at their current cost or lower recoverable amount at the balance sheet date or at the date of use or sale."[9]

(2) A method of revaluing elements of financial statements to the current cost of reproducing or repurchasing certain assets and expense items.

Current Liabilities

Liabilities expected to be discharged by using current assets within one year or the operating cycle, whichever is longer, or transferred to income in a relatively short period of time.

Current Operating Concept

A concept underlying the preparation of the income statement. Only those items that consist of revenues, expenses, gains, and losses that are ordinary and recurring are included in the income statement.

Current Ratio

See *ratios.*

Current Standards

Those basic standard costs that have been adjusted for changes in the business environment (e.g., fluctuating price levels and varying quality) as of or close to the date of presentation.

Current Value Accounting

An approach to accounting that combines aspects of economic theory with the conventional accounting method based on his-

---

[9]Statement of Financial Accounting Standards No. 33, "Financial Reporting and Changing Prices," Financial Accounting Standards Board, Stamford, Conn.

toric costs. Current value income models use current market prices which are incorporated in the traditional accounting format. Current value accounting takes two forms:

(1) *Replacement cost accounting*—based on the current acquisition value of assets; in effect, assets are valued at their current entry price.

(2) *Realizable value accounting*—based on the current realizable value of assets; that is, assets are valued at their current exit price.

Cursor

(1) (SC1) In computer graphics, a movable visible mark used to indicate a position on a display space. (2) A movable spot of light on the screen of a display device, usually indicating where the next character will be entered.

Cycle*

(1) An interval of space or time in which one set of events or phenomena is completed. (2) Any set of operations that is repeated regularly in the same sequence. The operations may be subject to variations on each repetition.

Cycle Count

A continuous counting of stock items throughout the year. The cycle count tests the condition of inventory records and provides a measure of record accuracy. A limited number of items are checked every day or at some other time interval.

Data

Facts which, by analysis and association, can be developed into useful information.

Data* (Data Processing)

(1) (ISO) A representation of facts, concepts, or instructions in a formalized manner suitable for communication, interpretation, or processing by humans or automatic means. (2) Any representation such as characters or analog quantities to which meaning is, or might be, assigned.

Data Bank*

(1) (ISO) A set of libraries of data. (2) A comprehensive collection of libraries of data. For example, one line of an invoice may form

an item, a complete invoice may form a record, a complete set of such records may form a file, the collection of inventory control files may form a library, and the libraries used by an organization are known as its data bank.

Data Base*

(1) (ISO) A set of data, part of the whole of another set of data, and consisting of at least one file, that is sufficient for a given purpose or for a given data processing system. (2) A collection of data fundamental to a system. (3) A collection of data fundamental to an enterprise.

Data Elements

An area in a record allotted to a group of characters containing one unit of information; synonymous with data field.

Data Encryption

A telecommunication security measure that involves the encoding of data, either through hardware or software, to "scramble" them or make them unintelligible during transmission. The data are decoded upon receipt.

Data Field

See *data elements.*

Data Management*

(1) The function of controlling the acquisition, analysis, storage, retrieval, and distribution of data. (2) In an operating system, the computer programs that provide access to data, perform or monitor storage of data, and control input/output devices.

Data Organization

The arrangement of information in a data set. For example, sequential organization or partitioned organization.

Data Processing*

(ISO) The execution of a systematic sequence of operations performed upon data, e.g., handling, merging, sorting, computing. Synonymous with information processing.

Data Processing System*

(ISO) A collection of methods, procedures, or techniques united by regulated interaction to form an organized whole.

Data Protection

As used in information processing, a safeguard against the loss or destruction of data.

Data Transmission*

(SC1) The conveying of data from one place for reception elsewhere by signals over a channel.

Days' Sales in Inventory

See *ratios.*

Days' Sales Outstanding

See *ratios.*

Debenture

A bond representing a general claim against all unencumbered assets rather than a specific claim against particular assets.

Debt Ratio

See *ratios.*

Debug*

(ISO) To detect, to trace, and to eliminate mistakes in computer programs or in other software.

Decentralized Management

An organizational approach in which the headquarters function maintains minimal direction and authority over operations and policies relating to a number of identifiable separate activities and operations. Decentralized management allows great freedom for decision making at the level of the separate units.

Decision Model

A formal framework, which may involve quantitative analysis, for making a choice among alternatives.

Decision Table*

(1) (ISO) A table of all contingencies that are to be considered in the description of a problem, together with the actions to be taken. (2) A presentation in either matrix or tabular form of a set of conditions and their corresponding actions.

Deductive Reasoning

A logical process of arriving at a conclusion that must be true if the premises are true. For example, "all books are educational; x is a book; therefore x is educational." Contrast with inductive reasoning.

Deferral Method

A method of accounting for the investment tax credit under which the ITC is reflected as a reduction of tax expense over the productive life of the asset acquired. See *flow-through method.*

Deferred Charges

The unamortized cost of acquiring an intangible asset, such as prepaid insurance.

Deferred Credits

(1) Generally applied to revenues received or recorded but which have not yet been earned; also called "deferred revenue." (2) The term also may refer to certain other balance sheet items with credit balances, such as deferred income taxes payable and premium on bonds payable.

Deferred Income Taxes

The estimated amount of income taxes that may become payable or receivable in future periods due to timing differences in recognizing items of revenue or expense. A timing difference occurs because of differences between financial reporting and reporting for income tax purposes.

Demographic Data

Data regarding personal characteristics of subjects as a group.

Department Budget

The expenditures and resource utilizations, classified in some detail for overall control and coordination, authorized for a department for a period of time.

Depletion

The process of allocating the cost of wasting assets (natural resources) to expense over the periods benefiting from the expenditure.

Depreciation

The process of allocating the cost of tangible assets to operations over periods benefited.

Descriptive Accounting Theory

A theory of accounting based on the belief that empirical research must be used to establish facts and relationships that can be used to build an empirically based theoretical structure of accounting thought. Contrast with normative accounting theory.

Development Costs

Economic sacrifices necessary to place in an operating state the results of a research effort. Only sacrifices necessary for the initial application of the operating process qualify as development costs.

Diagnostic Program*

(ISO) A computer program that recognizes, locates, and explains either a fault in equipment or a mistake in a computer program.

Dial-Up Line

A hookup that establishes a connection, through a public-switched telephone network, between two terminating devices.

Differential Cost

Changes in total costs which are attributable to alternative courses of action.

Digital Computer*

(1) (ISO) A computer in which discrete representation of data is mainly used. (2) A computer that operates on discrete data by performing arithmetical and logical processes on these data. (3) Contrast with analog computer.

Direct Access

(1) (ISO) The facility to obtain data from a storage device, or to

enter data into a storage device, in such a way that the process depends only on the location of those data and not on a reference to data previously accessed. (2) Contrast with sequential access.

Direct Access Storage

(ISO) A storage device that provides direct access to data.

Direct Access Storage Device

A device in which the access time is effectively independent of the location of data.

Direct Charging

The assignment of costs of goods and services to specific activities with a reasonable degree of certainty that the activities receiving the charge cause it. Although a degree of estimating may be tolerated, a strong aspect of observable economic reality is fundamental to the procedure.

Direct Costing

A type of product costing in which the cost assigned to a unit of inventory includes only the cost of inputs that vary directly with the number of units produced and that are used in the creation or modification of the unit. Only the directly variable product costs are chargeable to inventory. Contrast with full absorption costing.

Direct Financing Lease

See *lease.*

Direct Labor

The cost of labor that can be directly identified with specific products.

Direct Materials

The direct materials, by specific types of material, required to manufacture the finished goods.

Disclosure

The process of making available information about a business entity. Disclosures are generally through an explanation or exhibit attached to a financial statement or embodied in a report which is helpful in interpretation of the statement or report.

Discounted Cash Flow

A valuation of investment projects by adjusting cash flows for the time value of money using such techniques as internal rate-of-return or net-present-value.

Discovery Sampling

A statistical sampling plan which provides an assurance, at a prescribed confidence level, of finding at least one deviation from the normal expectation, if the deviations exist to a significant degree in the field. Also called exploratory sampling.

Discretionary Cost

A cost that a decision maker must periodically review to determine that it continues to be in accord with ongoing policies.

Disk Operating System (DOS)

An operating system that uses disks to assemble, edit, and execute programs.

Distributed Processing

A general term, usually referring to the use of intelligent or programmable terminals at sites remote from a company's main computer facility but linked to that facility via telecommunications.

Diversified Company

An organization which is engaged, at a significant level and on a continuing basis, in dissimilar lines of business concurrently. Such an enterprise may be organized into segments, such as subsidiaries, divisions, or departments, that operate in different industries.

Documentation

All of the physical evidence gathered to support a procedure or a conclusion.

Documentation* (Data Processing)

(ISO) The management of documents, which may include the actions of identifying, acquiring, processing, storing, and disseminating them.

Dollar Unit Method

The LIFO accounting method that uses dollars as the unit of measure rather than quantities of specific goods. Compares the investment in inventory by groups at the beginning of the year when LIFO was adopted with the investment at the end of the year stated in terms of dollars of the same price level. There is no comparison of quantities of individual items, and the relative inventory quantities are determined only by aggregate dollar amounts allocated to the inventories.

DOS

See *disk operating system.*

Due Audit Care

The care used by a prudent auditor—one whose degree of skill represents the standard of performance required of a practitioner—in the conduct of an audit. It is the care a prudent auditor would exercise in planning and performing an audit.

Due Diligence

The diligence of prospective buyers who obtain sufficient information on a securities offering. In general, "due diligence" meetings are held in the financial community in which most prospective buyers are located. The purpose of the meeting is to give prospective bidders an opportunity to meet with company officials and make sure that the bidders have used "due diligence" in obtaining all information affecting the securities which will be sold to the public.

Earnings

The excess (deficit) of revenue over expenses for an accounting period, which is the net increase (net decrease) in owners' equity (assets minus liabilities) of an organization for an accounting period from profit-directed activities. Sometimes used synonymously with net earnings, net income, and income.

Earnings Per Share

The amount of earnings for a period of time divided by the average number of shares of common stock or common stock equivalents outstanding.

Economic Life

The time period over which the use of an asset is economically justified. It is normally expressed as the period of time that revenues from the productivity of an asset exceed the cost of that productivity. Economic life is typically shorter than physical life and frequently shorter than useful life.

Economic Model

A symbolic, usually mathematical, representation of the activities of an entity. Variation in the assumptions and constraints can be used to predict or monitor actual operations.

Economic Order Quantity

The number of units of inventory that should be ordered at one time in order to minimize the expected annual costs of the inventory system.

Edit*

(ISO) To prepare data for a later operation. Editing may include the rearrangement or the addition of data, the deletion of unwanted data, format control, code conversion, and the application of standard processes such as zero suppression.

Efficiency Variance

See *variances.*

Empirical Analysis

An examination of data to determine relationships.

Empirical Research

Research consisting of the collection, examination, and analysis of "real world" data to draw inferences and make generalizations about the real world or to validate hypotheses.

Employee Stock Option

The rights of employees to acquire a specified number of shares of stock under specified conditions.

Emulation

The use of programming techniques and special machine features to permit a computing system to execute programs written for another system. Contrast with simulation.

End User

The ultimate source or destination of information flowing through a system. An end user may be an application program, an operator (such as a terminal user or a network operator/ administrator), or a data medium (such as cards or tapes).

Engineered Standards

Cost standards determined by use of engineered measurements and formula rather than by estimates or historic references as to cost.

Entity

An individual, partnership, corporation, or other organization that has a separate distinct identity and serves as a unit for which the accounting takes place.

Equity Method

See *consolidated financial statements.*

Error Control Procedure

(SC1) In data communication, that part of the link protocol controlling the detection, and possibly the correction, of transmission errors.

Error Detecting Code*

A code in which each expression conforms to specific rules of construction, so that if certain errors occur in an expression, the resulting expression will not conform to the rules of construction and, thus, the presence of the errors is detected. Synonym for self-checking code.

Estimated Standards

Cost standards determined by use of judgmental estimates and historic references that may not be highly correlated to specific engineering data. Often they are used to avoid the cost of preparing engineered norms or as a prelude to completing such effort.

Estimation Sampling

The use of techniques to collect samples that are representative of an entire population and that can be used to form an opinion about an estimate of certain population values.

Estimation Sampling for Attributes

A method of forming an opinion about the attributes or quality characteristics of items in the population under audit based on an estimation of the frequency of occurrence of this characteristic in the items in the statistical sample.

Estimation Sampling for Variables

The estimation of the value of a group of items using a sample which provides, at some confidence level, a range of upper and lower limits within which the true population mean falls.

Evaluation Period

A period of time during which a process is observed for purposes of comparing actual performance to planned performance.

Exception Message

In communicating with a logical unit, a message that indicates an unusual condition, such as a sequence number being skipped.

Exception Reporting

Reporting which calls to management's attention only those situations that violate predetermined standards or policies. Its essential characteristic is that it reports only events presumed to require action.

Excess Capacity

Productive capacity in excess, on a relatively long-term basis, of that needed to supply the demand. It should be distinguished from "idle capacity" which relates only to short-term imbalances in operational schedules.

Exchange Rate

The price of one national currency in terms of another.

Execution Time

The time during which an instruction is decoded and performed.

Expected Value

The weighted average of the outcomes of an action where the outcomes are weighted by their probabilities.

Expenditure

An outlay of cash or cash equivalent for goods or services or in settlement of an obligation.

Expenses

"[O]utflows or other using up of assets or incurrences of liabilities (or a combination of both) during a period from delivering or producing goods, rendering services, or carrying out other activities that constitute the entity's ongoing major or central operations."[10]

The cost of goods, services, and facilities used or absorbed in the generation of current revenue. Expenses are deducted from revenue in determining net earnings. The expenses of a period can be costs associated with the period on some basis other than a direct relationship with revenue and costs that cannot, as a practical matter, be associated with any other period.

Experimental Design

The plan for conducting a research experiment that will relate relevant variables in an experiment to each other.

Experimentation

A process of investigation characterized by the physical manipulation of certain variables while holding other variables constant and the observation of the impact of the manipulation on outcome variables.

Explanation

A goal of science involving a demonstration of the relationship among phenomena in a manner consistent with obtained evidence and verified laws or principles.

Exploratory Sampling

See *discovery sampling.*

---

[10]Statement of Financial Accounting Concepts No. 3, "Elements of Financial Statements of Business Enterprises," Financial Accounting Standards Board, Stamford, Conn.

Ex-Post Research

Research in which causal inferences are based on reasoning retrospectively from effects to causes.

External Validity

The extent to which the results of a research project can be used under situations and conditions beyond the experiment.

Extraordinary Items

Material items of gain or loss characterized by their infrequency of occurrence and their unusual nature.

Extraordinary Repairs

Substantial expenditures made to restore a fixed asset to productive capacity after a breakdown due to an accident, misuse, neglect, or excessive use. The effect of these expenditures is to restore excessive depreciation of assets over and above that covered by ordinary repairs. They restore an existing fixed asset to normal operating efficiency and are distinguished from betterments, additions, and improvements, which add to operating capacity.

Face Amount (or Value)

The amount of nominal value stated on the face of an instrument, such as a bond or share of capital stock. Such amount may differ from the fair market value.

Facsimile Equipment (FAX)

Terminal equipment for direct hard-copy transmission of images via telecommunications for reproduction at a remote site.

Factory Burden

See *burden*.

Factory Overboard

See *burden*.

Factory Overhead Budget

A prediction of all production costs for a budget period, except direct material and direct labor costs, classified by responsibility, function, or form.

Fair Market Value

The exchange price that would prevail for a good or service traded in an active market consisting of a large number of well-informed buyers and sellers.

Fairness

The idea that accounting procedures and resulting financial statements should be appropriate, provide adequate disclosure, and serve no special interests. A guideline of financial accounting and reporting which provides that the statements should conform to accepted principles and that no group should have undue influence on the procedures or reporting practices followed.

Fair Presentation

A general term indicating that financial statements are free from material misstatements and omissions and include the information necessary to interpret them properly.

Fair Value

A reasonable or equitable valuation based on all pertinent facts.

FASB

See *Financial Accounting Standards Board.*

FAX

See *facsimile equipment.*

Field

As used in information processing, a subdivision of a record, usually consisting of a single item of information related to the rest of the record. For example, a punched card often is divided into several fields.

Field Experiment

A type of experimental research in which the variables of interest are controlled and varied but the research context is taken as given.

Field Study

A type of research in which the researcher observes relationships as they occur without significantly intervening in the research setting.

FIFO

See *first-in, first-out.*

File*

(ISO) A set of related records treated as a unit; e.g. in stock control, a file could consist of a set of invoices.

File Maintenance

The process of updating, adding, and deleting records in a file to reflect changes.

File Protection

Prevention of the destruction of data recorded on a volume by disabling the write head of a unit.

File Safeguards

Controls that are concerned with safeguarding data files. These controls can be classified into five broad categories: (1) physical safeguards, (2) procedural controls, (3) retention plan, (4) reconstruction plan, and (5) protection against accidental or purposeful disclosure, modification, or destruction of information maintained on file.

Financial Accounting Standards Board (FASB)

Private sector agency established in 1973 and responsible for setting generally accepted accounting principles.

Financial Fixed Charge Coverage

See *ratios.*

Financial Information

That information, monetary or nonmonetary, necessary to interpret the cause and effect of actual or planned business and economic actions, activities, or asset and liability valuations.

Financial Leverage

The extent to which the assets of an entity are financed with debt.

Financial Reporting Release

See *Accounting Series Release.*

Finished Goods

Completed product, ready for sale or other disposition.

First-In, First-Out (FIFO)

An inventory flow assumption based on the movement of goods. The stock of merchandise or material that is acquired earliest is assumed to be used first; the stock acquired latest is assumed to be still on hand. Contrast with Last-In, First-Out.

Fiscal Year

Any accounting period of 12 successive calendar months, 52 weeks, or 13 four-week periods.

Fixed Assets

Noncurrent, nonmonetary tangible assets used in normal operations of a business.

Fixed Budget

A budget for a time period that assumes periodic expenses are not affected by the level of output or activity.

Fixed Cost

An operating cost that does not vary with changes in the level of activity over a relevant range of such activity.

Fixed-Length Record

A record having the same length as all other records with which it is logically or physically associated. Contrast with variable-length record.

Flexible Budgeting

A budget structure in which the budget amounts may be adjusted to any activity level. It may be a variable budget or a step budget, in which a series of detailed financial budgets is developed. From this series, a budget appropriate for any level of actual activity can be selected to evaluate actual expense and cost performance. See *variable budgeting.*

Floating-Point

A representation system in which the number to be represented is converted to a two-part number or expression, which is called the normalized form. The first part is the fractional part, called the mantissa because of the similarity to the mantissa in a logarithm. The second part is the exponent, which is the power to which the computer numbering system base is raised to make the expression equal to the original number. Using the exponent times a fraction method of expressing a number, the exponent can vary and then the point can float correspondingly, not changing the value of the number. When the point falls just to the left of the high-order one bit of the fraction, the expression is normalized.

Flowchart*

(ISO) A graphical representation for the definition, analysis, or method of solution of a problem, in which symbols are used to represent operations, data, flow, equipment, etc. Synonymous with flow diagram.

Flow Diagram

See *flowchart.*

Flow-Through Method

A method by which the investment tax credit is reflected as a reduction of tax expense in the financial statements in the year it is recognized. See *deferral method.*

Footnotes

Supporting detail regarding financial statement items, usually a narrative, and considered to be an integral part of the statements.

Forecasting

A process of predicting or projecting a future event or condition.

Foreign Corrupt Practices Act of 1977

A law enacted to regulate the conduct of American businesses and businessmen in foreign countries. There are two provisions to the Act:

(1) The antibribery provision makes it a criminal offense for any U.S. business enterprise—whether or not incorporated or publicly held—to offer a bribe to a foreign official, foreign political

party, party official, or candidate for foreign political office for the purpose of obtaining, retaining, or directing business to any person.

(2) The accounting standards provision establishes certain standards with respect to a company's books and records and, of significant importance, the system of internal accounting controls. Unlike the antibribery provisions, however, these standards apply to all companies subject to the reporting requirements of the Securities Exchange Act of 1934 (whether or not business is conducted in a foreign country).

Foreign Currency Transaction (Conversion) Gains and Losses

Gains and losses resulting from those transactions whose terms are stated in a currency other than the entity's functional currency. A change in exchange rates between the functional currency and the currency in which a transaction is denominated increases or decreases the amount of functional currency to be obtained upon settlement of foreign currency receivables or required to settle foreign currency payables. That increase or decrease in functional currency cash flows is an exchange gain or loss which would be included in determining net income for the period.

Foreign Currency Translation

The process of translating financial statement amounts expressed in different currencies to a common currency.

Foreign Currency Translation Gains and Losses

Gains and losses that result from the process of expressing, in the reporting currency of the entity, financial statements that are denominated or measured in a different currency. Adjustments that result from translating foreign entities' financial statements (whose functional currency is other than the U.S. dollar) would not be included in determining net earnings but would be accumulated, net of related tax effects, and reported as a separate component of stockholders' equity.

Formatted Display

On a display device, a display in which the attributes of one or more display fields have been defined by the user.

Free-Form

Pertaining to entry of data or the coding of statements without regard for predefined formats.

Fringe Benefit Rate

Fringe benefits expressed as a percentage of payroll.

Frequency Distribution

The grouping of all classes of the population by the number of elements in each class.

Full Absorption Costing

A costing system whereby direct materials, direct labor, and all elements of manufacturing overhead (fixed and variable) are absorbed into inventory. Contrasted with direct costing.

Full Consolidation

See *consolidated financial statements.*

Full Cost

The total direct and indirect sacrifice or effort applied to acquire, produce, or distribute a product or service.

Fully Diluted Earnings Per Share

The amount of earnings that may be attributed to each share of common stock given the maximum extent of potential conversions of convertible securities outstanding.

Function

A relation, frequently in equation form, that associates with each element of one group of things one or more elements in another group of things.

Functional Accounting

An accounting system (principally used by utilities) that accumulates costs and assets for each service provided or function performed.

Functional Budget

A budget in which expenses and revenues are classified according to functions of the enterprise.

Functional Costing

The measurement and identification of costs with the general type of economic activity in which the related sacrifices are made; e.g., manufacturing, selling, financing, and administrative expenses.

Functional Currency

"[T]he currency of the primary economic environment in which the entity operates; normally, that is the currency of the environment in which an entity primarily generates and expends cash."[11]

Functional Tests

The tests used to provide reasonable assurance that the controls necessary to assure the reliability of data are adequate in number and are functioning. Functional tests provide the basis for determining the nature, extent, and timing of substantive tests.

Function Key

(1) (SC1) In computer graphics, a button or switch that may be operated to send a signal to the computer program controlling the display. (2) A key on a terminal, such as the attention key, that causes the transmission of a signal not associated with a printable character. Detection of the signal usually causes the system to perform some predefined function for the user.

Funded

A reserve offset by segregated cash, securities, or other assets, available only for a stated purpose.

Future Costs

Estimations of the future prices and future quantities of goods and services necessary to attain a future, in-process, or completed objective. It is not the current cost of goods and services purchased for future delivery. For comparison with current or historical costs, future costs must be discounted to their present value.

GAAP

See *Generally Accepted Accounting Principles.*

---

[11]Statement of Financial Accounting Standards No. 52, "Foreign Currency Translation," Financial Accounting Standards Board, Stamford, Conn.

Gain

The net favorable effect of a nonoperating transaction or event. An increase in net assets (and equity) resulting from a nonoperating transaction or event in which the value of the consideration received exceeds the carrying value of any consideration given.

Generalizations

The process of making inferences about the entire population based on sample data collected and analyzed.

Generally Accepted Accounting Principles (GAAP)

The body of accounting rules, methods, and procedures that is sanctioned by the accounting profession, either by convention or by the authoritative literature, as a guide to the preparation of financial statements.

General Price-Level Adjusted Statements

Financial statements restated to eliminate the effect of changes in the general price level.

Goal

An objective established to coordinate and direct a group of individuals in the pursuit of desired activities.

Going Concern

The assumption that, in the absence of evidence to the contrary, a firm will continue to exist for the forseeable future.

Goodwill

Characteristics of a business entity, not individually identifiable, which permit it to earn some type of above-normal returns on the identifiable assets. An asset account which appears as the result of acquiring a business entity for an amount in excess of the fair value of the identifiable net assets. See also *negative goodwill*.

Gross Income

Total revenue, before deducting cost of goods sold or other expenses.

Gross Profit

Net sales less cost of goods sold.

Hardware Check

(1) A failure in a hardware unit that halts operation. (2)* Synonym for automatic check.

Hardware Controls

Controls that are built into the computer by the manufacturer. These controls are usually based on the concept of redundancy, in which an element is added to a code or a separate operation is added to a process merely for the purpose of error detection. These controls are all automatic and include: (1) redundant character, (2) duplicate processes, (3) echo check, (4) validity check, and (5) equipment check. The term is synonymous with machine controls.

Hardwired

Pertaining to a physical connection or characteristic; for example, the address of a console or I/O device.

Hash Total*

The result obtained by applying an algorithm to a set of data for checking purposes, e.g., a summation obtained by treating data items as numbers.

Header Record

A record containing common, constant, or identifying information for a group of records that follows.

Hedge

A form of price-fluctuation insurance, often built into a contract, that transfers the risk of fluctuating prices to other parties. It may also be achieved by a process of simultaneous sale and purchase of rights to goods and services for delivery at different dates.

High-Level Language

(ISO) A programming language that does not reflect the structure of any one given computer or that of any given class of computers.

Highly Inflationary Economy

An economy with "cumulative inflation of approximately 100 percent or more over a three-year period."[12]

---

[12]Statement of Financial Accounting Standards No. 52, "Foreign Currency Translation," Financial Accounting Standards Board, Stamford, Conn.

High-Order Position

The leftmost position in a string of characters.

Historical Cost

The amount originally. paid for an asset, unadjusted for subsequent changes in value.

Holding Gains or Losses

Unrealized gains or losses from holding assets or liabilities during a period of changing prices. See *current value accounting*.

Host Computer

(1) The primary or controlling computer in a multiple computer operation. (2) A computer used to prepare programs for use on another computer or on another data processing system; for example, a computer used to compile, link, edit, or test programs to be used on another system. (3) The primary or controlling computer in a data communication system.

Host Processor

The central or controlling processing unit in a multiple processing unit configuration.

Host System

(1) A data processing system used to prepare programs and the operating environments for use on another computer or controller. (2) The data processing system to which a communication system is connected and with which the system can communicate.

Housekeeping

(1) In data processing, operations or routines that do not contribute directly to the solution of the problem but do contribute directly to the operation of the computer. (2) Routine processing operations such as opening and closing of files and file maintenance.

Human Resource Accounting

The process of accounting for the investment in and benefits derived from the utilization of human resources in a business.

Hurdle Rate

The minimum acceptable rate of return that companies will consider from a prospective project or investment. The hurdle rate is generally in excess of a company's cost of capital and usually includes an inflation factor to be considered for the life of the project or investment.

Hypothesis

A declarative statement having some intuitive validity that attempts to explain or predict a relationship.

Ideal Capacity

The highest level of goods and services that can be provided by a specific set of resources operating under perfect conditions throughout a given time period.

Ideal Cost

The minimum cost that would result if all productive inputs combined to achieve an output level at the maximum end of the feasible range.

Because of its premise of technological perfection, such cost is meaningful only in a relative and not in a practical sense.

Idle Capacity

The practical level of operating capacity which exceeds, on a short-term basis, the current level of production.

Idle Capacity Variance

See *variances.*

Idle Time

A measure of wages paid for a period of unproductive time. Idle time results from circumstances or conditions that the worker cannot prevent and which therefore reduces the productive output of a plant or segment thereof for a specified period of time.

Imputed Cost

A cost properly attributed to a cost objective even though no actual transaction occurred which would be recognized in the accounting records. Imputed costs are not-ordinarily reflected in the accounting records.

Imputed Interest

An amount of interest assumed to be included in the face amount due on a note when the note does not carry an explicit rate of interest that is reasonable.

Income

See *earnings.*

Incremental Cost

The difference in cash flow, both as to amount and as to time of flow, between two alternative courses of action. Incremental cost is the additional cost caused by some specific project or group of projects as compared with some specific base case or reference standard.

Incremental Revenue

The additional revenue, either as to amount or as to timing, that results from pursuing an alternate course of action.

Independence

An auditor's mental attitude or state of mind of being unbiased and impartial in all professional activities. Independence ensures that a professional audit can be relied upon by users; it also enables the auditor to act and appear to act with integrity and objectivity.

Indirect Audit Evidence

Knowledge or facts that have objective properties and can be used by auditors to ascertain the degree of correspondence between economic actions and events and representations of such phenomena. Indirect evidence does not include facts that originate from the examination of the thing itself or facts that originate from the assertions of human beings.

Indirect Costs

Costs common to a multiple set of cost objectives and not directly assignable to such objectives in a specific time period. Such costs are usually allocated by systematic and consistent techniques to products, processes, or time periods.

Inductive Reasoning

The method of arriving at general conclusions from a series of specific facts. The process of generalization takes the following form:

Occurrence one of event A is accompanied by activity X.

Occurrence two of event A is accompanied by activity X.

Occurrence three of event A is accompanied by activity X—(Repetitive similar occurrences)—Therefore all occurrences of event A are accompanied by activity X [the generalization from particular facts].

Contrast with deductive reasoning.

Inference

A proposition derived by reasoning from other propositions or from evidence. The activity of developing propositions not included in facts but which may be deduced, postulated, or extracted from data.

Information Evaluation

The evaluation of alternative sets of data in terms of their costs and benefits where benefits reflect the information content of the data sets.

Initialize

To set counters, switches, addresses, or contents of storage to zero or other starting values at the beginning of, or at prescribed points in, the operation of a computer routine.

Initial Program Load

(1) The procedure that causes an operating system to begin operation. (2) The process by which a configuration image is loaded into storage at the beginning of a work day or after a system malfunction.

Input Controls

Control measures that relate to a specific data processing activity and that serve as controls over the inputs and the input phase of a data processing system. They include controls that relate to rejection, correction, and resubmission of data that were initially incorrect. They are designed to provide reasonable assurance that no data (including data transmitted over communications lines) have been omitted through loss or suppression and that the data received for processing by EDP are properly authorized, converted into machine-sensible form, and identified.

The possible areas where data input errors could occur are the following: (1) at the points of creation of input and conversion to machine-readable form, (2) at the point when data are first put into the computer, and (3) at the points where the data are moved or transmitted in the organization.

Input/Output Bound

A characteristic of a computer system that is restricted by the speed of its input/output devices, and in which the CPU stands idle a certain percentage of the time.

Input Stream

The sequence of job control statements and data submitted to an operating system on an input unit especially activated for this purpose by the operator. Synonymous with input job stream, job input stream.

Inquiry

A request for information from storage; for example, a request for the number of available airline seats, or a machine statement to initiate a search of library documents.

Installation

(ISO) A particular computing system, in terms of the work it does and the people who manage it, operate it, apply it to problems, service it, and use the results it produces.

Installment Sales

Sales in which the selling price is collected in several payments (installments).

Intangible Assets

Noncurrent assets lacking physical existence for which the service potential is expected to extend beyond the current period and for which the value derives from benefits conferred upon the owner.

Interactive

Pertaining to an application in which each entry calls forth a response from a system or program, as in an inquiry system or an airline reservation system. An interactive system may also be conversational, implying a continuous dialog between the user and the system. See *conversational mode.*

Interest

The cost incurred or amount earned for the use of borrowed capital.

Interface

As used in information processing, a shared boundary, e.g., the boundary between two systems or devices.

Interim Financial Reports

Reports on the financial aspects of activities and status of an entity between annual reporting dates. They may include complete financial statements, significant highlights of the organization's activities and status, and other data indicative of enterprise performance, risk, and changes. Information on revenue, expense, extraordinary items, and other accounting statement items is developed and disclosed according to principles and standards used in preparing conventional reports. The purpose of interim reports is to provide information indicative of attained enterprise progress and status and changes in process during the conventional reporting period. Interim reports reduce the lag between the time activities occur and their disclosure in accounting reports.

Internal Auditing

An appraisal activity within an organization that measures the extent to which organizational goals are met. Internal auditing is usually concerned primarily with financial and accounting matters and secondarily with other operations; it is performed by the employees of the organization under audit. Internal auditing is concerned with the effectiveness and reliability of operating reports to management and functions primarily as a service to management.

Internal Check

The coordinated methods and measures in an organization designed to check the accuracy and validity of organization data and to safeguard assets. It is part of the plan of internal control.

Internal Control

The plan of organization and all of the coordinate methods and measures adopted within a business to safeguard its assets, check the accuracy and reliability of its accounting data, promote operational efficiency, and encourage adherence to prescribed managerial policies.

Internal Rate of Return

That percentage of return on a specific investment which equates the present value of the projected net cash inflows of a project with that of the investment outlay.

Internal Storage

(ISO) Storage that is accessible by a computer without the use of input/output channels.

Internal Validity

The existence of an empirical research investigation under conditions such that the observed outcomes are caused by the specific experimental conditions.

Interperiod Tax Allocation

See *tax allocation.*

Interrupt

(1)* To stop a process in such a way that it can be resumed. (2) In data transmission, to take an action at a receiving station that casues the transmitting station to terminate a transmission. (3) (ISO) A suspension of a process, such as the execution of a computer program, caused by an event external to that process and performed in such a way that the process can be resumed.

Intraperiod Tax Allocation

See *tax allocation.*

Inventories

Goods held for sale, semifinished products, and materials and supplies not yet expensed or consumed.

Inventory Control

An approach to safeguarding and assuring the effective and

efficient acquisition and use of inventory. Inventory control systematically employs accounting documents and relates them to a physical review of factory and distribution operations.

Inventory Turnover

See *ratios.*

Investment

An expenditure to acquire property—real or personal, tangible or intangible—yielding income or services.

Investment Center

A unit responsible for expenses, revenues, and investment.

Investment Tax Credit (ITC)

A reduction of income taxes based upon the investment in specified depreciable assets acquired during the year.

ITC

See *investment tax credit.*

Job Control Language

A task-oriented language designed to express statements that identify a job or describe its requirements to an operation system. JCL is required for the following purposes: (1) to identify the job, (2) to identify the end of the source program, (3) to identify the end of the data, and (4) to identify the end of the job.

Job Cost Sheet

The detailed record for the accumulation of job costs, e.g., the material, labor, and overhead cost incurred on a job or specific production.

Job Order Costing

A method of cost accounting in which costs for material, labor and overhead (either actual or standard) are charged to a specific job or lot. The job or lot may consist of either a single unit or like units and pertains to either goods or services, such as check clearing in banks, mail sorting in post offices, food preparation in fast-food outlets, and premium handling in insurance companies.

Job Step

(1)* The execution of a computer program explicitly identified by a job control statement. A job may specify that several job steps be executed. (2) A unit of work associated with one processing program or one cataloged procedure and related data. A job consists of one or more job steps.

Job Stream

(ISO) The sequence of representations of jobs to be submitted to an operating system. Synonymous with input stream, run stream.

Joint Products

Two or more products so related that one cannot be produced without producing the others, each having relatively substantial value and being produced simultaneously by the same process up to a "split-off" point.

Joint Venture

A partnership between two or more persons, corporations, or other entities formed to carry out a single project and usually dissolved upon completion of the project.

Journal

A book of original entry that records transactions in chronological sequence.

Justification

The act of adjusting, arranging, or shifting digits to the left or right to fit a prescribed pattern.

Key

(ISO) One or more characters, within a set of data that contains information about the set, including its identification.

Keyboard

(1) A systematic arrangement of keys by which a machine is operated or by which data are entered. (2) A device for the encoding of data by key depression, which causes the generation of the selected code element.

Keyword

(1)* One of the predefined words of an artificial language. (2) One of the significant and informative words in a title or document that describe the content of that document. (3) A symbol that identifies a parameter. (4) A part of a command operand that consists of a specific character string (such as DSNAME=).

Laboratory Experiment

A type of experimental research in which both the variables of interest and the research setting are controlled by the researcher.

Labor Rate Variance

See *variances.*

Last-In, First-Out (LIFO)

A method of inventory valuation and costing based on the flow of costs theory, and the concept that a relatively permanent quantity of inventory is required to operate a business. It assumes that costs of the earliest purchases are applicable to the goods on hand, and the latest acquired stock is assumed to have been used immediately. It attempts to match current costs of obtaining inventory against current revenues. Contrasted with First-In, First-Out.

Last-In, First-Out Dollar Value

A form of LIFO inventory accounting with inventory quantities (layers) measured in dollars, rather than in physical terms. Adjustments to account for changing prices are made by use of a specific price index appropriate for the kinds of items in the inventory.

Last-In, First-Out Inventory Layers

When the ending inventory for a period is larger than the beginning inventory, this increase in physical quantities is given a value determined by the prices of the earliest purchases during the year (under a LIFO cost flow assumption). The LIFO inventory then consists of tiers, or layers, which typically consist of relatively smaller amounts of physical quantities from each of the past several years. Each layer carries the prices relative to the period of acquisition. The earliest layers will typically (in periods of rising prices) have prices very much less than current prices. If inventory quantities should decline in a subsequent period, the layers enter costs of goods sold first.

Last-In, First-Out Reserve

An unrealized holding gain in ending inventory; measured as the difference between LIFO and FIFO.

Learning Curve

The curve or line on a chart that shows the relationship between the level of output and some measure of learning or experience; the latter measure may be total number of units produced to date, time on the job, amount of training, and so forth.

Lease

Lease has been defined and reviewed in FASB Statement 13 and its amendments and interpretations. Definitions of specific related terms follow:

Capital lease—a lease that transfers substantially all the benefits and risks inherent in the ownership of the property to the lessee, who accounts for the lease as an acquisition of an asset and the incurrence of a liability. The lessor accounts for such a lease as a sale or financing arrangement.

Direct financing lease—a lease that does not result in a manufacturer's or dealer's profit (or loss) to the lessor, but does transfer substantially all the benefits and risks inherent in the ownership of the leased property to the lessee.

Leveraged lease—a lease in which a significant portion of the acquisition cost of the property to be leased is provided by a third party debt participant (lender). The lease is leveraged in the sense that the lessor, while borrowing most of the cost of the leased property, may deduct depreciation expense, interest on the loan, and perhaps an investment tax credit to offset the lease rental payments. Typically the lender could repossess the lease property.

Operating lease—a lease in which the risks or rewards of ownership remain with the lessor. The related rental payments are customarily recorded as an expense by the lessee and as rental income by the owning lessor during the time of use.

Sale leaseback—The sale of property by an owner and its subsequent lease back to the seller.

Sales-type lease—a lease that usually results in a manufacturer's or dealer's profit (or loss) to the lessor. This type of lease transfers substantially all the benefits and risk inherent in the ownership of the leased property to the lessee.

Ledger

A book in which transactions involving a particular account (i.e., cash) are recorded. A separate ledger is maintained for each balance sheet and income statement account.

Level of Statistical Significance

The probability that an obtained outcome of a research study could occur by chance. A .05 level would mean that in only 5 times in 100 repetitions of the experiment would it be probable for the outcome to be due to chance.

Leveraged Lease

See *lease.*

Liabilities

"[P]robable future sacrifices of economic benefits arising from present obligations of a particular entity to transfer assets or provide services to other entities in the future as a result of past transactions or events."[13]

LIFO

See *Last-In, First-Out.*

Light Gun

See *light pen.*

Light Pen

(SC1) In computer graphics, a photosensitive stylus used to identify display elements or to detect the light generated within an aiming symbol. Synonymous with light gun.

Linear Programming

A mathematical technique for allocating limited resources among activities for the attainment of goals. The measure of performance is a linear function of the controllable variables, and restrictions on the use of resources may be expressed as linear equations or inequalities.

---

[13]Statement of Financial Accounting Concepts No. 3, "Elements of Financial Statements of Business Enterprises," Financial Accounting Standards Board, Stamford, Conn.

Line Budgeting

The classification of budgeted expenses and revenue into account titles used in accounting reports, with separate detailed budgets explaining the content of each account or line in the list of budget items.

Line of Business

A set of operations directed to the production and distribution of a distinctive type of good or service to customers. A line of business need not be completely independent of other lines, but it must be separable at some point in the production and distribution process.

Closely related goods and services used by similar types of customers are combined into one line of business. Delivery of a good or service to customers is a prerequisite for a line of business.

Link*

(ISO) In computer programming, the part of a computer program, in some cases a single instruction or an address, that passes control and parameters between separate portions of the computer program.

Link-Chain Index

A method of determining an annual index for use in computing inventory amounts on the LIFO basis. The overall change in cost levels is measured first on an annual basis and then is multiplied by the last previously determined cumulative index.

Liquidating Dividend

(1) A pro rata distribution to stockholders or owners of an organization in liquidation, out of funds becoming available from winding up a business. (2) A pro rata distribution to stockholders representing a return of capital from a company that has wasting assets.

Liquidation Value

The market price in cash or cash equivalents that could be obtained in the event of an immediate requirement to discontinue ownership of an asset

Load

(1)* (ISO) In programming, to enter data into storage or working registers. (2) To bring a load module from auxiliary storage into main storage for execution. (3) In DOS, to bring a program phase from core image library into main storage for execution.

Local Terminal

A terminal connected by a cable rather than by a data link.

Long-Form Audit Report

A report normally prepared by independent auditors for use by management. It usually includes a statement of the scope of the examination and the auditor's opinion; the principal financial statements and accompanying footnotes; supplementary information comprising analytical schedules and ratios, comparative schedules, and statements; and other financial and accounting matters of interest to the client, as well as a discussion of the company's financial position, changes in financial position, and operating results.

Loop*

(1) (ISO) A set of instructions that may be executed repeatedly while a certain condition prevails. (2) In data communication, an electrical path connecting a station and a channel.

Loss

"[D]ecreases in equity (net assets) from peripheral or incidental transactions of an entity and from all other transactions and other events and circumstances affecting the entity during a period except those that result from expenses or distributions to owners."[14]

Lower of Cost or Market

A method of valuation that results in the asset's being valued at either acquisition cost or current replacement cost, whichever is lower.

Low-Order Position

The rightmost position in a string of characters

---

[14]Statement of Financial Accounting Concepts No. 3, "Elements of Financial Statements of Business Enterprises," Financial Accounting Standards Board, Stamford, Conn.

Machine Controls

See *hardware controls.*

Machine Language

See *computer language.*

Magnetic Ink Character Recognition (MICR)*

(ISO) The character recognition of characters printed with ink that contains particles of a magnetic material. Contrast with optical character recognition.

Maintenance

Expenditures necessary to achieve the originally anticipated useful life of a fixed asset. Maintenance is concerned with restoration or prevention of destruction of parts of a property that deteriorate at a rate faster than the whole property unit.

Maintenance (Data Processing)

(1)* (ISO) Any activity, such as tests, measurements, replacements, adjustments, and repairs, intended to eliminate faults or to keep a functional unit in a specified state. (2) Those activities intended to keep a machine in, or restore a machine to, good working order.

Major Control Field

The most significant control field in a record; the control field upon which sorting according to the collating sequence is first attempted.

Management Accounting

"[T]he process of identification, measurement, accumulation, analysis, preparation, interpretation, and communication of financial information used by management to plan, evaluate, and control within an organization and to assure appropriate use of and accountability for its resources. Management accounting also comprises the preparation of financial reports for non-management groups such as shareholders, creditors, regulatory agencies, and tax authorities."[15]

---

[15]Statement on Management Accounting No. 1A, "Definition of Management Accounting," National Association of Accountants, New York, N.Y.

Management Audit

An independent examination and evaluation of the actions of management according to various standards of good performance. It normally evaluates performance on bases other than profitability and is usually applied to all levels of management.

Management by Exception

An approach to management that requires that reports emphasize the deviation from some accepted basing point such as a standard, a budget, an industry average, or a prior-period experience.

Management Information System (MIS)

An organized method of providing past, present, and prospective information relating to internal operations and external intelligence. It supports the planning, controlling, and operational functions of an organization by providing information in the proper time frame to assist decision makers.

Managerial Budgeting

The use of incentive and control measures to develop a financial plan that will coordinate and control enterprise activities in an effective and efficient manner.

Marginal Cost

The total additional cost for one additional unit of activity at any specific activity level.

Marginal Revenue

The amount added to total revenue by the sale of one additional unit.

Matching

The concept of income determination that leads to recognizing related expenses and revenues in the same accounting period.

Materiality

A concept which specifies that, if it is expected that certain financial information may influence decisions based on financial statements, that information should be disclosed. The relative importance, when measured against a standard of comparison, of any item included in or omitted from books of account or financial statements.

Material Price Variance

See *variances.*

Material Quantity Variance

See *variances.*

Measurement

The process of assigning symbols, generally numbers, to objects, events, and properties according to rules.

Megabyte

One million bytes; 1,000 K bytes.

Merchandise Budget

The planning of sales, inventories, reductions, markdowns, employee discounts, stock shortages, purchases, freight-in, handling, storage, and gross margins for a merchandising enterprise.

Message Sink

(ISO) That part of a communication system in which messages are considered to be received.

Method Variance

See *variances.*

MICR

See *magnetic ink character recognition.*

Microfiche

(SC1) Microform whose medium is film, in the form of sheets that contain microimages arranged in a grid pattern. The microfiche usually contains a title that can be read without magnification. Microfiche with images reduced by a very high reduction factor usually is named ultrafiche.

Microfilm

(SC1) Microform whose medium is film, in the form of rolls, that contains microimages arranged sequentially.

Mips

Million instructions per second.

MIS

See *management information system.*

Mixed Cost

A cost composed of fixed and variable elements over various relevant ranges of operation.

Modem

(1) (SC1) A functional unit that modulates and demodulates signals. One of the functions of a modem is to enable digital data to be transmitted over analog transmission facilities. (2)* (Modulator-demodulator.) A device that modulates and demodulates signals transmitted over data communication facilities.

Moment (Statistics)

The various measures of central tendency of a probability distribution. The first moment is the mean, the second moment about the mean is the variance, and the third moment measures the degree of skewness of the distribution.

Monetary Items

Monetary assets or liabilities, fixed in terms of currency; usually contractual claims to fixed amounts of money. Examples of monetary assets and liabilities are cash, accounts and notes receivable, and accounts and notes payable. Under certain circumstances, a monetary asset or liability may become nonmonetary. For example, a marketable bond being held to maturity would qualify as a monetary asset because its face amount is fixed in terms of currency. However, if the same bond were being held for speculation, it would possibly be classified as a nonmonetary asset because the amount that would be received when sold is not determinable and therefore not fixed in terms of currency.

Monitor

(1) (ISO) A functional unit that observes and records selected activities within a data processing system for analysis. (2) Software or hardware that observes, supervises, controls, or verifies the operations of a system.

Motivation

The stimulation to action resulting from efforts (1) to attain goals

Multiple Budget

A budget spanning two or more budget periods that is continuously advanced one period as each time period passes. Synonymous with continuous budget.

Multiplex*

To interleave or simultaneously transmit two or more messages on a single channel.

Multivariate Analysis (Statistics)

A family of analytic methods that involves the simultaneous analysis of several variables.

Nanosecond

One-billionth of a second.

Negative Goodwill

"The excess of assigned value of identifiable assets (acquired) over cost of an acquired enterprise."[16] See also *goodwill*.

Net Assets

Total assets less total liabilities.

Net Book Value

See *book value*.

Net Earnings

See *earnings*.

Net Income

See *earnings*.

Net Present Value

The difference between the present value of all cash inflows from

---

[16]Accounting Principles Board Opinion No. 16. "Business Combinations," American Institute of Certified Public Accountants, New York, N.Y.

an investment and the present value of all cash outflows required to secure the investment at a given discount rate.

Net Profit Margin

See *ratios.*

Net Realizable Value

Estimated selling price in the ordinary course of business less reasonably predictable costs of completion and disposal.

Network

(1) (SC1) The assembly of equipment through which connections are made between terminal installations. (2) In data communication, a configuration in which two or more terminal installations are connected. (3) The interconnection of electrical components.

Net Working Capital

See *working capital.*

Node

(1) (SC1) In a data network, a point where one or more functional units interconnect data transmission lines. (2)* The representation of a state or an event by means of a point on a diagram.

Nonmonetary Items

Assets or liabilities other than monetary assets or liabilities. Examples of nonmonetary assets and liabilities are inventory; investments in common stock; property, plant and equipment; liability for advance rent collected; and common stock.

Nonparametric Statistics

A statistical test in which the model does not specify the distribution of the population data from which the sample is drawn. Nonparametric tests are also called distribution-free tests.

Nontheoretic Statements

Those statements resulting from accounting research not involving the use of a purely formal system.

Normal Capacity

An estimate of the long-range average measure of the rate at which a set of resources will be used to reach an objective.

Normal Costing

The process whereby products and activity units are assigned the sum of direct materials and labor resources consumed plus an allocation of overhead based on normal capacity.

Normal Distribution (Statistics)

A continuous probability distribution that is a symmetric bell-shaped curve when presented graphically.

Normal Production

The level of capacity utilization that will satisfy average consumer demand over a span of time long enough to include seasonal, cyclical, and trend factors.

Normative Accounting Theory

A theory that attempts to state what financial information should be collected, analyzed, and communicated. It is concerned with what ought to be.

Note Receivable Discounted

A note receivable that has been sold to a lender at a discount. Discounting notes receivable is a financing method used to improve cash flow.

Objectivity

A trait of financial reporting that emphasizes the verifiable, factual nature of events or transactions and minimizes the personal influence of the measurer in the measurement process.

Obsolescence

The decline in value of fixed assets due to changes in customer demand, new inventions, or technological progress. Known as functional depreciation, it may be ordinary, in the sense that it is anticipated, or extraordinary, when it is due to an unusual and significant change.

OCR

See *optical character recognition.*

Offline System

A system in which human operations are requried between the original recording functions and the ultimate data processing function. This includes conversion operations as well as the necessary loading and unloading operations incident to the use of point-to-point or data-gathering systems. Contrasts with online system.

Online System

(1) A system in which the input data enter the computer directly from the point of origin or in which output data are transmitted directly to where they are used. (2) In telegraph usage, a system of transmitting directly into the system.

Operating Budget

A schedule of the various production, administration, and distribution expenses, classified by the nature of the expense, of an organizational unit or subunit required to attain unit objectives during a period. Contrast with capital budget.

Operating Capacity

The number of units of output plants can produce when working on a normal operating schedule. The company's sales are often stated as a percent of operating capacity.

Operating Costs

Repetitive expenditures for material, labor, and other direct and indirect costs necessary for the performance of regular activities.

Operating Cycle

As used in financial reporting, the period between the acquisition of raw materials or finished goods by the expenditure of cash or its equivalent and the recovery of related amounts of cash through the sale of inventory for cash or receivables and the conversion of those receivables into cash.

Operating Lease

See *lease.*

Operating Leverage

See *ratios.*

Operating Plan

A plan made to implement the strategic plan. It is designed to determine what action is required in the current period to ensure adherence to the long-term strategic plan.

Operating System*

(ISO) Software that controls the execution of computer programs and that may provide scheduling, debugging, input/output control, accounting, compilation, storage assignment, data management, and related services.

Operational Auditing

A process of objectively obtaining and evaluating evidence regarding operating procedures and events compared to established criteria of good performance. It may result in recommendations to improve the effectiveness and efficiency of operations and internal controls.

Operations Research

The application of a scientific method to problems involving the control of organized systems so as to provide solutions which best serve the purposes of the organization as a whole.

Opinion Research

The use of survey research methods to obtain the beliefs, judgments, evaluations, and wishes of people about a research question.

Opportunity Cost

The maximum alternative earnings that might have been obtained if the productive good, service, or capacity had been applied to some alternative use.

Optical Character Recognition (OCR)

(1) (ISO) Character recognition that uses optical means to identify graphic characters. (2) Contrast with magnetic ink character recognition.

Out-of-Pocket Cost

The cash outflow related to carrying out an activity, producing a product, or completing a project.

Output Controls

Control measures that relate to a specific data processing activity and that serve as controls over the processing result and the output phase of a data processing system. Output controls are designed to ensure the accuracy or reasonableness of the processing result (such as updated master files in the form of punched cards, magnetic tapes, and discs in strips; reports; analyses; or documents of various types). These controls also ensure that only authorized personnel receive the output. Output controls should ensure the provision of a feedback mechanism through which these authorized persons may be able to report errors and/or suggest improvements.

Overabsorbed Overhead

The excess of manufacturing overhead applied to production over the actual expenses incurred; also referred to as *overapplied.*

Overhead Costs

Those costs which cannot, as a practical matter, be assigned to a firm's objectives in a direct fashion; overhead costs are, however, related to the accomplishment of those objectives. Customarily, a consistent method of cost allocation, which seeks to approximate the economic sacrifices incurred, is adopted in applying such charges to the cost objectives.

Overhead Efficiency Variance

See *variances.*

Overhead Rate

The ratio of overhead costs for a period of time related to the amount of some measurable associated causal factor in the same period of time. For example, the expected or standard overhead costs divided by the expected or standard productive effort.

Overhead Spending Variance

See *variances.*

Overhead Volume Variance

See *variances.*

Parameter

A characteristic that describes a state or limits the scope of a total population.

Parity Bit

(ISO) A binary check digit inserted in an array of binary digits to make the arithmetic sum of all the digits, including the check digit, always odd or always even.

Par Value

The value printed on the face of a security certificate.

Password

(1) A unique string of characters that a program, computer operator, or user must supply to meet security requirements before gaining access to data. (2) In systems with time-sharing, a one-to-eight character symbol that the user may be required to supply at the time the user logs on the system. The password is confidential, as opposed to the user identification.

Pay-Back Period

The period of time necessary to recoup the cash cost of an investment from the cash inflows attributable to the investment.

Pay-Back Ratio

See *ratios.*

Pension Expense[17]

The cost of a pension plan for a given period. The following terms are used in the definition of the annual provision for pension cost.

(1) Normal cost — The cost assigned, under the actuarial cost method in use, to each year subsequent to the inception of a pension plan.

(2) Prior service cost — "Pension cost assigned to years prior to the date of a particular actuarial valuation. Prior service cost includes any remaining past service cost."

---

[17]Accounting Principles Board Opinion No. 8, "Accounting for the Cost of Pension Plans," American Institute of Certified Public Accountants, New York, N.Y.

(3) Past service cost — The pension cost assigned to years prior to the inception of a pension plan.

(4) Vested benefits — Benefits that are not contingent upon the employee's continuing in the service of the employer.

(5) Actuarial Gains and Losses — The adjustments to the prior service cost because of (A) differences between actual experience and the actuary's assumptions or (B) revisions of the actuary's assumptions.

The annual provision for pension cost should be between the minimum and maximum stated below:

Minimum: The annual provision for pension cost should not be less than the total of (1) normal cost, (2) interest on any unfunded prior service cost, and (3) a provision for vested benefits.

A provision for vested benefits should be made if the actuarially computed value of vested benefits exceeds the assets and such excess is not at least 5% less than the comparable excess at the beginning of the year. The "assets" is the total of (1) the pension fund, (2) any balance-sheet pension accruals, less (3) any balance-sheet pension prepayments or deferred charges.

The provision for vested benefits should be the lesser of (A) the additional amount so that the excess at the beginning of the year will be reduced by 5% or (B) the amount necessary to make the provision for pension cost equal to the total of (1) normal cost, (2) 40-year amortization of the past service cost, (3) 40-year amortization of any change in prior service cost because of amendments, (4) 10-to 20-year amortization of actuarial gains or losses, and (5) interest on the difference between provisions and amounts funded.

Maximum: The annual provision for pension cost should not be greater than the total of (1) normal cost, (2) 10% of the past service cost (until fully amortized), (3) 10% of the amounts of any increases or decreases in prior service cost arising on amendments of the plan (until fully amortized), (4) 10-to 20-year amortization of actuarial gains or losses, and (5) interest difference between provisions and amounts funded.

The difference between the amount which has been charged against income and the amount which has been paid should be shown in the balance sheet as accrued or prepaid pension cost.

Percentage of Completion Method

A method used in financial reporting to recognize the revenue and costs related to a contract within a specific reporting period.

Such recognition should be based on the portion of the work completed, costs incurred in relation to the total work, or costs estimated to be required for the completion of the contract.

Perception

The feeling a person develops immediately or over time, based on both information and intuition, about a condition, person, or activity.

Performance

Together with facility, one of two major factors on which the total productivity of a system depends. Performance is largely determined by a combination of three other factors: throughput, response time, and availability.

Performance Budget

A budget classified by activities to be performed and by personal responsibility against which the results of actual performance are compared.

Performance Classification

The classification of resources and obligations according to functional responsibilities. Measures of efficiency and effectiveness can be developed to evaluate managerial performance in regard to these responsibilities.

Performance Measurement

A quantification of the degree and efficiency with which the objectives of a responsibility center have been accomplished.

Performance Report

A report comparing actual performance with expected or historic performance. The purpose of the report is to isolate deviations for prompt managerial consideration.

Period Costs

Those costs and losses incurred during an operating period that are not dependent on the volume level of activity.

Period Expenses

Those costs and losses that are charged against revenue during an operating period regardless of the volume level of activity.

Physical Control

The application of physical internal control procedures to the resources of an entity to ensure their efficient and effective use in accordance with policy.

Physical Inventory

A physical count (or other physical measure) of all inventories on hand. The physical inventory verifies the book balance and is usually done annually.

Physical Life

An estimate of the period over which an asset will maintain its functional capacity whether or not it will be so used by the organization.

Picosecond

One-thousandth of a nanosecond; one-billionth of a second.

Planning

The process of seeking out alternative courses of action, evaluating them by various techniques, and deciding which actions to take to attain goals.

Planning-Programming-Budgeting System (PPBS)

A comprehensive management system designed to improve policy making and the allocation of resources, especially in the public sector. The system provides for the determination of programs consistent with specific objectives, analysis of costs and effectiveness of programs, and continuous re-examination of program results in relation to anticipated outcomes to determine the needs for changes in established programs and objectives.

Plant

The production facilities and directly supporting resources of a manufacturing or service entity that are used in the physical creation of a good or service, as contrasted with the storage and distribution of goods and services.

Polling

(1)* Interrogation of devices for purposes such as to avoid contention, to determine operational status, or to determine readiness to send or receive data. (2) (SC1) In data communication, the process of inviting data stations to transmit, one at a time. The polling process usually involves the sequential interrogation of several data stations.

Pooling of Interests

A technique used for combining into one entity stockholder interests of previously independent, autonomous business entities through the exchange of voting common stock. Since the combination does not involve a cash remittance to individual shareholders but only a change in the form of their ownership right in net corporate assets, the book values of assets and equities as shown on the records of the combining entities are carried forward without revaluation into the books of the combined entity.

Population

The group of people or objects about which the researcher wishes to make statements.

Port

(1) (SC1) A functional unit of a node through which data can enter or leave a data network. (2) In data communication, that part of a data processor which is dedicated to a single data channel for the purpose of receiving data from or transmitting data to one or more external, remote devices. (3) An access point (for example, a logical unit) for data entry or exit.

Positive Accounting Theory

A theory of accounting based on the belief that empirical research must be used to establish facts and relationships that can be used to build an empirically based, theoretical structure of accounting thought.

Post-Statement Events

In financial reporting, an economic circumstance that occurs after the statement date but before publication of the related report. Where such events are of material nature or amount in relation to the specific report or to the future operations with which it is concerned, an appropriate adjustment should be made or a disclosure of the situation should be presented as a note to the report.

Postulates

Fundamental statements about the nature of a process that are ssumed to be true and from which all other theorems, principles, and rules for action can be derived by the logical rules of inference.

PPBS

See *planning-programming-budgeting system.*

Practical Capacity

A realistic expectation of the production level of an entity over a period of time. It may be measured as ideal capacity less an allowance for unavoidable operating interruption and maintenance.

Precision (Statistics)

A measure of the range of error of a statistical estimate of data.

Predetermined Overhead Rate

The rate at which manufacturing overhead is applied to production, based on the ratio of total budgeted overhead expenses for a period of time to the expected total of some relevant measure of activity for the same period, such as machine hours or direct labor hours.

Prediction

A scientific statement to the effect that a specific relationship will hold in the future.

Preferred Stock

Stock that has some priority over other shares regarding dividends or the distribution of assets upon liquidation.

Prepaid Expenses

Payments made for services to be received after the date of payment. Usually such services are consumed in the near future in the ordinary conduct of the business. Examples include prepaid rent, unexpired insurance, prepaid wages, and salaries.

Preprocessor

(1)* (ISO) A computer program that effects some preliminary computation or organization. (2) A program that examines the source program for preprocessor statements which are then executed, resulting in the alteration of the source program. (3) In emulation, a program that converts data from the format of an emulated system to the format accepted by an emulator.

Present Costs

In the context of past, present or future costs, those sacrifices necessary under the prevailing circumstances to achieve immediately an objective in process.

Present Fairly

To set forth information that is unbiased, unlikely to be misinterpreted, and sufficiently relevant to the needs of concerned users.

Present Value

The amount that is paid for the right to receive payment in the future, assuming that the rate of interest for ventures of similar risk is known and that payment is to be received at specific dates.

Price-Earnings Ratio

See *ratios.*

Price-Level Adjusted Statements

Statements that reflect changes in the general purchasing power of money and which are based on the same cost principles as historical-cost statements. In price-level adjusted statements the unit of measure is defined in terms of a single specified amount of purchasing power — the general purchasing power of the dollar at a specified date.

Primary Earnings Per Share

The amount of earnings that may be attributed to each share of common stock when the number of shares used in the calculation includes not only the weighted-average number of common shares actually outstanding but also the number of common shares represented by dilutive common stock equivalents. The earnings used in the calculation should be the net earnings minus preferred dividends plus the net interest and dividends related to the dilutive common stock equivalents.

Prime Cost

The cost of direct materials and direct labor.

Prior Period Adjustments

Adjustments of returned earnings as of the beginning of a fiscal period that relate to events of a prior period. These adjustements have been discussed in Accounting Principles Board Opinion

No. 9 and more recently in Statement of Financial Accounting Standards No. 16. In each case the controlling board sought to minimize the use of direct charges or credits to retained earnings. Currently, the only prior period adjustments which can be processed directly through retained earnings for public reporting purposes are those which correct an error in the financial statements of a prior period and those which result from the realization of income tax benefits of preacquisition operating loss carryforwards of purchased subsidiaries. (Certain additional usages of the term are possible in dealing with interim reports or with data organized for internal use.)

Probability

A measure between 0 and 1 that describes the likelihood of an event or set of events occurring.

Process Bound

A characteristic of a computer system that is restricted by the speed of the central processing unit and in which input/output devices stand idle a certain percentage of the time.

Process Costing

A method of cost accounting wherein costs (either actual or standard) are charged to processes, operations, or departments. This method of costing is used when there is continuous mass production of like units that usually pass in consecutive order through a series of production steps called operations or processes. Costs are accumulated by those operations or processes for a specified time period; an average cost per unit of output is developed for costing purposes.

Processing Controls

Control measures that relate to a specific data processing activity and that are designed to provide reasonable assurance that data processing has been performed as intended for the particular application.

Processor

(1) (ISO) In a computer, a functional unit that interprets and executes instructions. (2)* In hardware, a data processor. (3)* In software, a computer program that performs functions such as compiling, assembling, and translating for a specific programming language.

Product Costs

Those costs of raw materials, direct labor, and other costs that are directly or indirectly involved in the production of goods and services for sale to customers. Indirect costs include such items as factory depreciation, equipment maintenance, factory utilities, and wages for facilitating services in the plant. Indirect costs are customarily assigned to products or services by an appropriate allocation technique.

Production Budget

A prediction of the cost of producing the goods needed to meet the sales budget and maintain suitable inventories.

Productivity

(1) The relationship between "output" (the quantity of goods and services produced) and "inputs," (the amounts of labor, material, and capital needed to produce the goods and services). Usually measured in terms of output per worker per hour. (2) Simply stated, the quantity of output per unit of a factor of production.

Product Mix

A combination of outputs to be produced within the resource constraints of an entity.

Professional Ethics

The moral concepts and professional rules designed to guide individual members of a profession in a pattern of conduct that will assure acceptance of the results provided by a professional group.

Profit Center

A segment of business for which revenues and expenses caused or controllable by that segment are accumulated in the accounts. Such data are then used to evaluate segment performance and accountability.

Profit Margin

See *ratios*.

Profit Plan

A set of objectives, policy guidelines, and comprehensive detailed budgets for a period of time, together with a system of feedback reports for detecting variations from budget. This plan is intended to facilitate attainment of the profit objective for the entire enterprise for the year or shorter planning period.

Profit Planning and Control

A systematic and formalized approach for developing information used for planning, coordinating, and controlling enterprise activities to achieve profit objectives.

Pro Forma Budget

Projected financial statements based on various assumed facts.

Program Budget

A budget used for review and decision making at higher organizational levels to evaluate and coordinate program activities.

Programmed Costs

Planned costs that will be incurred for some particular time period as a result of a specific management policy decision. These costs may vary directly with volume, or they may increase or decrease at specific volume levels, such as upon addition of another shift. They also may vary with volumes of specific products, specific operations, or organization-wide activity.

Programming Language*

(ISO) An artificial language established for expressing computer programs.

Program Product

A licensed program that performs a function for the user and usually interacts with and relies upon system control programming or some other control program. A program product contains logic related to the user's data and is usable or adaptable to meet specific requirements.

Progress Payment

An advance payment on cost billed to and received from a customer in advance of delivery of the finished product or passage of title.

Project Budget

A budget of costs classified by resources and function for a specific and identifiable project over the project's life; this life may span several operating budget time periods.

Projections

Predictions of the outcome of events yet to occur based on specific forecasting techniques and an historical data base. Such forecasting is normally made within the constraints of an identified set of specific assumptions.

Property

The rights in resource objects that are recognized by law or social custom as belonging to a person or persons. Property may take several forms, but its essential characteristic is a tangible or intangible substance containing capacities which may be claimed legally or customarily by an individual or individuals to the exclusion of others.

Purchase Method

A method of accounting for a business combination that reflects the acquisition of one company by another. The difference, if any, between the fair value of the identifiable assets purchased and the amount paid is recorded as goodwill. The acquiring company reports the results of operations of the acquisition from the date it is acquired.

Purchasing Budget

A prediction, by types of material, of the cost and time needed to provide budgeted material requirements.

Purchasing Power Gains and Losses

In an inflationary period, the favorable effect (gain) from holding net monetary debt (monetary liabilities greater than monetary assets) or the unfavorable effect (loss) from holding net monetary assets (monetary assets greater than monetary liabilities). A net debtor position produces a gain because the debt will be paid off in cheaper dollars. A net creditor position produces a loss because the net monetary assets are worth less in terms of their purchasing power than they were at the beginning of the period. During a deflationary period, the effects would be just the opposite

Quality Control

A process, which may include statistical sampling, by which the quality of operation is monitored. Techniques include precise specifications, random inspection procedures, and disciplined reviews of deviations from specification.

Queue

As used in information processing, (1) A line or list formed by items in a system waiting for service; for example, tasks to be performed or messages to be transmitted in a message-switching system. (2) To arrange in, or form, a queue.

Random Access

(1)* In COBOL, an access mode in which specific logical records are obtained from or placed into a mass storage file in a nonsequential manner. (2) (ISO) Deprecated term for direct access.

Random Sample

A sample in which each element in the population of all elements has a known probability of being selected.

Ratio Analysis

Computation of significant financial and other ratios and the comparison of these ratios with those of prior years, and with industry averages; also includes discovering the trends of the ratios. The purpose of this analysis is to obtain indirect evidence about economic actions and events.

Ratios

A selective group of ratios used in financial analysis:

Acid test—determining the ratio of the total cash, trade receivables, and marketable securities of a business to its current liabilities.

Capacity ratio—the ratio of actual capacity of an enterprise or subunit thereof to the planned or budgeted capacity.

Current ratio—the ratio of current assets to current liabilities.

Days' Sales in Inventory—a measure of the age or adequacy of inventory, calculated by dividing the ending inventory balance by average daily cost of goods sold (or cost of goods used, if raw material inventory is being evaluated) for the preceding period

Days' Sales Outstanding—a measure of the age of receivables, calculated by dividing the ending receivables balance by average daily credit sales for the preceding period.

Debt Ratio—see *total debt to total assets.*

Financial fixed charge coverage—profit before taxes, interest charges, and lease obligations divided by interest charges and lease obligations. In filings with the Securities and Exchange Commission, fixed charges include preferred stock dividends.

Inventory turnover—cost of sales divided by average inventory during the period.

Net profit margin—the profit margin on sales, computed by dividing net earnings after taxes by sales. Indicates the profit per dollar of sales.

Operating leverage—the extent to which a firm's operations involve fixed operating expenses (fixed manufacturing, selling, and administrative expense). Being highly leveraged means that a relatively small change in sales results in a large change in net operating income.

Pay-back ratio—the initial cash cost of an investment divided by the calculated pay-back period.

Price-earnings ratio—the market price of a share of stock divided by earnings per share.

Profit margin—the percentage obtained by dividing pretax earnings by sales and transfers.

Receivable turnover—a measure of asset utilization determined by dividing total annual sales by the average receivable balance.

Reinvestment rate—the rate of return at which cash flows from an investment are reinvested.

Return on equity—the ratio of net profit after taxes to net equity (net worth). Indicates the rate of return on the stockholders' investment.

Return on investment—the ratio of the return (benefits less appropriate costs) from an investment to the amount of the investment. It may be computed for time periods or for projects or on specific investments by time periods.

Times-Interest-Earned—the ratio of pretax operating income to annual interest expense.

Total debt to total assets—generally called the debt ratio; measures the percentage of total funds provided by creditors

Reader

(1) A device that converts information in one form of storage to information in another form of storage. (2) A part of the scheduler that reads an input stream into the system.

Read-Only

A type of access to data that allows them to be read, but not copied, printed, or modified.

Read-Out Device

(ISO) Synonym for character display device.

Real Audit Evidence

Knowledge or facts directly available to an auditor from an examination of the subject. This information is sufficient (a measure of quantity) and competent (a measure of quality) and enables the auditor to know the relative truth or falsity of the facts asserted.

Realization

"[I]n the most precise sense,...the process of converting non-cash resources and rights into money;...most precisely used in accounting and financial reporting to refer to sales of assets for cash or claims to cash. The related terms *realized* and *unrealized* therefore identify revenues or gains or losses on assets sold and unsold, respectively."[18]

Realtime

(1) (ISO) Pertaining to the processing of data by a computer in connection with another process outside the computer according to time requirements imposed by the outside process. The term "realtime" is also used to describe systems operating on conversational modes and processes that can be influenced by human intervention while they are in progress. (2) Pertaining to an application in which response to input is fast enough to affect subsequent input, such as a process control system or a computer-assisted instruction system.

---

[18]Statement of Financial Accounting Concepts No. 3, "Elements of Financial Statements of Business Enterprises," Financial Accounting Standards Board, Stamford, Conn.

Receivables

Claims of an entity for money, other goods, or services.

Receivable Turnover

See *ratios.*

Recognition

"[T]he process of formally recording or incorporating an item in the financial statements of an entity. Thus, an asset, liability, revenue, expense, gain, or loss may be recognized (recorded) or unrecognized (unrecorded)."[19]

Recomputation

An auditing procedure that involves recalculation to verify arithmetical accuracy.

Record

(1)* (ISO) A collection of related data or words, treated as a unit; for example, in stock control, each invoice could constitute one record. (2) In Virtual Telecommunications Access Method (VTAM), the unit of data transmission for record-mode. A record represents whatever amount of data the transmitting node chooses to send. (3)* Variable-length record.

Recovery Procedure

(SC1) In data communication, a process whereby a specified data station attempts to resolve conflicting or erroneous conditions arising during the transfer of data.

Recovery Routine

As used in information processing, a routine that is entered when an error occurs during the performance of an associated operation. It isolates the error, assesses the extent of the error, indicates subsequent action, and attempts to correct the error and resume operation.

Register

(ISO) A storage device, having a specified storage capacity such as a bit, a byte, or a computer word, and usually intended for a special purpose.

---

[19]Statement of Financial Accounting Concepts No. 3, "Elements of Financial Statements of Business Enterprises," Financial Accounting Standards Board, Stamford, Conn.

Regression (Statistics)

A statistical method used to determine relationships among variables.

Reinvestment Rate

See *ratios.*

Related-Party Transactions

A transaction between parties in which one party has the ability to apply significant influence on the economic decisions of the other party. Common owners, employers, officers, financial rights, or obligations may imply the existence of related parties.

Relation

A bond or connection between two or more elements or between elements in one group and those in other groups, such as between grades earned in college and success on the CMA examination.

Relevant Cost

A cost that should be considered in choosing among alternatives. Only those costs yet to be incurred (i.e., future costs) that will differ among the alternatives (the differential costs) are relevant in decision making.

Relevant Range

The range of economic activity within which estimates and predictions are valid.

Reliability (Statistics)

The degree of confidence that a sample estimate of a population parameter is within a certain range of the result that would be obtained from a complete census of the entire population.

Remote Access*

Pertaining to communication with a data processing facility through a data link.

Remote Terminal

(1) A terminal attached to a system through a data link. (2) In telephony, a terminal attached through a trunk or tieline.

Repairs

The cost of restoring to normal operating condition parts, service capacity equivalent, or assets damaged or worn out.

Replacement

The exchange or substitution of one fixed asset for another having the capacity to perform the same function. Within reasonable limits, the new asset may perform the function more or less efficiently than the retired asset, and it may have the capacity to perform the function for a longer or shorter period of time, but the intent of the exchange must be to substitute assets having similar service capacity.

Replacement Cost

The cost required to replace the service capacity of an existing asset. Physical replacement of an identical asset is not required. The emphasis is on replacing the services to be provided by an asset rather than on replacing the asset itself.

Reporting Currency

"The currency in which an enterprise prepares its financial statements."[20]

Reproduction Cost

The cost required to restore an existing asset to its original condition.

Research and Development Costs

Outlays made in an attempt to discover new knowledge (research) or to utilize the results of research to develop new or improved products (development). Unless such costs are incurred under contractual arrangements for others, they must be charged to expense when incurred.

Research Design

An outline of the activities to be carried out by the researcher. The design includes the development of hypotheses, the methods to be used to gather and analyze data, the scheme for controlling and manipulating the variables, and the preparation of the research report.

---

[20]Statement of Financial Accounting Standards No. 52, "Foreign Currency Translation," Financial Accounting Standards Board, Stamford, Conn.

Residual Income

The net income which an investment center is able to earn above a specified rate of return on assets. It is the operating income of a profit center or investment center less the imputed interest on the assets used by the center.

Response Time

(1)* (ISO) The elapsed time between the end of an inquiry or demand on a data processing system and the beginning of the response, e.g., the length of time between an indication of the end of an inquiry and the display of the first character of the response at a user terminal. (2) See *turnaround time.*

Responsibility Accounting

A system of reporting tailored to an organizational structure so that costs and revenues are reported at the level having the related responsibility within the organization.

Retained Earnings

Net earnings over the life of a corporation less dividends and earnings capitalized due to stock dividends. Thus, the retained earnings account represents the total earnings of a corporation which have been retained in the business and not transferred to contributed capital because of stock dividends. Appropriations of retained earnings do not diminish the amount of retained earnings; they merely subdivide the existing amount.

Return on Equity

See *ratios.*

Return on Investment

See *ratios.*

Revenue Realization

The point or time when it is appropriate to recognize revenue, usually when an exchange transaction has occurred and no significant uncertainty remains with respect to the collectibility of the sales price or the costs yet to be incurred.

Revenues

"[I]nflows or other enhancements of assets of an entity or settlements of its liabilities (or a combination of both) during a period from delivering or producing goods, rendering services, or other activities that constitute the entity's ongoing major or central operations."[21]

Risk

A decision setting in which the decision maker can calculate the probability that a given outcome will be associated with a particular course of action.

Risk Analysis

Various methods for identifying, disclosing possible consequences of, quantifying, and placing an economic cost on various types of risks associated with various economic projects and objectives.

Run Stream

See *job stream*.

Safety Stock

An inventory cushion meant to absorb deviations from expected maximum demand and unplanned variations in the length of lead-time requirements.

Sale/Leaseback

See *lease*.

Sales Budget

A prediction, classified by responsibility, product, and area, of the net revenue expected to be available to an entity in a period of time.

Sales Forecast

A prediction of sales for the budget period using various data and methods such as trend projections, correlation analysis, operations research techniques, and computer simulation, or less rigorous prediction procedures.

---

[21]Statement of Financial Accounting Concepts No. 3, "Elements of Financial Statements of Business Enterprises," Financial Accounting Standards Board, Stamford, Conn.

Sales Mix

The relative combination of quantities of the various products which make up the total sales of a company.

Sales Mix Variance

See *variances.*

Sales-Type Lease

See *lease.*

Sales Volume Variance

See *variances.*

Salvage Value

The net cash inflow expected from the sale of resources no longer useful to the firm.

Sample

A subset of a total population having characteristics similar to the total population to such an extent that knowledge about the population may be inferred from the sample.

Sampling

A method of forming an opinion about a group of items on the basis of an examination of fewer than all of the items, with or without the use of mathematical procedures.

Sampling Techniques

Methods of obtaining information about a population by analyzing a portion of the population.

Satellite Computer

(1) A computer that is under the control of another computer and performs subsidiary operations. (2) An offline auxiliary computer.

Scaling

(1) The process of extrapolating certain criteria from an item or activity; the process normally involves constructing and employing measurement methods for the assessment of the criteria or

criterion. (2) The assignment of numbers to attributes of items or activities in such a way that the relationship among the numbers reflects the relationship among the items with respect to the attribute being measured.

Scheduler*

A computer program designed to perform functions such as scheduling, initiation, and termination of jobs.

Scientific Method

The process of inquiry, for the purpose of obtaining knowledge, involving (1) observing a problem, (2) developing a hypothesis of a solution, (3) developing a research design, (4) making observations and testing the results of experiments, and (5) drawing inferences from the investigation.

Scratch

To erase data on a volume or delete their identification so that they can be used for another purpose.

Scrolling

(1) (SC1) In computer graphics, the continuous vertical or horizontal movement of the display elements within a window in a manner such that new data appear at one edge of the window as old data disappear at the opposite edge. The window may include the entire display surface. (2) Transcribing data, usually annually, from a source document into a format for data entry.

SEC

See *Securities and Exchange Commission.*

Second-Generation Computer

A computer utilizing solid state components.

Securities and Exchange Commission

A regulatory agency of the United States government that has jurisdiction over the securities and financial markets, including financial reporting by publicly held companies.

Security

(1) Prevention of access to or use of data or programs without authorization. (2) The evidence of a debt or ownership or related/

right. It includes stock options and warrants, as well as debt and stock.

Segment

(1)* (ISO) A self-contained portion of a computer program that may be executed without the entire computer program necessarily being maintained in internal storage at any one time. (2)* (ISO) To divide a computer program into segments. (3) In telecommunications, a portion of a message that can be contained in a buffer.

Segment Margin

The contribution margin for each segment of a business less all separable fixed costs, both discretionary and committed. A measure of long-run profitability.

Segment of a Business

An identifiable collection of related resources and activities. Operationally it is a significant strategic or organizational component of an entity enterprise—a subsidiary, division, department, the entity itself, or other units—having distinctive resources and activities which can be treated as an entity for planning and control purposes.

Segment Reporting

The process of presenting financial and other information for components of a business entity.

Self-Checking Code*

See *error detecting code.*

Semivariable Cost

A cost that includes both variable and fixed elements.

Sensitivity Analysis

The study of the way changes or errors in assumptions affect the output of a decision model. It seeks to determine how incremental changes in the various input variables in the decision model affect the responsiveness of the output.

Separable Cost

In joint product costing, a cost directly identifiable with a specific product beyond a common cost cut-off point.

Sequential Access

(1) (ISO) The facility to obtain data from a storage device or to enter into a storage device in such a way that the process depends on the location of those data and on a reference to data previously accessed. (2) An access mode in which records are obtained from, or placed into, a file in such a way that each successive access to the file refers to the next subsequent record in the file. The order of the records is established by the programmer when creating the file. (3) In systems with Virtual Storage Access Method (VSAM), the retrieval or storage of a data record in either its entry sequence, its key sequence, or its relative-record sequence, relative to the previously retrieved or stored record.

Sequential Sampling

The process of selecting items for a sample by starting with an initial random selection and taking subsequent items at equal intervals.

Service Capacity

As used in regard to accounting for replacement costs, the capacity to perform at the same level the function or functions that an existing asset normally performs.

Service Departments

Those departments that exist solely to aid the production departments by rendering specialized assistance with certain phases of the work.

Service Program

See *utility program.*

Session

(1) The period of time during which a user of a terminal can communicate with an interactive system; usually, the elapsed time from when a terminal user logs on the system until he logs off the system. (2) The period of time during which programs or

devices can communicate with each other. (3) In SNA, a logical connection established between two network addressable units (NAUs) to allow them to communicate. The session is uniquely identified by a pair of network addresses, identifying the origin and destination NAUs of any transmissions exchanged during the session.

Set

Any well-specified collection of distinct objects or symbols.

Setup

(1)* (ISO) In a computer that consists of an assembly of individual computing units, the arrangement of interconnections between the units and the adjustments needed for the computer to operate upon a particular problem. (2)* An arrangement of data or devices to solve a particular problem. (3) The preparation of a computing system to perform a job or job step. Setup is usually performed by an operator and often involves performing routine functions, such as mounting tape reels and loading card decks.

SFAS

See *Statement of Financial Accounting Standards.*

Shared File

A direct access device that may be used by two systems at the same time; a shared file may link two systems.

Short-Form Audit Report

A document in which the independent accountant sets forth the scope and nature of his examination and expresses his independent expert opinion regarding the fair presentation of the information accompanying the report.

Short-Run Performance Margin

The contribution margin for each segment, less separable discretionary costs.

Shutdown Cost

Periodic expenses that will continue to be incurred if the activity does not operate. They do not include those costs incurred prior to the point of no activity.

Significant Variance

A variance of actual performance from the budget that indicates a high probability that the operation or activity is out of control (and is not being performed as planned). See *variances*.

Sign-On

The procedure performed at a terminal while it is in initial mode. This procedure can include entering only the sign-on command or entering the sign-on command with a password or other user-specified security data. See *password*.

Simulation

A method of studying problems whereby a model of a system or operational process is subjected to a series of assumptions and variations in an effort to find one or more acceptable solutions.

Small Group Behavior

The behavior of small groups of individuals both among themselves and toward individuals and groups outside their group.

SNA

See *systems network architecture*.

Social Accounting

An aspect of the field of management accounting that measures and reports the impact of an organization's activities in its social environment. It includes effects such as pollution, discrimination, and product safety as well as financial effects.

Software*

(1·) (ISO) Computer programs, procedures, rules and possibly associated documentation concerned with the operation of a data processing system. (2) Contrast with hardware.

Source Statement

A statement written in symbols of a programming language.

Span of Control

The number of employees or organizational components that report to a specific manager.

Spending Variance

See *variances*.

Split-Off Point

In connection with joint products, that point in the production process at which individual products become identifiable and beyond which separate costs are recognized.

Spot Rate

"The exchange rate for immediate delivery of currencies exchanged."[22]

Standard Cost

A forecast of the cost of performance that should be attained under projected conditions as determined by reasonable estimates or engineering studies.

Standard Cost System

An accounting technique whereby costs are recorded on the basis of predetermined standards while deviations from such standards are identified separately for analysis and control.

Standard Deviation

A measure of the dispersion in a frequency distribution.

Standby Capacity

The capacity to provide service from existing resources or organizations during periods when normal capacity is impaired. It is the ability to assure continuance of production by the substitution of alternative means of performance.

Statement

(1)* (ISO) In a programming lanaguage, a meaningful expression that may describe or specify operations and is usually complete in the context of that programming language. (2)* In computer programming, a symbol string or other arrangement of symbols.

Statements of Financial Accounting Standards (SFAS)

Final statements of generally accepted accounting principles on some aspect of financial accounting or reporting. These statements are issued by the Financial Accounting Standards Board.

---

[22]Statement of Financial Accounting Standards No. 52, "Foreign Currency Translation," Financial Accounting Standards Board, Stamford, Conn.

Statements of International Accounting Standards (SIAS)

Pronouncements issued by the International Accounting Standards Committee (IASC) in an effort to encourage consistency in financial reporting throughout the world. IASC is an autonomous part of the 11-nation body known as the International Coordination Committee for the Accounting Profession.

Statements on Management Accounting (SMA)

Pronouncements issued by the National Association of Accountants to provide guidance on management accounting concepts, policies, and practices. These statements are developed by the Association's Management Accounting Practices Committee.

Station

(1) One of the input or output points of a system that uses communication facilities; for example, the telephone set in the telephone system or the point where the business machine interfaces with the channel on a leased private line. (2) One or more computers, terminals, or devices at a particular location.

Statistical Inference

The use of a limited quantity of observed data, generally from a sample, as a basis for generalizing on the characteristics of a larger, unknown universe or population.

Statistical Sampling

A method of forming an opinion about a group of items by examining a few items and applying mathematical procedures. The primary purpose of the statistical approach is to obtain objective results from a sample and to measure the reliability of the estimate so obtained. See *sampling.*

Statistics

(1) The theory and methods of collecting, classifying, analyzing, and interpreting quantitative data. (A statistic is a measure calculated from a sample, while a parameter is a population value.) (2) The study of sample data to compare sources of variations of phenomena, to accept or reject hypothesized relations between the phenomena, and to aid in indexing reliable inferences from empirical observations.

Step Budget

See *flexible budgeting.*

Step Variable Costs

Those variable costs that change abruptly at intervals of activity because their acquisition comes in indivisible segments.

Stock Dividend

A pro rata distribution of shares of capital stock to existing shareholders. The shareholders contribute nothing to the corporation in exchange for the additional shares. The distribution is accounted for by transferring, from retained earnings to contributed capital, an amount equal to either the par value or the market value of the shares issued.

Stockholders' Equity

The excess of assets over liabilities. Stockholders' equity is the claim of the stockholders to their share in the entity's assets after its obligations have been met.

Stock Right

The right to participate in a future stock issuance under specified terms with respect to price and time.

Stock Split

A process whereby existing outstanding shares of capital stock are replaced by a larger number of shares sufficient to maintain the same total par value or stated value outstanding as existed prior to the split.

Storage Capacity

(ISO) The amount of data that can be contained in a storage device, measured in binary digits, bytes, characters, words, or other units of data.

Strategic Plan

A plan that summarizes and articulates the basic operational tasks, objectives and goals, and strategies for the organization. The basic operational tasks are simply shorthand for what the organization's basic business(es) or function(s) are, stated in terms of what the company wants to be. An objective implies a long time sequence and need not be measurable in numbers; it is likely to be just beyond an organization's grasp, but the organization can work toward the objective regardless of intermediate achievements. Goals imply a shorter measurable time sequence and an accomplishment that can be measured in numerical terms; for example, a goal might be to achieve a 15 percent ROI within five years. A strategy is a broader course of action—a major action, and usually one implying a relatively long time span. A strategy is what one is going to do and not how one is going to do it. See *tactical plan.*

Stratification (Statistics)

The process of classifying accounting data into separate sampling strata for making estimates. These estimates may be combined to make an overall estimate of a population parameter or moment.

Structured Programming

A technique for organizing and coding programs that reduces complexity, improves clarity, and makes the programs easier to debug and modify. Typically, a structured program is a hierarchy of modules, each of which has a single entry point and a single exit point; control is passed downward through the structure without unconditional branches to higher levels of the structure.

Subsidiary Ledger

A book in which transactions involving particular customers, creditors, inventory items, etc. are recorded. The sum of the balances in the subsidiary ledger for a particular account (i.e., accounts receivable) should agree with the control account figure for that account that appears in the income statement or balance sheet.

Substantive Tests

The types of auditing procedures used to obtain evidence as to the validity and propriety of the accounting treatment of transactions or balances or, conversely, of errors or irregularities therein. They include tests of details of transactions and balances and analytical review of significant ratios and trends. Although the purpose of substantive tests differs from that of compliance tests, both purposes often are accomplished concurrently through tests of details.

Sunk Cost

An expenditure for equipment or other productive resources which cannot be reversed and, thus, one which has no economic relevance in the subsequent decision-making process.

Surrogate

A substitute variable having characteristics or attributes similar to a real variable or phenomenon such that the substitute variable can be used to represent the real variable phenomenon.

Survey Research

A type of descriptive research in which data are gathered from a sample in order to make generalized observations about the population of interest.

System Control Programming

Programming that is fundamental to the operation and maintenance of the system. It serves as an interface with program products and user programs.

Systems Network Architecture (SNA)

The total description of the logical structure, formats, protocols, and operational sequences for transmitting information units through the communication system. Communication system functions are separated into three discrete areas: the application layer, the function management layer, and the transmission subsystem layer. The structure of SNA allows the ultimate origins and destinations of information—that is, the end users—to be independent of, and unaffected by, the specific communication-system services and facilities used for information exchange.

Table*

(1) (ISO) An array of data, each item of which may be unambiguously identified by means of one or more arguments. (2) A collection of data in which each item is uniquely identified by a label, by its position relative to the other items, or by some other means.

Tactical Plan

A plan that encompasses a short time span, generally one year, and which is more detailed than is a strategic plan, which extends over a longer period of time and is broader in scope. A tactical plan is oriented toward the means of attaining goals, whereas a strategic plan is oriented toward the objectives and goals themselves. For example, the tactical budget plan is the sum of the annual sales forecast, production plan, and various expense budgets. See *strategic plan.*

Task

(ISO) A basic unit of work to be accomplished by a computer. The task is usually specified to a control program in a multiprogramming or multiprocessing environment.

Tax Allocation

Interperiod tax allocation—the process of allocating income taxes among time periods. This allocation is made necessary by timing differences between (a) reporting revenue and expenses for financial accounting and (b) for tax returns.

Intraperiod tax allocation—the process of allocating income tax expense applicable to a given period to the items that gave rise to the expense. The allocation is required because of the various locations of income and loss items in the financial statements. The basic rule for intraperiod tax allocation is that the tax follows the item.

Telecommunications System

The devices and functions concerned with the transmission of data between the central processing system and the remotely located users. The system uses the telephone and telegraph lines or microwave for transmitting data to a computer center and/or a remote terminal.

Teleprocessing

Synonym for telecommunications system.

Terminal

(1)* A point in a system or communication network at which data can either enter or leave. (2) A device, usually equipped with a keyboard and some kind of display, capable of sending and receiving information over a communication channel.

Testimonial Audit Evidence

Indirect knowledge formally provided by individual assertions about the existence of a thing or event that is accepted as audit evidence because it has objective properties.

Tests of Compliance

Tests that provide reasonable assurance that internal control methods and procedures are operating effectively.

Theory

A set of explanations that are logically consistent and that describe relationships among phenomena. The explanations may be of different levels of quality ranging from what might be (speculative) through what is (tested empirical proof) to what should be (normative theory).

Throughput

The total amount of useful work performed by a computer system during a given time period.

Time-Series Analysis

The study and analysis of the behavior patterns of various variables or objects over a period of time.

Time-Sharing

(1) (ISO) A mode of operation of a data processing system that provides for the interleaving in time of two or more processes in one processor. (2) A method of using a computing system that allows a number of users to execute programs concurrently and to interact with the programs during execution. (3) (ISO) Deprecated term for conversational mode.

Times-Interest-Earned

See *ratios.*

Total Debt to Total Assets

See *ratios.*

Transfer Price

The price at which goods and services are transferred from one segment of a business to another segment.

Troubled Debt Restructuring

A change in the terms of a debt in which some concession or advantage is granted by the creditor (lender) to the debtor (borrower). For example, the creditor may agree to stretch out the payment terms, temporarily defer some required payments, or accept a smaller payment than is legally due. To be considered a "troubled" debt restructuring, the concession, for legal or economic reasons, must be one that the creditor would not otherwise consider.[23]

Turnaround Time

(1) (ISO) The elapsed time between submission of a job and the return of the complete output. (2) In data communication, the actual time required to reverse the direction of transmission from send to receive or vice versa when using a half-duplex circuit. For most communication facilities, there will be time required by line propagation and line effects, modem timing, and machine reaction. A typical time is 200 milliseconds on a half-duplex telephone connection. (3) See also *response time.*

Ultrafiche

See *microfiche.*

Uncertainty

The condition of not knowing which of a wide-open-ended range of conditions or events will occur and to be unable to assign probability thereto.

Unconsolidated Subsidiary

A subsidiary presented on the parent company's financial statements as an investment, utilizing the equity method of accounting for the investment. Certain types of subsidiaries are often not consolidated, such as foreign subsidiaries in certain countries and financing susidiaries of manufacturing concerns.

Underabsorbed Overhead

The excess of actual manufacturing expenses incurred over the amount of manufacturing overhead applied to production. Synonymous with underapplied overhead.

---

[23]Statement of Financial Accounting Standards No. 15, "Accounting by Debtors and Creditors for Troubled Debt Restructurings," Financial Accounting Standards Board, Stamford, Conn.

Uniformity

The notion that like economic events should be reflected in the same manner by all entities.

Useful Life

The service capacity, normally expressed in time periods or production units, of an asset used in its original form for entity activities, whether or not the use is economically justifiable.

User Profile Table

In systems with time-sharing, a table of user attributes built for each active user from information gathered during log on.

Utility

The relative satisfaction or need gratification derived from a good or service.

Utility Program*

(1) (ISO) A computer program in general support of the processes of a computer; for instance, a diagnostic program, a trace program, a sort program. Synonymous with service program. (2) A program designed to perform an everyday task such as copying data from one storage device to another.

Utilization Cost

The economic sacrifice involved in using an available resource or service to perform some act.

Validation Procedures

The use of confirmation, physical inspection, replication, vouching, reconciliation, account analysis, and other procedures to afford reasonable assurance that an accounting record reflects reality.

Validity

The determination of whether a test yields desired results with the necessary elements of accuracy, precision, reliability, and relevance.

Validity Check

A check that a code group is actually a character of the particular code in use.

Variable (Statistics)

A property or construct that takes on different values.

Variable Budgeting

The budgeting of costs and expenses by areas of activity within time periods into fixed and variable categories, where the amounts of the budgeted variable costs vary with the level of activity. See *flexible budgeting*.

Variable Cost

A cost that increases as the volume of activity increases and decreases as the volume of activity decreases.

Variable-Length Record

(1) A record having a length independent of the length of other records with which it is logically or physically associated. Contrast with fixed-length record. (2)* Pertaining to a file in which the records are not uniform in length.

Variance

A deviation of actual from a standard, goal, or expectation strongly emphasized in applying budgetary and standard cost approaches.

Variance Analysis

The classification of budgetary or standard cost variances so as to reveal price changes, inefficiencies, and other elements resulting from variations in experience.

Variances

A representative list of variances used in variance analysis:

Budget revision variance—the variance of actual performance from budget performance that is due to a change in the budget.

Budget variance—a measure of the variation of actual expenses, revenues, assets, and liabilities from budgeted amounts, normally classified by individual responsibility for the variation.

Capacity variance—see *volume variance*.

Efficiency variance—the difference between actual and standard quantities of labor or variable overhead for units of goods produced, multiplied by the standard price per unit.

Idle capacity variance—a measure of the cost of idle plant capacity.

Labor rate variance—the difference between actual wages and standard wages, multiplied by the actual hours of direct labor used.

Material price variance—the difference between the actual unit price for purchased parts and materials and the established unit price standard, multiplied by the actual number of units acquired (or used in production).

Material quantity variance—the difference between the actual unit usage of parts and materials and the established unit usage standard, multiplied by the standard unit price for the material.

Method variance—a change in production method or technique that occasions a variance from standard cost.

Overhead efficiency variance—the difference between actual direct labor hours incurred and the standard direct labor hours of production, multiplied by the standard variable overhead rate per direct labor hour or per some alternate appropriate basis.

Overhead spending variance—the difference between actual overhead costs incurred and the sum of the actual number of units (multiplied by the variable overhead rate) plus the budgeted fixed overhead costs.

Overhead volume variance—the difference between actual and budgeted units produced in a time period, multiplied by the fixed overhead rate. See *volume variance.*

Sales mix variance—the variance in the actual versus the forecasted sales mix, due to a change in sales pattern with products having varying profit ratios.

Sales volume variance—the difference between actual and forecasted sales due to changes in sales volume.

Spending variance—an average price variance for variable overhead which may be broken down into component parts.

Volume variance—the difference between fixed cost assigned to products in a specified time period and budgeted fixed manufacturing overhead. In substance it is the amount of under-or over-absorbed fixed manufacturing overhead that is due to a variation in the level of use of fixed plant assets from the budgeted or scheduled level of use in a specified time period. Also referred to as capacity variance.

Verifiability

The attribute of information that allows duplication, by qualified individuals working independently of one another, of a measure or conclusion.

Virtual Storage

(ISO) The storage space that may be regarded as addressable main storage by the user of a computer system in which virtual addresses are mapped into real addresses. The size of virtual storage is limited by the addressing scheme of the computing system and by the amount of auxiliary storage available, and not by the actual number of main storage locations.

Virtual Storage Access Method

An access method for direct or sequential processing of fixed- and variable-length records on direct access devices.

Virtual Telecommunications Access Method

A set of programs that control communication between terminals and application programs running under DOS/VS, OS/VSI, and OS/VS2.

Voice Grade Line

The common communications line used in normal telephone communications. It is an essential part of most communications systems involving computers and data transmission. The voice grade line has a bandwidth of 2,400 bps (bits per second).

Volume Variance

See *variances.*

Vouching

The process of establishing the accuracy and authenticity of entries in ledger accounts or other records by examining such supporting evidence of transactions as invoices, paid checks, receiving reports, and other original papers.

VSAM

See *virtual storage access method.*

VTAM

See *virtual telecommunications access method.*

Wand Leader

A device used to read magnetically encoded information on merchandise tickets, credit cards, and employee badges.

Warranty Cost

A cost incurred in connection with the sale of goods or services that requires a further performance by the seller after the sale has taken place.

Working Capital

(1) The excess of current assets over current liabilities.

(2) Sometimes used to mean current assets, when the excess of current assets over current liabilities is referred to as net working capital.

Zero Base Budgeting

The process of developing a periodic budget on the assumption that the enterprise is initiating operations at the beginning of the budget period; thus total budget must be developed rather than an increment-over-last-period type of budget.

NATIONAL ASSOCIATION OF ACCOUNTANTS
MANAGEMENT ACCOUNTING PRACTICES COMMITTEE
1982-83

Chairman
John F. Chironna
Director of Accounting Practices
International Business Machines Corp.
Tarrytown, N.Y.

Dennis R. Beresford
Partner
Ernst & Whinney
Cleveland, Ohio

James Don Edwards
J. M. Tull Professor of Accounting
University of Georgia, School of
Accounting
Athens, Ga.

Penny A. Flugger
Auditor
Morgan Guaranty Trust Co.
New York, N.Y.

William J. Ihlanfeldt
Assistant Controller
Shell Oil Company
Houston, Tex.

Earl R. Milner
Vice President and Controller
A. O. Smith Corporation
Milwaukee, Wis.

Bryan H. Mitchell
Controller
A. C. Nielsen Co.
Northbrook, Ill.

Stanley R. Pylipow
Vice-President / Finance &
Administration
Fisher Controls International, Inc.
St. Louis, Mo.

Allen H. Seed, III
Senior Consultant
Arthur D. Little, Inc.
Cambridge, Mass.

Howard L. Siers
Assistant Comptroller
E.I. du Pont de Nemours &
Company, Inc.
Wilmington, Del.

Robert B. Sweeney
Director—School of Accountancy
University of Alabama
University, Ala.

Armin C. Tufer
Partner
Deloitte Haskins & Sells
Chicago, Ill.

SUBCOMMITTEE ON MAP STATEMENT PROMULGATION
1982-83

*Robert B. Sweeney, *Chairman**

*John F. Chironna

*Allen H. Seed, III

*Howard L. Siers

Herbert C. Knortz
Executive Vice President & Comptroller
International Telephone & Telegraph
Corporation
New York, N.Y.

Herbert H. Seiffert
Assistant Treasurer
Johnson & Johnson
New Brunswick, N.J.

Donald J. Trawicki
Partner
Touche Ross & Co.
New York, N.Y.

* Also member of MAP Committee

NAA STAFF

Louis Bisgay, *Director,* Management Accounting Practices
Robert W. McGee, *Manager,* Management Accounting Practices
Rosemary A. Schlank, *Manager,* Management Accounting Practices

Statements on Management Accounting

Statement Number 4A
November 1, 1984

PRACTICES AND TECHNIQUES

Cost of Capital

In accordance with the charge to the Management Accounting Practices (MAP) Committee to issue statements on management accounting principles and practices, Statements on Management Accounting are promulgated to reflect official positions of the National Association of Accountants (NAA). The work of the MAP Committee is based on a framework for management accounting, whose principal categories are:

1. Objectives
2. Terminology
3. Concepts
4. Practices and Techniques
5. Management of Accounting Activities

Statements on Management Accounting

Statement Number 4A
November 1, 1984

Practices and Techniques:
Cost of Capital

National Association of Accountants

Acknowledgments

The National Association of Accountants is grateful to the many individuals who contributed to the publication of Statement 4A, *Cost of Capital.* Appreciation is extended to members of the Management Accounting Practices Committee and its Subcommittee on MAP Statement Promulgation and also to former MAP Committee members: Dennis R. Beresford, partner, Ernst & Whinney; Penny A. Flugger, senior vice president and auditor, Morgan Guaranty Trust Company; Earl R. Milner, vice president and controller, A.O. Smith Corporation; and William J. Shannon, corporate controller, Ingersoll Milling Machine Company. Special thanks are extended to Professor Robert A. Howell (clinical professor of management and accounting, Graduate School of Business, New York University, and president of Howell Management Corporation), Mr. Kenneth Brown (consultant, Howell Management Corporation), and Professor Jonathan B. Schiff (Pace University and NAA staff) for their research and writing associated with this project.

Introduction

1. This Statement is intended to be a practical guide to understanding and computing the cost of capital. In keeping with this goal, much of the theory behind various concepts has been omitted. A wealth of literature has appeared on this subject; it is partially referenced at the end of this Statement. This Statement should be particularly beneficial to those desiring a basic familiarity with the subject or to those seeking a brief overview of its salient aspects.

2. The reader will not find a standard formula that he or she can apply to all problems. Several ways of computing and using the cost of capital are discussed. This Statement does not express a view in favor of any one method; rather, it describes several alternatives and discusses their differences. Judgment is required to decide the best way to compute the cost of each component as well as the overall cost of capital. These decisions depend on the data available and how the calculated cost is to be used.

Definition

3. The cost of capital is a composite of the cost of various sources of funds comprising a firm's capital structure. It is the minimum rate of return that must be earned on new investments that will not dilute the interests of the shareholder.

4. Management often makes decisions that affect the firm's capital structure. Sources of financing may be different, costs may vary, or the proportion of each source in relation to the entire capital structure may change. Each of these variations affects the firm's cost of capital.

Uses of the Cost of Capital

5. The cost of capital may be of assistance in three major uses: in making capital investment decisions, in managing working capital, and in evaluating performance.

6. In making capital investment decisions, the cost of capital can be used as a discount rate of return in evaluating the present value of project cash flows or as a "hurdle" or "threshold" rate when evaluating the internal rate of return. The hurdle rate used

may differ from the calculated cost of capital to reflect the relative risk attributed to a specific project, division, or business unit.

7. In managing working capital, the cost of capital may be used to calculate the cost of carrying the firm's investment in receivables and to evaluate alternative policies and practices with regard to receivables. When deciding on an inventory management strategy, the cost of capital can be used as a guide to evaluate the financial costs of carrying inventory.

8. The cost of capital may also be employed as a benchmark for the evaluation of performance. The reported return on capital or return on net assets may be compared with the cost of capital for this purpose.

9. The cost of capital may also be used in acquisition analysis, liquidation studies, research and development decisions, and source-of-financing decisions. In regulated industries the cost of capital is used to set rates that will generate the allowable profit for the firm.

Financing Alternatives

10. Capital can be obtained in several ways: various forms of debt, such as notes, bonds, or loans, may be issued; new shares of preferred or common stock may be issued; or the firm may retain earnings instead of distributing these earnings as dividends. Each of these sources of capital has its own cost, and the cost of each component may vary as the mix of the components changes. Of course, cost is not the only factor considered when choosing among financing alternatives. Control, risk, timing, and flexibility must be considered, as well as the relevant planning horizon involved, be it two, three, five or more years into the future. However, this Statement deals only with the cost of capital.

Cost of Capital Calculation

11. The cost of capital is found by determining the costs of the individual types of capital and multiplying the cost of each by its proportion in the firm's total capital structure. The cost of capital is therefore a weighted average.

12. If a firm uses "n" different types of financing, each with its own cost and proportion in the capital structure, and "k" represents the cost of an element in the capital structure, and "p" is the

proportion that element comprises of the total capital structure, a general formula for the cost of capital (k_a) is:

$$k_a = p_1 k_1 + p_2 k_2 \ldots + p_n k_n \qquad \text{(eq. 1)}$$

13. For example, assume XYZ Corporation uses three types of financing: debt, preferred stock, and common equity, with after-tax costs of 6%, 12%, and 16%, respectively. If the debt comprises 30% of the capital structure, the preferred stock 20%, and the common equity 50%, the cost of capital would be:

$$
\begin{aligned}
k_a &= p_1 k_1 + p_2 k_2 + p_3 k_3 \\
&= .30\,(6\%) + .20\,(12\%) + .50\,(16\%) \\
&= 12.2\%
\end{aligned}
$$

14. For the purpose of investment decisions, the cost of capital should be based on the current or prospective cost of the various capital components rather than on their historical costs. Two problems must be considered when computing the weighted average cost of capital:

a. How to determine the cost (k) of each of the various components, and
b. How to determine their respective weights (p) in the capital structure of the firm.

This Statement discusses various approaches to solving these problems.

Capital Components and Their Costs

15 The first step in determining the cost of capital is to calculate the cost of each component in the capital structure (the k's in eq. 1). Three types of financing are commonly used by firms: debt, including that portion of short-term debt considered permanent; preferred stock, and common equity. While many similar steps are involved in calculating the cost of each component, each financing method has its own attributes.

The Cost of Debt

16. The after-tax cost of debt is the interest rate, k_d, multiplied by

(1–t), where "t" is the firm's applicable tax rate. Questions which must be answered in applying this method are:

a. What interest rate should be used for k_d?
b. How should different issues or types of debt be handled?
c. What effect do income taxes have on the interest rate?

17. Usually debt has specific, stated interest cost provisions. Interest is paid either during the term of debt, or at the end of it, deducted from the principal in advance (discounting), or treated using a combination of these methods. The amortization of the premium or discount should be considered part of the cost of debt. In the event that debt is discounted or requires compensating balances, appropriate adjustment should be made to the stated interest rate.

18. The effective cost of debt is lower than the stated interest rate because the firm can deduct interest payments when determining taxable income. The higher the tax rate, the lower the effective after-tax cost of debt. In order to equate the tax treatment of debt and equity, the interest rate net of the applicable tax rate is used in the cost of capital formula.

19. For example, if the firm's debt consists of 12% bonds and it anticipates a 45% tax rate, the cost of debt would be:

$$\text{Effective after-tax rate} = k_d\ (1–t) \qquad \text{(eq. 2)}$$
$$= 12\%\ (1–.45)$$
$$= 6.6\%$$

20. While regulators often use an average stated actual cost for k_d to determine allowable rates of return for pricing purposes, it is preferable to use the current replacement cost (market value) of debt for calculating a cost of capital for the purpose of assessing the present value of future cash flows or for evaluating alternative investment proposals of financial policies if the policies or proposals involve debt financing. Cash flows associated with new investments should be matched with the current or prospective cost of all capital associated with such investments.

21. If one or more issues of debt are involved, yields to maturity should be used to calculate the cost of debt. The average cost of debt would therefore appear as shown in Table 1.

4

Table 1
Weighted Average Cost of Debt
using Yield to Maturity

1	2	3	4	5 = (3×4)
Debentures	Market value	% of total	Yield to maturity[1]	Weighted cost
Issue A	45	10.0	11.2%	1.12
Issue B	125	27.8	12.4%	3.45
Issue C	280	62.2	13.1%	8.15
Total	450	100.00		

Weighted average cost of debt before taxes	12.7%
Adjustment for income taxes (1−.45)	.55
Weighted average cost of debt after income taxes	6.99%

[1]The yield to maturity on a bond is the rate of discount that equates the present value of all interest and principal payments with the proceeds of the bond. If interest payments are made at the end of each year and the face value of the bond is $1,000, we solve the following equation for r, the yield to maturity:

$$p = \frac{I}{(1 + r)} + \frac{I}{(1 + r)^2} + \cdots + \frac{I}{(1 + r)^n} + \frac{1,000}{(1 + r)^n}$$

Where:

p = proceeds
I = annual interest and payment per coupon rate
n = number of years to bond maturity

Convertible Debt

22. When a firm issues debt convertible into common stock, it is in reality issuing a bond plus a call option on the equity of the firm. Convertible debt is a security that is exchangeable into common stock at the option of the holder under specified terms and conditions. Because of this conversion feature, the coupon rate on an equivalent convertible debt issue is less than that of the straight debt issue. The actual cost of convertible debt is higher than the cost of debt that is not a convertible issue because equity has a higher cost than debt.

23. In determining the cost of capital, convertible debt should be treated as though it has been converted to equity if the conversion price of the debt is close to the market value of the firm's common stock. Otherwise, convertible debt should be treated as debt. In such cases, a premium may be imputed and added to the interest rate to reflect the value of the conversion privilege.

Preferred Stock

24. The general formula for the component cost of preferred stock (k_p) used to calculate the firm's cost of capital is the preferred dividend (D_p) divided by the proceeds (actual cost) or current price per share (P_p) (current or prospective cost):

$$k_p = \frac{D_p}{P_p} \qquad \text{(eq. 3)}$$

25. Preferred dividends are not tax deductible and represent an outflow of after-tax funds. For example, if a $100 share of a firm's preferred stock has an 11% dividend, it costs the firm $11 in after-tax earnings. If XYZ has a 45% tax rate, the company must earn $1.82 before taxes for each dividend dollar paid.

26. A firm may have more than one issue of preferred stock outstanding. In this case, the weighted average rate on all preferred stock should be used.

Deferred Items

27. Deferred items may be classified in various ways depending on the source of the item. With respect to the cost of capital, an item such as deferred income taxes may be treated as "free capital" if the source of such capital is the federal government or other third parties. However, if the source is considered attributable to shareholders, deferred items may be classified as part of equity. In practice, some firms omit deferred items in the calculation of the cost of capital, some treat them as zero cost items, and some treat them as part of equity.

28. Foreign currency translation and similar noncash adjustments to common equity that are not included in the company's target capital structure should ordinarily not be included in the calculation of the cost of capital.

Common Equity

29. Common shareholders' equity consists primarily of common stock, paid-in capital, and retained earnings. The cost of equity capital is the most difficult component to calculate. In theory, it is the expected, required, or actual rate of return on the firm's

common stock which, if earned, will leave the market value of the stock unchanged. This rate is difficult to estimate because there are no fixed contractual payments for common stock as there are for other securities issued by the firm. This Statement presents several methods of estimating the cost of equity ranging from simple to complex. Each method has advantages and disadvantages. More than one method may be used to provide a reasonable estimate of the cost of equity capital.

Historical Rate of Return

30. One method used to determine the cost of equity capital is the historical rate of return to the stockholder. This method is applied by calculating the rate of return earned by an investor who is assumed to have purchased the stock some time in the past, held it until the present, and sold it at current market prices.

31. For example, assume that five years ago the price of a share of XYZ Corporation's common stock was $100. Dividends of $10 were paid each year, and today the stock sells for $110. The average rate of return for an investor who purchased a share at $100 was 12% per year ($10 dividend plus $2 average annual capital gain/$100) using this historical method. Twelve percent is the estimate of the current rate of return on the stock, or the firm's cost of equity capital.

32. If used as an estimate of future cost of capital, this procedure assumes that:

   a. There will be no significant change in the firm's future performance.
   b. No significant changes in the level of interest rates will occur.
   c. Investor attitudes toward risk will not change.

33. This method should be used with a great deal of caution because such conditions rarely, if ever, exist. The historical method is not relevant for future decisions unless the future is expected to be like the past.

Earnings/Price Ratio

34. The earnings/price ratio is calculated by dividing earnings per share by the average price per share. This method is illustrated below.

35. For example, if a share of XYZ is selling for $100 and the expected earnings per share is $12, which is used to approximate the earnings per share, the earnings/price ratio is computed as follows:

$$k_s = \frac{EPS}{P_o} = \frac{12}{100} = 12\% \qquad \text{(eq. 4)}$$

36. It matches two unrelated factors, earnings based on historical experience (EPS) with a price (P_o) that is determined by the investors' perception of the present value of the future cash flows.

Dividend Growth Model

37. The dividend growth model reflects a market value approach to determining the cost of equity capital. The basic logic of this method is that the market price of a stock equals the cash flow of expected future incomes, both dividends and market price appreciation, discounted to their present value. Looked at in another way, this means that when the present value of the future flow of incomes is equal to the market price, the discount rate is equal to the cost of equity capital. A simplifying assumption is made that incomes will grow at a constant compound rate.

38. The dividend growth model projects the cost of equity as the dividend yield plus the expected dividend growth rate (g). If D_1 is the dividend, then the cost of equity capital (k_s) is:

$$k_s = \frac{D_1}{P_o} + g \qquad \text{(eq. 5)}$$

39. Like all methods for determining the cost of equity capital, it requires an estimate, in this case, of the value of "g." However, for entities in which dividend flow is relatively certain, such as some utilities, this model may be used reliably. For example, assume XYZ Corporation's stock is currently selling at $50 a share, the dividend at the end of year 1 is expected to be $6, and dividends are projected to grow at about 5% per year. For this company, the cost of equity capital (k_s) is:

$$k_s = \frac{6}{50} + 5\% = 17\%$$

The dividend in this case one year hence would be: $6 + $6 (.05) = $6.30, which is the initial dividend plus the growth in dividend.

40. This equation is useful only if market expectations are that dividends per share will grow at the rate "g." Therefore, the important factor is estimating investors' perception of the growth in dividends per share. If investors believe that the past trend in earnings per share will continue, this trend expressed as a percent may be used as the dividend growth rate.

The Capital Asset Pricing Model (CAPM)

41. The capital asset pricing model was developed in connection with portfolio management. Some writers believe that it also can be useful to measure the cost of equity capital for an individual firm.

42. The capital asset pricing model is based on the premise that the required rate of return on any security equals the riskless rate of interest plus a premium for risk, the latter designated as Beta. It is the expected or required rate of return on the firm's common stock, and the CAPM can be used to obtain an estimate of this cost.

43. Usually the riskless cost is the current or anticipated rate on long-term U.S. Treasury bonds or short-term Treasury bills. The amount added for risk of a given firm is found by calculating its Beta.

44. Formulas for computing Beta are used principally to describe the risk of a portfolio of securities rather than the risk characteristics of an individual firm. Moreover, studies have shown that calculations of Beta based on historical data may not produce reliable results. Investment firms calculate Betas for individual firms whose stock is traded publicly.

45. The CAPM, when used to estimate the cost of equity capital, requires the following steps:

   a. Estimate the riskless rate, R_F (either the rate on U.S. Treasury bonds or the 30-day Treasury bill rate).
   b. Estimate the stock's Beta (b) or obtain this estimate from a brokerage firm or investment advisory service.
   c. Estimate the return on the market as a whole, or on an average stock value (k_M). Studies have indicated that the rate of return for the market as a whole has historically been gener-

ally 5-7% higher than the risk-free rate of return. Thus, some firms add 6% to the Treasury bond rate to approximate the rate of return for the market as a whole.

d. Estimate the firm's cost of equity (k_s) as:

$$k_s = R_F + b\,(k_M - R_F)$$

For example, if the Treasury bond rate is 8%, XYZ's Beta is 0.9, and the expected return for the market is 14%, XYZ's cost of equity calculated using CAPM would be:

$$k_s = 8 + 0.9\,(14 - 8) = 8 + 5.4 = 13.4\%$$

e. While the CAPM appears to produce a precise calculation of the firm's cost of equity, each term in this equation is, in fact, an estimate. Factors affecting the estimate are:

- The decision whether to use long-term or short-term Treasury bonds for R_F.

- The difficulty in estimating the Beta that investors expect the company to have in the future.

- The problems in arriving at the expected return for the market as a whole.

Bond Yield Plus Risk Premium

46. Another approach to estimating a firm's cost of equity is the addition of a risk premium to the interest rate on the firm's long-term debt. A firm's cost of equity is somewhat greater than the interest rate on debt.

47. A rough approximation based on historical patterns is obtained by adding the risk premium to the firm's bond rate. The risk premium is estimated to be 4%. For example, if XYZ's bonds are yielding 12% return, an estimate of its cost of equity (k_s) might be:

$$k_s = \text{Pretax bond yield} + \text{risk premium} = 12\% + 4\% = 16\%$$

48. The 4% spread is judgmental and varies depending on market conditions and other factors. Therefore the value of k_s calculated in this manner should be viewed as a quick rule-of-thumb approximation.

Weighting Methods

49. Once the costs of the various capital components have been determined, it is necessary to weight them to calculate the cost of capital. Any of three methods can be used to determine these weights (the p's in eq. 1): the existing proportions of the capital components on the firm's balance sheet, the current proportions of the market values of the firm's outstanding securities, or the proportions that should be maintained in the firm's target capital structure. For retrospective evaluation of the company, the existing capital structure may be appropriate. For prospective evaluation, the target capital structure is more relevant.

50. One method for determining weights is to use the book value of each capital component as recorded on the balance sheet. Those who advocate a book value weight approach argue that it corresponds to the amounts shown for the assets on the balance sheet; therefore, using this method preserves consistency with published data. However, this method poses problems. The company's securities, if traded publicly, sell at market values that may be quite different from those stated on the balance sheet.

51. Some authorities support the use of market value proportions to calculate the cost of capital. This approach is consistent with using market values to determine the cost of the individual components of capital.

52. The differences between the relative weights derived from using book and market values are presented in XYZ's partial balance sheet (Table 2). In this illustration, there is a relatively large difference between the two weighting methods. The effect of this difference on the cost of capital is shown in Table 2, page 12.

53. Another approach is to use the weights that exist in the firm's target capital structure. Theoretically, each firm has a capital structure, i.e., a mix of its capital components, that provides the optimum balance of risk and return. Firms establish target capital structures and raise new capital in a manner that will keep the actual capital structure in the desired proportions over time. Proponents of this approach argue that the target proportions of debt, preferred stock, and common equity should be used to calculate the firm's future cost of capital.

Computing the Cost of Capital

54. Once the cost of each component and its proportion in the capi-

Table 2
XYZ Corporation Partial Balance Sheet

Year ended December 31, 19XX
(Dollar figures in millions)

	Book value	Book proportions	Market value	Market proportions
Debentures, Issue A (11%)	$ 50	0.05	$ 45	0.03
Debentures, Issue B (12%)	127	0.12	125	0.08
Debentures, Issue C (13%)	276	0.26	280	0.19
Total debt	$ 453	0.43	$ 450	0.30
Preferred stock				
($11 dividend, $100 par)	50	0.05	39	0.03
common equity[1]	540	0.52	1,015	0.67
Total capital	$1,043	1.00	$1,504	1.00

[1]This example ignores deferred items. Equity includes common stock outstanding and retained earnings.

tal structure have been determined, they can be used to compute the firm's cost of capital. As shown in eq. 1, this is done by multiplying the cost of each source of capital by its proportion in the capital structure to obtain a weighted cost for each element. The sum of these weighted costs is the weighted average cost of capital. As an example, the weighted average cost of capital for XYZ Corporation is computed using market values.

55. The yields to maturity of the three debentures A, B, and C are 11.2%, 12.4%, and 13.1%, respectively. If the market proportions of debt from Table 1 are applied, the weighted average or overall cost of debt is 12.7%. (See Table 1 for computations.)

Effective cost of debt = 12.7 (1 − 0.45) = 6.99%

The market price of preferred stock is $78 per share. Its component cost is then calculated from eq. 3:

$$k_p = \frac{D_1}{P_p} = \frac{11}{78} = 14.1\%$$

56. Because the cost of retained earnings is considered the same as the cost of common stock, these two components are combined and referred to as common equity. Assume XYZ's common stock dividend expected next year is $12 and dividends have

Cost of Capital

grown at a rate of 5% per year. If the stock is currently selling at $100, the cost of common equity is:

$$k_p = \frac{D_1}{P_0} + g = \frac{12}{100} + 5\% = 17\%$$

(If all these data are not available, one of the other methods can be used to compute the cost of common stock.)

Table 3 shows a sample weighted-average cost of capital calculation.

Table 3

	Cost	Weight (Table 2)	Composite
Debt	7.0%	0.30	2.1
Preferred stock	14.1%	0.03	0.4
Common equity	17.0%	0.67	11.4
Cost of capital		1.00	13.9%

Divisional Costs of Capital

57. A single company-wide cost of capital may not be an acceptable criterion in capital budgeting analysis, especially for a diversified business. In such a case, the use of a divisional cost of capital may be warranted for a unit of the company that has different risk and return characteristics than the company as a whole.

58. One way of estimating divisional cost of capital is to compute with the costs of various fund sources for the firm as a whole, then allow for divisional risk characteristics by changing the proportion of debt and equity in the divisional capital structure accordingly.

Another alternative involves regarding the division as typical of its industry with debt/equity ratios and costs similar to those of the industry. These data are available from the investment firms.

Summary

59. The cost of capital can be a useful management tool for evaluating alternative investments. It is an estimation that is reliable

only to the extent of the reliability of its component parts. The measurement of the cost of equity is usually the most troublesome element. Additionally, in formulating the cost of capital, estimates and assumptions are made that affect the accuracy of this measure and the degree upon which it can be relied. With respect to prospective decision making, historical information used as inputs in the cost of capital formulation is relevant only to the extent that it represents current cost.

60. Cost of capital is one criterion that should be examined with other data with respect to a business decision and should not be the sole criterion.

Appendix: Annotated Bibliography— Cost of Capital

The following annotated bibliography includes both published articles and texts and is designed to provide the reader with additional information regarding the cost of capital. The selection criterion for this reference listing was the usefulness of the individual references to the reader.

Articles

a. Abdelsmad, Moustafa and Tai S. Shin, "What You Should Know About the Cost of Capital," *Management World*, November 1981, pp. 31-35. The authors provide an introductory overview of the cost of capital. This brief piece avoids financial jargon and is a good introduction for a nonfinancial manager.

b. Corcoran, Patrick J. and Leonard G. Sahling, "The Cost of Capital: How High Is It?" *Federal Reserve Bank of New York Quarterly Review*, Summer 1982, pp. 23-31. The authors offer a method to remove the distorting effects of inflation from the relevant rates upon which investment decisions are made. The analysis discriminates between the effects of expected inflation and the uncertainty relative to expected inflationary impact.

c. Elliot, Grover S., "Analyzing the Cost of Capital," MANAGEMENT ACCOUNTING, December 1980, pp. 13-24. The author presents a case study and develops the component costs of long-term debt, preferred stock, and common equity. He also discusses problems associated with the cost of capital computation resulting from uncertain future behavior and the impact of inflation.

d. Geyikdagi, Y.M., "The Cost of Capital and Risk of 28 U.S. Multinational Corporations vs. 28 U.S. Domestic Corporations: 1965-1978," *Manage-*

ment International *Review - 1981*, Vol. 21, pp. 89-93. This paper presents a comparison of the cost of equity capital of U.S. multinational firms with the cost of equity capital of U.S. domestic firms over a 13-year period. An extensive bibliography also is provided.

e. Gup, Benton E. and Samuel W. Norwood, III, "Divisional Cost of Capital: A Practical Approach," *Financial Management*, Spring 1982, pp. 20-24. This article reviews previous work on divisional cost of capital and presents an alternative to the application of the capital asset pricing model (CAPM) for this purpose. The alternative was based on practices at Fuqua Industries. The authors also supply a useful bibliography.

f. Hayes, Robert H. and David A. Garvin, "Managing as if Tomorrow Mattered," *Harvard Business Review*, May-June, 1982, pp. 70-79. Contained in this critical piece is a section on the use of the "hurdle rate" derived from the cost of capital. The authors argue that an artificially high rate is employed for capital budgeting decisions which does not reflect current economic realities.

g. Maus, William J., "How to Calculate the Cost of Capital in a Privately-Owned Company," MANAGEMENT ACCOUNTING, June 1980, pp. 20-24. This article presents a method for computing cost of capital when a sound value for stock is not readily available. A case study is used to illustrate the suggested method.

Handbooks

a. Altman, Edward I., *Financial Handbook*, 5th edition, John Wiley & Sons, New York, N.Y., 1981.

b. Hagin, Robert L., *The Dow Jones-Irwin Guide to Modern Portfolio Theory*, Homewood, Ill., 1979.

Textbooks

a. Brigham, Eugene F., *Fundamentals of Financial Management*, 3rd edition, Dryden Press, Hinsdale, Ill., 1983.

b. Gitman, Lawrence J., *Principles of Managerial Finance*, 3rd edition, Harper & Row, New York, N.Y., 1982.

c. Schall, Lawrence D. and Charles W. Haley, *Introduction to Financial Management*, 3rd edition, McGraw-Hill Book Co., New York, N.Y., 1983.

d. Van Horne, James C., *Financial Management & Policy*, 6th edition, Prentice-Hall Inc., Englewood Cliffs, N.J., 1983.

e. Weston, Fred J. and Eugene F. Brigham, *Essentials of Managerial Finance*, 5th edition, Dryden Press, Hinsdale, Ill., 1979.

SUBCOMMITTEE ON MAP STATEMENT PROMULGATION

Robert B. Sweeney, *Chairman*
Memphis State Chair of Accountancy
Memphis State University
Memphis, Tenn.

*Robert N. Anthony

John F. Chironna
Director of Accounting Practices
IBM Corporation
Tarrytown, N.Y.

Richard A. Curry
Senior Vice President-Finance
The Coleman Company
Wichita, Kans.

Robert A. Howell
*Clinical Professor of Management
and Accounting*
Graduate School of Business
New York University
New York, N.Y.

Herbert C. Knortz
Executive Vice President & Comptroller
ITT Corporation
New York, N.Y.

*Allen H. Seed, III

Herbert H. Seiffert
Assistant Treasurer
Johnson & Johnson
New Brunswick, N.J.

Donald J. Trawicki
Partner
Touche Ross & Company
New York, N.Y.

*Also a member of MAP Committee

NATIONAL ASSOCIATION OF ACCOUNTANTS
MANAGEMENT ACCOUNTING PRACTICES COMMITTEE
1984-85

Statements on Management Accounting

Statement Number 4B
June 13, 1985

PRACTICES AND TECHNIQUES

Allocation of Service and Administrative Costs

In accordance with the charge to the Management Accounting Practices (MAP) Committee to issue statements on management accounting principles and practices, Statements on Management Accounting are promulgated to reflect official positions of the National Association of Accountants (NAA). The work of the MAP Committee is based on a framework for management accounting, whose principal categories are:

1. Objectives
2. Terminology
3. Concepts
4. Practices and Techniques
5. Management of Accounting Activities

Statements on Management Accounting

Statement Number 4B
June 13, 1985

Practices and Techniques: Allocation of Service and Administrative Costs

National Association of Accountants

Acknowledgments

The National Association of Accountants is grateful to the many individuals who contributed to the publication of Statement 4B, "Allocation of Service and Administrative Costs." Appreciation is extended to members of the Management Accounting Practices Committee and its Subcommittee on MAP Statement Promulgation. Special thanks are extended to Jonathan B. Schiff (Pace University and NAA staff) for his research and writing associated with this project.

Introduction

1. This Statement is intended to help management accountants deal with problems associated with the allocation of service and administrative costs. It is the position of the National Association of Accountants (NAA) that allocations are appropriate in certain circumstances and that some approaches to allocating these costs are superior to others. A summary of NAA recommendations may be found in paragraphs 33-37.
2. The allocation of service and administrative costs is of concern to operating executives as well as to management accountants because these costs often are substantial and have a significant impact on segment profitability, product cost finding, government contract pricing, and the valuation of assets.
3. Problems in allocating service and administrative costs have been highlighted by recent court cases, often in situations involving rate-regulated industries. The decisions of the courts are a reflection of common and case law. They lack consistency with regard to the allocation of corporate costs to cost objects.
4. Under various circumstances, some or all of the elements of service and administrative costs are allocated to cost objects. This Statement suggests the circumstances under which these costs should be allocated and the methods of allocation that are appropriate in each of these circumstances.

Statement Scope

5. Costs assigned to a given cost object are either direct costs or indirect costs of that cost object. A cost item is a direct cost if it can be identified specifically with a cost object in an economically feasible manner. A direct cost, therefore, is a cost that is assigned directly to a cost object.

   A cost item is an indirect cost if it cannot be identified specifically with a cost object in an economically feasible manner. An indirect cost is allocated to the applicable cost objects on some reasonable basis. This Statement is limited to allocated costs.
6. There are two types of cost allocations: (a) the allocation of costs to time periods (for example, the allocation of the cost of plant to the periods for which the plant is used, via the

depreciation mechanism) and (b) the allocation of the costs of a time period to the cost object whose costs are measured during that period. This Statement is limited to allocations of the latter type.

7. There are three general types of cost construction: full costs, responsibility costs, and differential costs. Because the cost allocation problem for each is considerably different, the types are discussed separately.

8. The Statement applies only to allocations that are material in amount, that is, to practices that might make a difference in the actions of the person who uses the cost information.

9. This Statement relates primarily to broad cost objects such as divisions, or similar responsibility centers, and product lines within a larger entity. Service and administrative costs collected in production cost centers are assigned to products flowing through these cost centers. The allocation of such costs to products is not addressed in this Statement.

Definitions

10. Service and administrative costs are costs that are incurred by headquarters staffs or other central units, as contrasted with costs that are incurred in production, marketing, or other operating units. In general. service units exist to provide services to other units, and administrative costs are incurred for the entity as a whole. For the purpose of this Statement, there is no need to make a precise distinction between them.

A cost object is a product, contract, project, organizational subdivision, or other unit for which costs are measured or estimated.

Full Costs

11. The full cost of a cost object is the sum of its direct costs plus a fair share of applicable indirect costs. Therefore, if the purpose of assigning costs is to measure full costs, a fair share of service and administrative costs should be allocated to those cost objects to which they are applicable.

12. The circumstances in which the measurement of full costs may be appropriate include: (a) external reporting per Financial Accounting Standards Board (FASB) and Securities & Exchange Commission (SEC) guidelines; (b) analysis of

Allocation of Service and Administrative Costs

the economic profitability of a division, or other subdivision of an entity, or product line; (c) measurement of the cost of providing a service (for example, the cost of operating a company's cafeteria); (d) calculation of a price that is based on full cost, such as the rates charged by regulated companies, the price of a cost-type contract, and prices usually charged for goods and services in many companies; and (e) allocation of state income taxes.

13. Service and administrative costs are allocated to divisions to satisfy the external reporting requirements of the Financial Accounting Standards Board and the Securities & Exchange Commission. Statement of Financial Accounting Standards (SFAS) No. 14, "Financial Reporting for Segments of a Business Enterprise," requires that operating expenses not traceable directly to an industry segment be allocated on a reasonable basis to those segments deriving benefits. (Certain expenses, however, are not to be allocated for FAS 14 purposes: general corporate expenses, interest expense, and income taxes.) For SEC purposes, in filings that for the first time include separate financial statements of a subsidiary, division, or lesser component of a corporate entity, historical income statements may have to be revised to include an allocation of corporate costs not allocated previously. Examples include cases of initial registration statements for spinoffs or significant acquisitions.

14. If the objective is to measure full costs, the preferable method of allocating service and administrative costs is based on a hierarchy of alternatives, arranged in the order of how closely they are related to the cause of the cost's incurrence:

   a. To the extent feasible, elements of these costs should be allocated by measuring the amount of resources consumed by the cost center receiving the service. For example, if a division uses a measured number of hours of the corporate legal staff for a problem that relates to that division, the legal cost should be assigned on the basis of a cost per hour used.

   b. If a direct measure of the amount of services provided to a cost center is not available or is not cost-effective to produce, the costs should be allocated on some basis that reflects the relative amount caused by the various cost centers. Examples of such bases of allocation are given in paragraph 15.

   c. If no causal connection for the amount of cost applicable to cost centers can be found, service and administrative costs should be allocated on the basis of the relative overall activity of the cost center. Activity may be measured by a single criterion, such as the total costs incurred in each cost center, or by an average of several criteria. A commonly used measure is the three-factor "Massachusetts Formula," which is a simple average of the cost center's payroll, revenue, and assets as a proportion of the company's total payroll, revenue, and assets.

15. In allocating costs on the basis of a presumed causal connection, the costs first are grouped into relatively homogeneous pools, then allocated to cost centers on bases such as the following:

a. *Personnel-related costs.* Costs such as personnel department costs, payroll preparation costs, cafeteria losses, and medical department costs may be allocated on the basis of the relative number of employees of the cost object.

b. *Payroll-related costs.* Costs such as pensions, other fringe benefits, and payroll taxes may be allocated on the basis of the relative labor costs of the cost object.

c. *Material-related costs.* Costs such as purchasing, material handling, and storage may be allocated on the basis of the relative material cost of the cost object or, in some circumstances, on the basis of physical quantities.

d. *Space-related costs.* Costs such as insurance, depreciation, and maintenance of physical facilities may be allocated on the basis of the relative square footage (or cubic footage) of the cost object.

e. *Energy-related costs.* Costs such as electricity and steam may be allocated on the basis of the relative amount of installed horsepower or other measure of utility consumption of the cost object.

16. In deciding on the number of cost pools, the benefit of a more detailed calculation should be compared with the record-keeping cost of such detail. At one extreme, a single overhead rate may provide an adequate measure. At the other extreme, a large number of cost pools may be warranted.

17. If costs initially are allocated on the basis of a standard cost and the result does not approximate actual cost, variances between standard and actual cost should be allocated to the responsible cost center.

18. If cost allocation methods are prescribed by a regulatory

body or by the terms of a contract, these requirements take precedence over any of the statements made above. For full costing guidance, firms should consider the promulgations of the Cost Accounting Standards Board (CASB) on allocation methodology, where appropriate. The CASB Standards provide a systematic approach of particular value for the full costing objective. (See Appendix A for a summary of relevant CASB Standards.)

Responsibility Costs

19. Responsibility costs are cost constructions designed to motivate the managers of responsibility centers to act in the best interests of the company. The comparison of actual costs incurred with budgeted or planned costs provides the mechanism to accomplish this purpose.
20. For responsibility costing, service and administrative costs should be allocated to a responsibility center only if (a) they can be influenced, perhaps only indirectly, by actions of the center's manager, (b) they are believed to be helpful in indicating the amount of resources that headquarters provides as support to the responsibility center, (c) they improve the comparability of the performance of a responsibility center with that of an independent company that incurs these costs directly, and/or (d) they are used in product pricing decisions.
21. In order to encourage the use of certain staff services, such as consulting, audit, or legal services, the costs of these services often are not charged to responsibility centers or are charged at less than full cost even though they can be traced to responsibility centers.
22. In general, noncontrollable elements of service and administrative costs should be reported separately from elements of cost that the manager can control. Thus standard predetermined rates should be used where applicable.

Differential Costs

23. Differential costs are elements of cost that are expected to be different if one course of action is adopted as compared with the costs of an alternative course of action and are used in the decision-making arena. The alternatives range in mag-

Table 1
Criteria for Selecting Allocation Bases
as Illustrated by Various Taxation Policies
(see paragraph 28 for corresponding text)

Criterion	Taxation allocation method
Benefits	Tax rate is the same for all citizens, and taxes increase in proportion to wealth — for example, real estate tax. Increased property translates directly into increased need for police, fire, defense, and other services.
Cause	Original gasoline tax which funded highway construction and maintenance; tax increases in relation to use.
Fairness	Flat tax; all citizens are equal, so tax is the same for all, such as a poll tax.
Ability to bear	Progressive tax — for example, income-based tax; individuals with higher income are taxed at a higher rate (redistribution of income — not benefit related).

Table 2
Sample Allocation Bases Reflective
of the Criteria of Table 1
(see paragraph 28 for corresponding text)

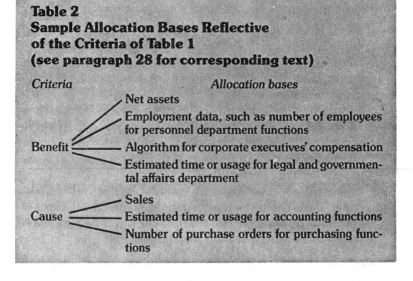

Criteria	Allocation bases
Benefit	Net assets
	Employment data, such as number of employees for personnel department functions
	Algorithm for corporate executives' compensation
	Estimated time or usage for legal and governmental affairs department
Cause	Sales
	Estimated time or usage for accounting functions
	Number of purchase orders for purchasing functions

nitude from a proposal to accept a lower-than-normal price on an individual order to a proposal to enter a new type of business involving the construction of new plants and the development of production and marketing organizations.

24. Differential costs always result from estimates of what costs

would be in the future. Historical costs, therefore, are irrelevant except as they help indicate what future costs will be.

25. Differential costs always relate to the specific alternatives being considered. Therefore, no general statements can be made about which, if any, elements of service and administrative costs are differential in the analysis of a given proposal.

26. In general, the larger the differences among the alternatives being considered, the more elements of service and administrative costs are likely to be different. Also, the longer the time period involved, the more elements of service and administrative costs are likely to be different.

Allocation Criteria

27. Four criteria are used in selecting a specific allocation base: (a) benefit, (b) cause, (c) fairness, and (d) ability to bear the costs. These criteria serve as the theoretical underpinning for allocation practices.

28. Of the four, the two most commonly employed are benefit and cause. For example, the "benefits" criterion can be applied to corporate administrative costs because it is felt that cost objects benefit from these costs and should share responsibility for them. Additionally, the "cause" criterion can be applied to corporate service costs when the user cost objects precipitate the costs involved. There is a good deal of ambiguity regarding the use of the terms "benefit" and "cause;" often they are used interchangeably.

Fairness is an often-discussed criterion, but it is difficult to use operationally because it is so broad.

Ability to bear the costs generally is tied to an allocation based on profit and is used in the context of an embryonic division or product line. This criterion is of limited use because of its dysfunctional effect on management behavior.

In order to demonstrate the criteria for selecting allocation bases, an analogy may be drawn between these criteria and taxation policy (allocation of tax burden). Table 1 illustrates this point. This table is provided solely for instructional purposes. Many managers perceive allocation of central costs as a charge against cost object earnings.

Table 2 provides a list of sample allocation bases and their related criteria.

Table 3
Examples of Service and Administrative
Costs and Related Allocation Bases
Frequently Used in Industry
(see paragraph 31 for corresponding text)

Service and administrative costs	Acceptable allocation bases
Research and development	Estimated time or usage, sales, assets employed, new products developed
Personnel department functions	Number of employees, payroll, number of new hires
Accounting functions	Estimated time or usage, sales, assets employed, employment data
Public relations and corporate promotion	Sales
Purchasing function	Dollar value of purchase orders, number of purchase orders, estimated time or usage, percentage of material cost of purchases
Corporate executives' salaries	Sales, assets employed, pre-tax operating income
Treasurer's functions	Sales, estimated time or usage, assets or liabilities employed
Legal and governmental affairs	Estimated time or usage, sales, assets employed
Tax department	Estimated time or usage, sales, assets employed
Income taxes	Net income
Property taxes	Square feet, real estate valuation

29. Use of different allocation bases varies widely in practice. Some companies use one allocation base for all central service and administrative costs and for all purposes. Most frequently used is a broad measure of activity or size or a combination of these factors, including sales, operating revenue, net assets, and total direct expense. In a multidivisional setting, some firms use sales as the allocation base for simplicity as well as for consistency.

30. Other firms use a single allocation base for all expenses for a single purpose. The bases used in this context are also broad and include net assets, net sales, and number of employees.

31. Some firms use a single allocation base for one expense type

Table 4
Reasons for Allocating and Not Allocating per the Three Allocation Objectives (see paragraph 32 for corresponding text)

Allocation objective: To compute income and asset valuation and to obtain a mutually agreeable price. (Full cost)

Reasons for allocating
a. Recover fair share of shared corporate costs.
b. Sensitize managers to the existence of shared corporate costs, which must be covered.
c. Allocation methods fairly reflect each cost object's share of necessary common costs.
d. When prices are governed by regulation, the allocation of service and administrative costs is required by those regulations.

Reasons for not allocating
a. Prices are determined by forces beyond management's control. Allocation methods will not affect them.
b. Allocations are arbitrary, and the resultant "full costs" are not reliable bases for pricing in certain strategic or tactical decision frameworks.
c. Product line managers are free to establish their own prices, and their profit margins are adequate to cover all costs.
d. The pricing policy is designed to provide a contribution margin from each product sufficiently high to cover all shared costs.

Allocation objective: To motivate managers. (Responsibility cost)

Reasons for allocating
a. Remind business unit managers that shared costs exist and that business unit profit must be sufficient to cover some portion of those costs.
b. Relate business unit profit to total company profits.
c. The method of allocation fairly reflects each business unit's usage of essential common services.
d. Stimulate business unit managers to participate in the control of shared costs.
e. Encourage the use of shared services.

Reasons for not allocating
a. Service and administrative costs are not related to individual business units, so allocations are arbitrary and tend to distort divisional profits.
b. Business unit managers object to charges for costs that are not within their control.
c. The allocation of service and administrative costs would not materially affect reported business unit profit.
d. There is a lack of agreement among business unit managers regarding an appropriate allocation method.
e. The cost of making allocations exceeds the potential benefits derived.

Table 4
**Reasons for Allocating and Not Allocating
per the Three Allocation Objectives**
(continued)

Allocation objective: To predict the economic effects of planning
decisions. (Differential cost)

Reasons for allocating
a. Shared costs are relevant in determining the effect of the proposed decision on the company as a whole.
b. An allocation of service and administrative costs provides the
best available approximation of expected changes in these costs.

Reasons for not allocating
a. Shared costs are not expected to be affected by the planning
decisions made.
b. The allocation of service and administrative costs is arbitrary
and presents a distorted view of prospective cash flows or profit
resulting from a decision.

for all purposes. Table 3 provides examples of shared service
and administrative costs and related allocation bases. The
bases are listed sequentially by frequency of use in industry.

32. Table 4 summarizes the three allocation objectives and the
reasons for allocating or not allocating to achieve each
objective.

Summary of NAA Recommendations

33. Service and administrative cost allocations may or may not
be appropriate for management accounting purposes depending on (a) the objective of the decision to be made and
(b) the reasons that apply to each case. Management accountants therefore should determine which rationale, on
balance, best fits the circumstances depending on the principal objectives of the prospective allocation.

34. In order to provide objective measurements of economic
performance, allocation criteria should reflect cause or
benefit.

35. For full costing purposes, costs should be allocated based
upon a hierarchy of alternatives. Firms should consider the
guidance provided by the CASB in this matter.

36. For the purposes of responsibility accounting:

a. Allocation should be applied where appropriate with the use of predetermined or standard rates or amounts because business unit managers should not be held responsible for variances in certain shared service and administrative costs not traceable to their actions.

b. Allocated corporate expense should be separated from nonallocated expense in order to focus the cost object manager's attention on the expense that he or she can control directly.

37. For differential costing purposes, the only relevant costs are those future costs that relate to the specific alternatives being considered.

Appendix A
CASB Standards

1. When market prices are not appropriate or available, an alternate method of obtaining a "fair" price is used. Cost Accounting Standards promulgated by the Cost Accounting Standards Board (CASB) outline acceptable methods of cost allocation with a view toward arriving at a "fair" price for government contracts. For example, an aircraft manufacturer produces both commercial and military products. The price of a new military product for the United States government will include an allocation of service and administrative costs within the constraints of CASB rulings. CASB standards continue to have the force of law, and these standards, originally intended for use by defense contractors, now are required by virtually all nondefense contracts with the federal government in excess of $100,000. CASB Standards concerning the allocation of central corporate costs therefore provide guidance as to the methodologies that may be applied in situations not involving government contracts. References from relevant standards follow.

2. *No. 403 – Allocation of Home Office Expenses to Segments*
This Standard establishes criteria for allocating home office expenses to cost objects based upon the beneficial or causal relationship between such expenses and the cost objects. Three steps are delineated for this purpose:

a. *Direct Allocation:* Expenses are identified for direct allocation to the maximum extent possible. For example, legal services are allocated based on the time devoted to a specific cost object's affairs.

b. *Indirect Allocation:* Expenses that are not directly allocable but that are material in amount in relation to total home office expense should be pooled into logical and homogeneous groups and allocated on bases that reflect the relationship of expenses to the segment. For example, marketing policy costs may be allocated based on sales or segmental marketing costs.

c. *Residual Expenses:* Expenses that remain unallocated by direct or indirect allocation should be allocated based on overall activity. For example, the expenses of top corporate officers are difficult to allocate based upon the criteria of a beneficial relationship. Sales or the Massachusetts formula[1] are used to allocate these expenses because they represent overall activity of a segment.

The Standard stresses the importance of minimizing the amount of residual expenses.

3. *No. 410 — Allocation of Business Unit General and Administrative Expenses to Cost Objectives*

This Standard provides criteria for allocating business unit general and administrative expenses and home office expenses to business unit final cost objects based on their beneficial or causal relationship.

Business unit general and administrative expenses should be included in a separate indirect cost pool and allocated only to final cost objects. The bases for allocation are total cost, value-added input, or a single cost element such as direct labor hours.

4. *No. 418 — Allocation of Indirect Cost Pools*

This Standard provides criteria for the inclusion of indirect costs in cost pools, including service centers, and offers suggestions for the selection of allocation bases. Indirect costs are included in homogeneous groups based upon the similarity of beneficial or causal relationships, but only if the resultant allocation would have been equivalent if individual items were allocated separately.

---

[1] The Massachusetts formula is an allocation base that employs three elements: payroll, revenue, and assets. This base is commonly used by contractors with the federal government in conformance with CASB standards. This formula is an algorithm based upon a division's causal or beneficial relationship with central costs. The formula's major benefits are its ease of application and its three-factor construct.

5. The preferred allocation basis is one that measures resource consumption, such as labor hours or machine hours. The second order of preference is measure of output, such as units produced or documents processed. If neither of the first two measures is usable, a surrogate measure of output or activity may be applied. Variances, material in amount and arising from the use of forecasted or standard costs, should be allocated to cost objects in proportion to the costs allocated previously using predetermined rates.

Annotated Bibliography — Allocation of Service and Administrative Cost

The following annotated bibliography includes published articles, reports, and texts and is designed to provide additional information regarding the allocation of service and administrative costs. The selection criterion for this reference listing was the usefulness of the individual references to the reader.

Articles

a. Blanchard, Garth A. and Chee W. Chow, "Allocating Indirect Costs for Improved Management Performance," *Management Accounting*, March 1983, pp. 38-41. The authors take a positive view of cost allocation from a behavioral and responsibility accounting standpoint. They also provide a comprehensive and useful list of references.

b. Singhvi, Surendra S., "Corporate Budgeting and Financial Management," *Journal of Accounting, Auditing, and Finance*, Spring 1978, pp. 290-293. The author reports and analyzes the results of a survey of 32 corporations regarding their allocation of central costs. Various allocation methods used by the surveyed firms are discussed and contrasted.

c. Smith, Alan F., "Central Overhead Allocation Makes Sense," *Management Accounting* (British), May 1978, pp. 206-207, 221. The author summarizes the arguments related to the efficacy of allocating or not allocating. While the author views allocation favorably, he does review the economist's negative view of allocating central corporate costs.

d. Zimmerman, Jerold L., "The Cost and Benefits of Cost Allocation," *The Accounting Review*, July 1979, pp. 504-521. In this award-winning article, the author provides a rigorous and comprehensive evaluation of the benefits and costs related to various types of cost allocation, including service and administrative cost allocation. A complete reference section also is provided.

Reports

a. *Toward Common Concepts of Cost Allocations in Cost Accounting,* The Boeing Company, Seattle, Washington, 1978.
b. *Allocating Corporate Expenses,* Business Policy Study No. 108, The National Industrial Conference Board, New York, 1963.
c. *The Allocation of Corporate Indirect Costs,* National Association of Accountants, New York, 1981.
d. *How Companies Allocate Corporate Expenses,* Information Bulletin No. 17, The Conference Board, February 1977.

Textbooks

a. Anthony, Robert N., James S. Reece, and Glenn A. Welsh, *Fundamentals of Management Accounting,* fourth edition, Richard D. Irwin, 1985.
b. Horngren, Charles T., *Cost Accounting: A Managerial Emphasis,* fifth edition, Prentice-Hall, 1983.
c. Mautz, Robert K., *Financial Reporting by Diversified Companies,* Financial Executives Research Foundation, 1968.
d. Shillinglaw, Gordon, *Managerial Cost Accounting,* fifth edition, Richard D. Irwin, 1982.

SUBCOMMITTEE ON MAP STATEMENT PROMULGATION

*Allen H. Seed, III, *Chairman*

*Raymond H. Alleman

*Robert N. Anthony

Richard A. Curry
Senior Vice President — Finance
The Coleman Company
Wichita, Kan.

Robert A. Howell
*Clinical Professor of
Management and Accounting*
Graduate School of Business
New York University
New York, N.Y.

Arthur D. Lyons
Vice President — Controller
FMC Corporation
Chicago, Ill.

Daniel McBride
*Director of Financial
Accounting Policy*
Honeywell, Inc.
Minneapolis, Minn.

J. Charles Stracuzzi
Controller
Blount AgriProducts Group
Grand Island, Neb.

Donald J. Trawicki
Partner
Touche Ross & Company
New York, N.Y.

*Also a member of MAP Committee

NATIONAL ASSOCIATION OF ACCOUNTANTS
MANAGEMENT ACCOUNTING PRACTICES COMMITTEE
1984-85

Chairman
Bernard R. Doyle
Manager-Corporate Accounting Services
General Electric Company
Fairfield, Conn.

Raymond H. Alleman
Vice President & Deputy Comptroller
ITT Corporation
New York, N.Y.

Henry R. Anderson
Director
School of Accounting
University of Central Florida
Orlando, Fla.

Robert N. Anthony
Professor Emeritus
Harvard Business School
Boston, Mass.

William J. Ihlanfeldt
Assistant Controller
Shell Oil Company
Houston, Tex.

Eugene H. Irminger
Senior Vice President of Finance
Centel Corporation
Chicago, Ill.

James J. Latchford
Assistant Vice President &
Assistant Controller
W. R. Grace & Company
New York, N.Y.

Bryan H. Mitchell
Controller
A. C. Nielsen Company
Northbrook, Ill.

Allen H. Seed, III
Senior Consultant
Arthur D. Little, Inc.
Cambridge, Mass.

Norman N. Strauss
Partner
Ernst & Whinney
New York, N.Y.

Edward W. Trott
Partner
Peat, Marwick, Mitchell & Co.
Tampa, Fla.

Robert G. Weiss
Vice President & Controller
Schering-Plough Corporation
Madison, N.J.

NAA STAFF

Louis Bisgay, *Director*, Management Accounting Practices
Jonathan B. Schiff, *Manager*, Management Accounting Practices

Statements on Management Accounting

Statement Number 4C
June 13, 1985

PRACTICES AND TECHNIQUES

Definition and Measurement of Direct Labor Cost

In accordance with the charge to the Management Accounting Practices (MAP) Committee to issue statements on management accounting principles and practices, Statements on Management Accounting are promulgated to reflect official positions of the National Association of Accountants (NAA). The work of the MAP Committee is based on a framework for management accounting, whose principal categories are:

1. Objectives
2. Terminology
3. Concepts
4. Practices and Techniques
5. Management of Accounting Activities

Statements on Management Accounting

Statement Number 4C
June 13, 1985

Practices and Techniques: Definition and Measurement of Direct Labor Cost

National Association of Accountants

Acknowledgments

The National Association of Accountants is grateful to the many individuals who contributed to the publication of Statement 4C, *Definition and Measurement of Direct Labor Cost.* Appreciation is extended to members of the Management Accounting Practices Committee and its Subcommittee on MAP Statement Promulgation. Special thanks are extended to Michael J. Sandretto, Price Waterhouse & Co., Columbus, Ohio, for his research and writing associated with this project.

Definition and Measurement
of Direct Labor Cost

1. The term "direct labor cost" as used in practice, in literature, and in litigation has a wide variety of meanings. Unless the meaning intended in a given context is clear, confusion and misunderstanding are likely to result. The purpose of this Statement is to provide a conceptual definition of direct labor costs that, in the absence of a specified alternative, should be taken as the meaning of this term.
2. In a manufacturing company, direct labor cost is an element of inventory cost and of cost of sales. Differences in the way companies define this term result in variations in the amount recorded as direct labor and the amount recorded as overhead. Differences in the way labor costs are accounted for in cost-type contracts and differences in the way labor costs are measured for responsibility centers, for projects, for functions (such as marketing, administration), and for other purposes also lead to differences in the distinction between direct labor costs and overhead costs and hence in differences in the amount of total costs recorded. If users do not understand what elements are included in direct labor cost in such situations, their interpretations of the numbers may be erroneous.
3. This Statement makes the conceptual definition more concrete by describing how direct labor costs should be measured. Measurement has two aspects: (a) the quantity of labor effort that is to be included as direct labor, that is, the types of hours or other units of time that are to be counted, and (b) the unit price by which each of these quantities is multiplied to arrive at a monetary cost.

Definitions

4. *Direct Labor Cost.* Labor quantities that can be specifically identified with a cost object in an economically feasible manner, priced at the unit price of direct labor.
5. *Cost Object.* A product, contract, project, organizational subdivision, function, or other unit for which costs are measured or estimated.
6. *Direct Cost.* Any cost that can be specifically identified with a cost object in an economically feasible manner.

7. *Labor Quantity.* A unit of labor time, such as a minute, hour, week, or month.
8. *Nonproductive Labor.* Labor quantities that do not contribute directly to the production of goods or services. Examples include coffee-break time, downtime, and personal time.
9. *Cost Element.* A subdivision of cost, such as basic compensation, employer's FICA tax, or health and life insurance costs.
10. *Unit Price of Direct Labor.* Compensation and compensation-related cost elements that can be specifically identified with the direct labor quantity in an economically feasible manner and that can be measured with reasonable accuracy.

Measurement

11. Estimates of direct labor quantities and unit prices may be sufficiently accurate to be considered "specifically identified" with a cost object. The following are examples of estimates that are sufficiently accurate to be considered direct labor costs in most circumstances:
    a. A manufacturing firm establishes standard labor times for its products, but its system does not trace variances from these standards to individual products. Nevertheless, there is a reasonable expectation that variances are proportional to the standard quantities and thus that the actual labor quantities are proportional to the standard quantities.
    b. A manufacturing firm uses a plant-wide predetermined labor rate in its cost system. Its average direct labor unit prices are approximately the same for all products. Wage rate variances are written off as period expenses and cannot be assigned to products.
    c. Break time and personal time relate to all productive time in a day. Nevertheless, break time and personal time are assigned to standard labor time as an average percentage of productive time.
    d. Health insurance premium is added to direct labor cost as a percentage of direct labor cost or as a fixed amount per hour of direct labor.

Labor Quantities

If the cost object is a manufactured or processed product, its direct labor cost normally includes all labor directly associated with transforming or adding value to the product. Such labor includes fabrication, processing, process or machine tending, assembly, packaging, and on-line inspection labor.

13. If the cost object is a service, its direct labor cost normally includes all labor that can be specifically identified with providing the service.

14. If the cost object is a project, its direct labor cost normally includes all labor that can be specifically identified with the project. For a large project, direct labor cost typically includes far more categories of direct labor because it is relatively easy to specifically identify employees with such a project. Examples include the time of janitors, material handlers, maintenance personnel, draftsmen, managers, and engineers. If a large project is broken down into a series of smaller projects, products, or subassemblies, the labor categories listed in this paragraph typically are not included in the direct labor cost of these subdivisions.

15. Costs classified as direct labor costs must be excluded from costs used in calculating overhead rates. For example, if one project is large enough to require the full-time services of a janitor, but other projects share janitorial services, the costs of the shared janitorial services should not be included in the overhead rate applied to the first project.

Nonproductive Labor Quantities

16. Nonproductive time may be a normal and unavoidable part of total labor time. In such cases, a pro rata share of nonproductive time should be classified as direct labor time. For example, coffee breaks and personal time may be established by custom, specified in labor contracts, or legislated. An employee who works seven and one-half hours might be given an additional one-half hour of paid time for coffee breaks and for personal time. If so, and if 15 hours of productive time are associated directly with a cost object, the direct labor quantity should include one hour of nonproductive time, making a total of 16 direct labor hours for the cost object.

17. Other categories of nonproductive labor, such as downtime, clean-up, and training, are less likely to be direct labor

quantities. The amount of downtime usually cannot be specifically identified with a particular cost object; it may result from a parts shortage or a broken machine. Similarly, clean-up or training may be a fill-in for a shortage of work. In these cases, nonproductive time is not a direct labor cost because it cannot be specifically identified with a cost object.

Unit Price of Labor:
Cost Elements in Direct Labor Cost

18. The following cost elements should be included in the unit price of direct labor because they can be specifically identified with a quantity of labor and because they can be measured accurately for the direct labor quantity that is used on a cost object:
    - Basic compensation
    - Individual production efficiency bonuses
    - Group production efficiency bonuses
    - FICA (employer's portion)
    - Cost of living allowances (COLA)

19. The following cost items usually should be included in the unit price of direct labor quantity by firms with relatively stable operations. Although the relationship between direct labor quantities and these cost elements is less certain than the relationship of the cost elements listed in paragraph 17, these costs are incurred because an organization uses a quantity of labor. These elements can be specifically identified with direct labor quantities over a period of approximately one year or less:
    - Health insurance
    - Group life insurance
    - Holiday pay
    - Vacation pay
    - Pension costs and other post-retirement benefits
    - Worker's compensation insurance expense
    - Unemployment compensation insurance — state and federal

20. Premium pay for overtime, holidays, and second- or third-shift work sometimes is considered direct labor cost and sometimes indirect labor cost. If a premium is incurred because of a particular product or other cost object, the premium

is considered a direct labor cost of the cost object causing the premium to be paid, even if that cost object is not produced by premium labor time. If the premium is earned only occasionally and if it is not clear which product caused its incurrence, the premium usually should be considered an indirect labor cost. If premiums are a significant and usual part of compensation, they usually should be included in direct labor cost as an average cost per hour or as an average percentage of direct labor cost.

21. The following items usually are excluded from the unit price of direct labor because they cannot be identified with direct labor quantities, except over the long term:

   - Wage continuation plans (for example, separation allowances)
   - Contributions to Supplemental Unemployment Benefit (SUB) plans
   - Membership dues
   - Safety-related items
   - Company-sponsored cafeteria
   - Recreational facilities

22. Some firms grant employees sick leave credit based on time worked — one day of sick leave for each two months worked, for example. That credit can be accumulated, then taken as vacation or as additional pay after a certain length of time. In such cases, the cost should be considered part of the unit price.

23. Certain activities are related to direct labor quantities. However, except in the case of large cost objects, these activities relate to more than one cost object and are not a part of direct labor cost. Examples are:

   - Payroll department
   - Personnel department

24. Some firms have profit-sharing plans or other bonus plans based on income. In many such firms, the relationship between a labor quantity and the bonus is not specific enough to have the bonus qualify as a part of the unit price of direct labor. The bonus is identified with the firm's overall profitability rather than with the direct labor cost of individual cost objects.

25. An exception to the above profit plan principle is a bonus plan that is limited to, for example, 15% of basic compen-

sation and where profit is almost always greater than needed to pay the maximum bonus. In such cases, the bonus should be considered an element of the unit price of labor.

Cost Systems

26. The cost accounting systems of many firms treat labor costs as consisting only of payroll costs and define direct labor cost as only the payroll cost associated with operations that physically transform or add value to a product. Other labor quantities and other elements of the unit price of labor are treated as overhead. In such systems, direct labor cost is defined more narrowly than in this Statement. Nevertheless, if the relevant overhead is allocated on the basis of direct labor, the resulting product costs may be substantially the same as those resulting from application of the concepts in this Statement. The identification of direct payroll costs in such systems provides information that is needed for many management accounting purposes. However, it should be recognized that direct labor cost as measured in such systems — and for other purposes — may be different from direct labor cost as measured according to the concepts of this Statement.

NATIONAL ASSOCIATION OF ACCOUNTANTS
MANAGEMENT ACCOUNTING PRACTICES COMMITTEE
1984-85

Chairman
Bernard R. Doyle
Manager-Corporate Accounting Services
General Electric Company
Fairfield, Conn.

Raymond H. Alleman
Vice President & Deputy Comptroller
ITT Corporation
New York, N.Y.

Henry R. Anderson
Director
School of Accounting
University of Central Florida
Orlando, Fla.

Robert N. Anthony
Professor Emeritus
Harvard Business School
Boston, Mass.

William J. Ihlanfeldt
Assistant Controller
Shell Oil Company
Houston, Tex.

Eugene H. Irminger
Senior Vice President of Finance
Centel Corporation
Chicago, Ill.

James J. Latchford
Assistant Vice President &
Assistant Controller
W. R. Grace & Company
New York, N.Y.

Bryan H. Mitchell
Controller
A. C. Nielsen Company
Northbrook, Ill.

Allen H. Seed, III
Senior Consultant
Arthur D. Little, Inc.
Cambridge, Mass.

Norman N. Strauss
Partner
Ernst & Whinney
New York, N.Y.

Edward W. Trott
Partner
Peat, Marwick, Mitchell & Co.
Tampa, Fla.

Robert G. Weiss
Vice President & Controller
Schering-Plough Corporation
Madison, N.J.

NAA STAFF

Louis Bisgay, *Director*, Management Accounting Practices
Jonathan B. Schiff, *Manager*, Management Accounting Practices

Statements on Management Accounting

Statement Number 4D
January 3, 1986

PRACTICES AND TECHNIQUES

Measuring Entity Performance

In accordance with the charge to the Management Accounting Practices (MAP) Committee to issue statements on management accounting principles and practices, Statements on Management Accounting are promulgated to reflect official positions of the National Association of Accountants (NAA). The work of the MAP Committee is based on a framework for management accounting, whose principal categories are:

1. Objectives
2. Terminology
3. Concepts
4. Practices and Techniques
5. Management of Accounting Activities

Statements on Management Accounting

Statement Number 4D
January 3, 1986

Practices and Techniques:
Measuring Entity Performance

National Association of Accountants

Acknowledgments

The National Association of Accountants is grateful to the many individuals who contributed to the publication of Statement 4D, "Measuring Entity Performance." Appreciation is extended to members of the Management Accounting Practices Committee and its Subcommittee on MAP Statement Promulgation. Special thanks are extended to James D. Brown and Faith F. Madigan, Howell Management Corp., and to Jonathan B. Schiff, Pace University and NAA staff, for their research and writing associated with this project.

Introduction

1. This Statement is intended to help management accountants deal with the issues associated with measuring entity performance. It is the position of the National Association of Accountants (NAA) that specific measures are appropriate in certain circumstances and that some entity performance measurement approaches are preferable to others. A summary of NAA recommendations appears in paragraphs 45-47.

2. The question "How well is a business entity performing?" is of interest to a number of parties: present and prospective shareholders, bankers and other creditors, financial analysts, senior executives, unit managers, prospective employees, and executives and employees within the firm. Some are interested for investment/disinvestment purposes, others for the purpose of determining creditworthiness, and others for the evaluation of one's own or a subordinate's performance. Managers also may use performance information to correct management problems and to identify opportunities. Not all parties use the same yardstick to measure performance. In this Statement, the primary emphasis is on information useful to management in evaluating an entity's economic performance.

Statement Scope

3. The underlying assumption of this Statement is that an important objective of management is to increase the real economic value of the entity. The Statement describes several commonly used performance measures that are derived from the traditional historical accounting system. It also suggests the use of other quantitative and qualitative performance measures that can provide management with a more realistic reflection of entity performance for a company, division, product line, or territory.

Definitions

4. The following financial statement components have specific definitions for the purposes of this Statement. It is understood that modifications to these definitions may be appropriate

with respect to other reporting objectives and specific business contexts.

a. "Working Capital" consists of current assets less current liabilities excluding interest-bearing debt. Working capital as reconstituted is made up primarily of cash, accounts receivable, inventory, accounts payable, and income tax liability. Working capital is a net asset or investment of the entity that tends to be a function of revenues. Generally, as revenues increase, management is forced to invest additional financial resources in working capital. Interest-bearing debt, such as debt notes, bank loans, and debt securities, is excluded from working capital because (a) the amount of short-term debt is discretionary, as entities can often use short- and long-term debt interchangeably, and (b) the type of debt used is a financing, not an operating, decision.

b. "Property, Plant, and Equipment (PP&E) and Other Assets" consists of all long-term assets. PP&E and other assets are discretionary investments in the sense that outlays generally are not a function of current-period revenues. Management evaluates proposed investments in PP&E separately, and the gross level of PP&E often rises in a step function.

c. "Net Assets Employed" or "Total Capital," which is mathematically equal to working capital plus PP&E and other assets, equals debt (long-term and current plus deferred items) and equity. Net assets employed measures the total funds committed to an entity; changes in the balance are caused only by net cash flow into or out of the entity.

   Investment in working capital, because it is driven by revenues, behaves like a variable cost. The primary components of working capital—cash, accounts receivable, inventory, and accounts payable—are the balance sheet assets and liabilities that support revenues, materials, and direct labor. Investments in PP&E and other assets, on the other hand, are largely discretionary, require management intervention, generate fixed costs, and behave like a fixed cost.

d. "Net Income" is the difference between revenues and expenses after providing for income taxes. Most business entities have various sources of revenue and various types of expenses that can be categorized by function, variability, or timing of recognition.

e. "Noncash Items" are depreciation, amortization, and deferred taxes. In certain instances, other significant noncash items may arise.

f. "Cash from Operations" is defined as the sum of net income and noncash items.

g. "Operating Cash Flow" equals cash flow from operations less increases (plus decreases) in investments in working capital; property, plant, and equipment; and other assets. A negative amount means that additional capital, in the form of debt and/or equity, must be raised for the entity; a positive amount means that debt was reduced, equity repurchased, and/or dividends paid.

Types of Performance Measures

5. A number of performance measures are used by business organizations. The following section provides an overview of major methods currently employed, moving from the narrowest and most traditional to the most comprehensive and least traditional.

Net Income and Earnings Per Share

6. Accounting net income either expressed as a dollar amount or related to the number of shares is a widely used measure of entity performance. Net income and earnings per share attempt to measure value creation based on the accounting transactions that took place in a prior period.

7. Net income is calculated in accordance with generally accepted accounting principles (GAAP). While entities often place an extremely high emphasis on this measure, its value is reduced because it does not consider asset management or the impact of inflation in many circumstances. Furthermore, accounting net income ignores the effect of many value-creating activities that do not meet its stringent requirements of certainty and ability to be estimated. For example, a successful new product development or the loss of key managers has no immediate impact on net income although it may have a significant impact on future net

incomes. Finally, if used as the sole measure of performance, net income may be managed to improve short-term results to the potential detriment of long-term net income. Examples are reductions in outlays for current research and development and the failure to dispose of obsolete assets solely to avoid loss recognition.

8. Net income per share uses net income as its numerator and therefore is subject to the problems mentioned above. Similarly, the complexity of a specific company's capital structure affects the denominator (and often the numerator) of this index. Given these circumstances, comparability often is difficult.

9. Net income, therefore, should be used with an understanding of its limitations and in conjunction with other accounting and nonfinancial measures of performance.

Cash Flows

10. Cash flows may be used to assess entity performance as well as to evaluate the entity's capacity to service debt, pay dividends, and remain solvent. Cash flows also may be a useful measure of cash management performance. Because cash flows are less bound to accounting estimates and allocations than is net income, they aid in understanding the dynamics of an entity's operating, investing, and financing activities.

11. Cash flows alone, however, may not present an adequate picture of performance or a reliable predictor of future performance unless the reasons for the cash flows are understood. For example, a young, growing entity with very good prospects may have large negative cash flows; an entity in a declining industry may produce strong, positive cash flows.

Return on Investment

12. Return on investment (ROI) relates the income an entity has earned to the assets that it employed. It measures the degree of efficiency with which the entity's assets were used and takes into account the cost of tying up capital necessary to support operations. ROI is, therefore, a useful tool for monitoring the effectiveness of asset management and business strategies.

13. When ROI is used to measure an entity's performance, the net assets employed represent the historical cost to the firm of producing the cash flows and income. To arrive at the ROI, the earnings or cash flows realized during a period are divided by the net assets employed.

14. The investment base of the entity may be total assets, net assets employed (debt, deferred items, and equity), or equity. If used consistently, the ratio calculated with each base may be useful to the decision makers in the firm.

15. Return on total assets measures the utilization of assets, but it fails to take into account the extent to which short-term liabilities, such as payables, reduce financing requirements. Managers usually are concerned with generating a satisfactory return on both debt and equity financing, and they typically use return on total capital (debt, deferred items, and equity), which is the same as return on net assets employed. Return on equity is the measure most consistent with the important long-term objective of increasing an entity's economic value.

16. Accounting assumptions, notably depreciation and inventory valuation methods, affect income, net assets employed, and, consequently, ROI.

    ROI also can be influenced by management decisions to defer maintenance or to reduce research or marketing expenditures. In addition, the balance sheet may significantly understate the economic worth of physical assets in times of inflation, thereby overstating the return generated by older plants and divisions. The return ratio also should be evaluated in light of the entity's stage of development, whether it be a start-up or declining operation. Also, caution should be applied in employing ROI for an interdivisional or an interperiod comparison of performance.

17. Another limitation of ROI is that an entity manager may be motivated to divest assets that are yielding less than the average return to the entity but that are still yielding a return in excess of the corporation's cost of capital.

Residual Income

18. Residual income is an alternative to net income that recognizes the cost of capital and replaces a ratio (ROI) with a dollar amount. To calculate residual income, net assets

employed is multiplied by the cost of financing the net assets employed (a cost of capital[1] rate). Different rates may be used to reflect different risks. For example, a turnaround entity may be more expensive to finance than a more stable entity; the turnaround entity would be charged at a higher financing rate. This capital charge is subtracted from adjusted income (net income plus after-tax interest) to arrive at residual income. If residual income is positive, returns exceed the cost of financing the entity.

19. Residual income explicitly incorporates the relative risk associated with the assets or operations being measured. With this measure the unit manager knows the return criteria to be applied to the entity's investment base. Use of residual income eliminates the situation confronting the manager who, if measured by ROI, is motivated to increase average ROI and may discard investment opportunities that yield less than the average return to the entity but more than its cost of capital.

20. A shortcoming of residual income is that the ability to compare entities of different sizes via ratios is lost because different entities may have different costs of capital. Residual income also has many of the same motivational deficiencies as the ROI calculation, and it does not resolve the question of what to include in the investment base.

21. At present, the residual income measure is not used widely in performance evaluation. However, its conceptual base is employed by many entities that assign a cost of capital or interest charge to subunits.

Market Value

22. A comprehensive measure of the future income potential of an entity is, in theory, the value of the entity determined by the market. Generally, financial theorists assume that in an organized, efficient stock market, changes in owners' expectations about future cash flows are reflected in changes in the market price of the entity's stock. To the extent that the owners' expectations of future returns from dividends and

---

[1] See Statement on Management Accounting 4A, "Cost of Capital," for guidance on the computation of the cost of capital.

stock appreciation are based on the real value or cash-generating ability of the entity, market price changes may be an appropriate indicator of entity performance.

Economic Income

23. In economic terms, the primary measure of entity performance is economic income. Economic income is defined as the change in the present value of future cash flows expected to accrue to owners from one period to the next less net investments by the owners of the entity.

24. Discounting estimated future cash flows to arrive at present values often is used to value businesses, evaluate acquisition candidates, and make capital investment decisions. For purposes of measuring entity performance, economic income may be thought of as the increase in value of the entity due to the strategies implemented, the management team developed, the efficiencies gained, and so on during the measurement period.

25. The amount and timing of a business entity's net future cash flows are based on forecasts that may be unreliable. The correct discount rate also is uncertain. In practice, therefore, measures of economic income are imprecise and are not readily verifiable.

26. Comparisons between competitive entities are employed in evaluating entity performance. Caution should be exercised in such an evaluation because of differences in capital structure, allocation policies,[2] and other entity-specific factors.

Inflation-Adjusted Performance Measurement

27. The impact of inflation in assessing the performance of an entity may be substantial even during a period of relatively low general inflation. The cumulative effect of even low levels of inflation over several years may be material to certain accounts. Additionally, the reported amounts for subsidiaries

---

[2]See Statement on Management Accounting 4B, "Allocation of Service and Administrative Costs," for guidance on this practice issue.

operating in highly or hyperinflationary foreign countries are affected significantly.

28. All the measures of performance mentioned above (net income, earnings per share, return on investment, residual income) can be adjusted to correct for changes in general or specific price levels. In times of inflation, the dollar, which is the yardstick of financial performance measurement, has different values at different points in time. Some inflation-adjusted financial statements attempt to replace nominal dollars with a dollar of constant value or measure the impact of inflation on changes in specific prices on nonmonetary assets (current cost).

29. Generally, inflation adjustments to the balance sheet write up last-in, first-out (LIFO) inventories and fixed assets. Monetary assets and liabilities also are affected. Net income is adjusted to reflect the replacement cost of inventory sold and assets used as well as monetary gains and losses.

30. Inflation-adjusted performance measures attempt to reflect more accurately the replacement value of resources consumed and of assets employed in the creation of wealth. On the other hand, this type of inflation accounting is more subjective and therefore more prone to manipulation than are historical accounting measures.

Limitations of Financial Measures

31. Financial measures of performance may be short-term oriented and, if used as part of an incentive system, may encourage activities and behavior that do not have long-term value. Because of changing price levels, accounting measures using historical costs combine different units of measure. Accounting measurements might be modified to show how the present period's events will influence future cash flows; in practice, however, this modification may be problematic. Additionally, behavioral considerations must be evaluated if a measurement system is to support the objective of goal congruence.

Stages of Growth and Financial Patterns

32. The primary financial performance measures — revenues, income, cash flows, returns on assets and capital — tend to

exhibit specific patterns that can be associated with stages of an entity's growth. The stages are (a) the start-up, or entrepreneurial stage; (b) a period of rapid growth; (c) maturity, when growth slows and may flatten; and (d) a period of decline (Table 1). These patterns can be traced to the economic conditions and business objectives that typically prevail at the stages in an entity's life cycle.

33. The start-up stage is typically one of revenue growth, negative or negligible profitability, negative cash flows, and negative or negligible return on net assets employed. The ratio of investment to revenues is at its highest level.

34. In the growth stage, the business entity is growing rapidly, and net income and cash from operations are positive. Investment requirements for working capital and PP&E and other assets often are large enough, however, to keep operating cash flow negative. Later, investment requirements slacken relative to the cash from operations, and positive operating cash flows result. Return on net assets employed also improves at this stage.

35. In the entity's mature stage, revenues slow or flatten, but net income remains positive. Although the entity may continue to invest in PP&E and other assets, the investments tend to be for replacement rather than for new capacity. The result is a high return on net assets employed.

36. Finally, in the decline stage, revenue reductions are more severe. Operations remain profitable, but net income as a percent of revenues declines. However, operating cash flows tend to accelerate because of a reduction in working capital. The entity may continue to make modest investments in PP&E and other fixed assets, but the drop in net assets employed is significant. The effect on return on net assets employed depends upon how rapidly net income declines relative to the base of net assets employed.

37. As portrayed in Table 1, accounting patterns of a normal business change over time, with losses in the early stages turning to profits in later periods and with the negative cash flows of the early stages continuing beyond the point when net income turns positive. Return on net assets employed runs the gamut from a negative figure to a positive, upward trend. A single measure of performance, such as net income, earnings per share, cash flow, or return on investment, is insufficient to evaluate financial performance over all stages. All financial measures do not work together; for example,

Table 1
Stages of Growth and Economic Patterns

	1A Start-up	1B Start-up	1C Start-up	2A Growth	2B Growth	3 Mature	4 Decline
Income statement							
Revenues	+	+	+	+	+	+	+
Expenses	–	–	–	–	–	–	–
Net income	–	–	+	+	+	+	+
Cash flows							
Net income	–	–	+	+	+	+	+
Adjustments for noncash items	+	+	+	+	+	+	+
Cash from operations	–	+	+	+	+	+	+
Investments in working capital	–	–	–	–	–	0	+
Investments in PP&E and other assets	–	–	–	–	–	–	0
Operating cash flows	–	–	–	–	+	+	+
Return on net assets employed	negative		improving		high		declining

positive net income can accompany negative operating cash flow. Therefore, a set of measures that includes all the measures discussed in the Statement should be considered.

Implications for Financial Measures of Performance

38. A manager should be aware of the growth stage of the entity when evaluating financial results.
    a. During the early stages of an entity's life cycle, non-financial events, such as developing a product, building an organization, or locating investors, may far outweigh the importance of any financial measures. Gaining a position in the marketplace with limited financial resources is usually of paramount concern to start-up companies. Therefore, revenue growth and operating cash flows generally are the more important financial performance measures during the early stages of the entity's life cycle.
    b. A growth entity continues to monitor revenue growth, but it balances this measure with profitability measures and asset management (return on investment, residual income). As capital resources become more accessible, operating cash flow takes on relatively lesser importance.
    c. A mature entity is primarily concerned with return on assets employed and equity and must closely manage the asset base and related cash flows and profitability to achieve high returns. It is at this stage, especially, that all financial performance measures must be monitored by management with the objective of possible entity rejuvenation.
    d. When an entity is declining, cash flow is critical again, and managers must carefully weigh investments to improve profitablity with the objective of "harvesting" the firm's assets. Longer-term measures of performance, such as ROI or residual income, may become relatively less important.

Budgets

39. The diverse patterns of revenue growth, income, cash flows, and asset requirements illustrate the need for budgets as a

tool for performance measurement. There is no one "best" net income amount which applies to all entities at all times. Budgets provide a basis for absolute measures of performance such as net income, return on investment, and operating cash flows.

40. Budgets should reflect the strategies of the entity. Even a mature entity may decide to invest large sums temporarily in marketing, research and development, or other efforts, resulting in lower, but acceptable, levels of income.

41. Budgets also should incorporate all major categories of measurement: revenues, income, cash flows, and returns. As stated earlier, net income is not a good proxy for all aspects of performance; the various dimensions can move independently. Without targets for all the categories, no context is developed for overall entity evaluation.

Nonfinancial Measures of Performance

42. Financial measures traditionally have dominated the measurement of entity and management performance. However, as the competitive environment increasingly demands management's understanding of and involvement in operating decisions, nonfinancial performance measures such as market share, innovation, quality and service, productivity, and employee development should take on a larger role in performance measurement.

43. Nonfinancial indicators provide two advantages over strictly quantitative financial measures:

   a. Nonfinancial indicators directly measure an entity's performance in the activities that create shareholder wealth, such as manufacturing and delivering quality goods and services and providing service for the customer. Nonfinancial measures can better fulfill the diagnostic (operational audit) function of performance measurement.

   b. Because they measure productive activity directly, nonfinancial measures may better predict the direction of future cash flows. For example, the long-term financial viability of some industries rests largely on their ability to keep promises of improved product quality at a competitive price.

44. Nonfinancial performance measures provide a rich oppor-

tunity for managers to improve entity evaluations and operations. Such measures direct management's attention to the entity's operations and, in the long run, may better reflect the financial returns generated by an entity than do the short-term historical financial measures.

Summary of NAA Recommendations

45. This Statement summarizes current practices in the measurement of entity performance and suggests that:
    a. Many measurement practices are incomplete or too narrow; that is, they focus principally on one or a few measures rather than on a more comprehensive set of measures.
    b. Some measures rely too heavily on historical-cost-based calculations rather than on making appropriate adjustments to compensate for real economic changes.
    c. Performance evaluation that utilizes only financial measures may tend to focus too narrowly on the short term. Including some broader, nonfinancial measures provides a more comprehensive picture of the entity's performance.
46. Therefore, the NAA makes the following recommendations:
    a. Financial measures of entity performance should be comprehensive and should include aspects of growth, income, cash flows, and return on investment simultaneously.
    b. At each stage of growth in an entity's life cycle, different measures of financial performance take on varying degrees of importance. Therefore, neither growth nor net income nor cash flows nor return on investment should be emphasized to the exclusion of other meaningful measures.
    c. The measurement of performance by a multiple set of financial measures should be enhanced by the development and use of a budgeted set of expectations against which actual results are compared.
    d. Historical-cost-based accounting calculations, especially in times of significant inflation, should not be relied upon exclusively in entities that are affected by inflation.
    e. An entity also should consider appropriate nonfinancial, longer-term measurements pertaining to such facets of

the business as market, product, operations, new product development, and human resources rather than strictly short-term financial measures of performance.

47. An important objective of a business entity is to improve its long-term value to shareholders as well as its utility to employees and to society at large. A number of performance measures should be used to keep management on the track of reaching this objective. These measures should include revenues, net income, return on assets employed, and cash flows as the principal measures of financial performance and should include such nonfinancial measures as market share, quality and service, productivity, and innovation.

Bibliography

Textbooks

a. Anthony, R. N., J. Dearden and N. Bedford. *Management Control Systems: Text and Cases*, fifth edition, Homewood, Ill.: Richard D. Irwin, Inc., 1984.
b. Solomons, David. *Divisional Performance: Measurement and Control*. Homewood, Ill.: Richard D. Irwin, Inc., 1965.
c. Vancil, Richard F. *Decentralization: Managerial Ambiguity by Design*. Homewood, Ill.: Dow Jones-Irwin, 1979.

Articles

a. Dearden, A. "The Case Against ROI Control," *Harvard Business Review*, May-June 1969.
b. Greiner, Larry E. "Evolution and Revolution as Organizations Grow," *Harvard Business Review*, July-August 1972.
c. Kaplan, Robert A. "The Evolution of Management Accounting," *The Accounting Review*, Vol. LIX, No. 3, July 1984.
d. _____ . "Measuring Manufacturing Performance: A New Challenge for Managerial Accounting Research," *The Accounting Review*, Vol. LVIII, No. 4, October 1983.
e. Rappaport, Alfred. "Selecting Strategies that Create Shareholder Value," *Harvard Business Review*, May-June 1981.
f. _____ . "Do You Know the Value of Your Company?" *Mergers & Acquisitions*, Spring 1979.
g. Reece, James S., and William R. Cool. "ROI Is Still Viewed as the Most Useful Measure of a Division's Performance," *Harvard Business Review*, May-June 1978.

SUBCOMMITTEE ON MAP STATEMENT PROMULGATION

*Allen H. Seed, III, *Chairman*

*Raymond H. Alleman

*Robert N. Anthony

Richard A. Curry
Senior Vice President — Finance
The Coleman Company
Wichita, Kan.

Robert A. Howell
*Clinical Professor of
Management and Accounting*
Graduate School of Business
New York University
New York, N.Y.

*Arthur D. Lyons

Daniel McBride
*Director of Financial
Accounting Policy*
Honeywell, Inc.
Minneapolis, Minn.

J. Charles Stracuzzi
Controller
Blount AgriProducts Group
Grand Island, Neb.

Donald J. Trawicki
Partner
Touche Ross & Company
New York, N.Y.

*Also a member of MAP Committee

NATIONAL ASSOCIATION OF ACCOUNTANTS
MANAGEMENT ACCOUNTING PRACTICES COMMITTEE
1985-86

Chairman
Bernard R. Doyle
Manager-Corporate Accounting Services
General Electric Company
Fairfield, Conn.

Raymond H. Alleman
Vice President & Comptroller
ITT Corporation
New York, N.Y.

Robert N. Anthony
Professor Emeritus
Harvard Business School
Boston, Mass.

Patricia P. Douglas
Professor of Accounting and Finance
University of Montana
Missoula, Mont.

William J. Ihlanfeldt
Assistant Controller
Shell Oil Company
Houston, Tex.

Eugene H. Irminger
Senior Vice President of Finance
Centel Corporation
Chicago, Ill.

James J. Latchford
*Assistant Vice President &
Assistant Controller*
W. R. Grace & Company
New York, N.Y.

Arthur D. Lyons
Vice President-Controller
FMC Corporation
Chicago, Ill.

Allen H. Seed, III
Senior Consultant
Arthur D. Little, Inc.
Cambridge, Mass.

Norman N. Strauss
Partner
Ernst & Whinney
New York, N.Y.

Edward W. Trott
Partner
Peat, Marwick, Mitchell & Co.
Tampa, Fla.

Robert G. Weiss
Vice President & Controller
Schering-Plough Corporation
Madison, N.J.

NAA STAFF

Louis Bisgay, *Director*, Management Accounting Practices
Jonathan B. Schiff, *Manager*, Management Accounting Practices

Statements on Management Accounting

Statement Number 4E
June 3, 1986

PRACTICES AND TECHNIQUES

Definition and Measurement of Direct Material Cost

In accordance with the charge to the Management Accounting Practices (MAP) Committee to issue statements on management accounting principles and practices, Statements on Management Accounting are promulgated to reflect official positions of the National Association of Accountants (NAA). The work of the MAP Committee is based on a framework for management accounting, whose principal categories are:

1. Objectives
2. Terminology
3. Concepts
4. Practices and Techniques
5. Management of Accounting Activities

Statements on Management Accounting

Statement Number 4E
June 3, 1986

Practices and Techniques:
Definition and Measurement of
Direct Material Cost

National Association of Accountants

Acknowledgments

The National Association of Accountants is grateful to the many individuals who contributed to the publication of Statement 4E, *Definition and Measurement of Direct Material Cost.* Appreciation is extended to members of the Management Accounting Practices Committee and its Subcommittee on MAP Statement Promulgation. Special thanks are extended to Michael J. Sandretto, Price Waterhouse & Co., Columbus, Ohio, for his research and writing associated with this project.

Definition and Measurement of Direct Material Cost

1. The term "direct material cost" as used in practice, in literature, and in litigation has a wide variety of meanings. Unless the intended meaning in a given context is clear, confusion and misunderstanding are likely to result. The purpose of this Statement is to provide a conceptual definition of "direct material cost" that, in the absence of a specified alternative, should be taken as the meaning of this term.
2. This Statement makes the conceptual definition more concrete by describing how direct material costs should be measured. Measurement has two aspects:
   a. The quantity of material that is to be included as direct material, that is, the inputs that are to be counted.
   b. The unit price by which each of these quantities is multiplied to arrive at a monetary cost.
3. Many of the examples used in this Statement refer to the direct material cost of goods produced in manufacturing companies. The examples apply equally well to the same or similar transactions for projects, services, and other cost objects. The allocation of joint product or by-product costs is not addressed in this Statement.
4. In a manufacturing company, direct material cost is an element of inventory cost and of cost of sales. Differences in how companies define this term result in variations in the amount recorded as direct material cost and the amount recorded as overhead or expense. Differences in the way material costs are accounted for in cost-type contracts, in projects, and for other cost objects also lead to differences in the amounts recorded as direct material cost and the amounts recorded as overhead or expense. If users do not understand what items are included in direct material cost in such situations, their interpretation of the information may be erroneous, and they may make unsound decisions.

Definitions

5. *Direct Material Cost*—Quantities of material that can be specifically identified with a cost object in an economically feasible manner, priced at the unit price of direct material.

6. *Cost Object*—A product, contract, project, organizational subdivision, function, or other unit for which costs are measured or estimated.

7. *Direct Cost*—A cost that can be specifically identified with a cost object in an economically feasible manner.

8. *Material Quantity*—A physical amount of material, such as a pound of copper, a 50-gallon drum of a chemical, or a batch of 100 semiconductors.

9. *Scrap*—Material residue from manufacturing operations that has some value. Examples of scrap include border material from stamping operations, shavings, filings, borings, and turnings. Scrap may have relatively minor recovery value, as in the case of steel, or it may be of significant value, as in the case of gold.

10. *Waste*—Material that is lost, evaporates, or shrinks in a manufacturing process or is a residue that has no significant recovery value in excess of its disposal costs.

11. *Defective Units*—Production that does not meet quality standards. Defective units may be reworked and sold, or they may be rejected and disposed of for salvage value.

12. *Material-Related Costs*—Costs, other than direct material costs, that are incurred as a result of the acquisition, inspection, storage, or movement of direct material quantities.

13. *Cost Item*—A subdivision of cost, such as freight, duty, insurance, sales tax, or outside processing costs.

14. *Unit Price of Direct Material*—Invoice price and acquisition-related cost items that can be specifically identified with direct material quantities in an economically feasible manner and that can be measured with reasonable accuracy.

Materiality

15. If a cost item is immaterial, it should be accounted for in a manner that is economically feasible.

Material Quantities

16. If the cost object is the production of a manufactured or processed product, its direct material cost normally should include quantities of material that become a physical part of the cost object and those materials that are consumed in the

manufacturing process that can be specifically identified with that cost object.

17. If the cost object is the production of a service, its direct material cost normally should include all quantities of material that can be specifically identified with producing the service.

18. If the cost object is the production of a project, its direct material cost normally should include all quantities of material that can be specifically identified with the project. For a large project, direct material cost typically includes far more categories of direct material quantities than in a product because it is relatively easy to identify quantities of material specifically with a large project. Examples include fasteners, adhesives, lubricants, and other items whose unit costs are too low to be considered direct material costs for many manufactured products. If a large project is broken down into a series of smaller projects, products, or subassemblies, the material categories listed in this paragraph typically are not included in the direct material cost of these subdivisions.

19. Costs classified as direct material costs must be excluded from costs used in calculating overhead rates. For example, if one project is large enough to include fasteners and lubricants in direct material quantities, but those items are included in overhead for other projects, the cost of fasteners and lubricants should not be included in the overhead rate applied to the first project. It follows that entities that define direct material costs differently for different cost objects will have two or more overhead rates.

20. Material quantity should include the cost of packaging material to the extent it is included in the finished product. Examples include bottles for liquor and perfume and containers for cosmetics and medical products.

21. Material quantity should include packing supplies necessary to deliver goods to customers, to the extent that the goods are packed with these supplies as part of the production process.

Material Lost in the Production Process

22. Direct material cost should include the material cost of scrap, waste, and normally anticipated defective units that occur in the ordinary course of the production process. The

following examples depict situations in which such costs should be classified as direct material costs:

a. A part is stamped from a roll of strip steel, or a finished unit is produced by turning a casting. The amount of material lost in these processes through ordinary scrap usually can be predicted with reasonable accuracy. The cost of the predicted scrap should be included in the direct material cost of the part.

b. A quantity is lost in the production process through evaporation, dehydration, spoilage, shrinkage, or similar causes. The amount of material that is lost in these processes usually can be predicted with reasonable accuracy. The cost of the predicted amount of lost material should be included in the direct material cost.

c. Engineering estimates are developed for the percentage of defective units expected from a given production process, and they are reasonably accurate. The cost of material in the estimated percentage of defective units should be included in the direct material cost of completed production.

d. In most cases, the net salvage value of estimated scrap, waste, and defective units should reduce the direct material cost. However, the direct material cost should be increased if the related costs exceed the salvage value, as in the case of certain chemical or nuclear wastes.

23. Unanticipated quantities of scrap, waste, or defective units should not be included in direct material cost. These quantities should be included in manufacturing overhead or should be expensed.

Samples, Prototypes, and Initial Production Runs

24. Routine quality assurance samples that are tested to destruction should be included in direct material cost. Nonroutine quality assurance samples taken due to quality problems should not be included in direct material cost.

25. The material cost of marketing samples and prototypes should not be included in direct material cost.

Unit Price of Direct Material

26. The unit price of direct material should include the invoice

price and other costs paid to vendors to deliver the material quantity to the production facility or to a point of free delivery. The following costs are included in the unit price of direct material:

- Invoice price for direct material quantity,
- Invoice price for outside processing,
- Shipping costs (inward freight) paid or owed to outside vendors,
- Sales tax,
- Duty, and
- Cost of delivery containers and pallets, net of return refunds.

27. Trade discounts, refunds, and rebates should be deducted in calculating the unit price of direct material.

28. If cash discounts offered by the vendor exceed reasonable interest rates, the price of direct material should be reduced by the excess.

29. Demurrage charges should not be included in direct material cost.

30. Royalty payments and licenses should be included in direct material cost if they are functions of direct material quantities used in producing the cost object.

Use of Estimates

31. Estimates of direct material quantities and unit prices may be used if they are sufficiently accurate to be considered "specifically identified" with a cost object. The following situations are examples of estimates that are sufficiently accurate to be considered direct material costs in most instances:

   a. A manufacturing firm establishes standard material quantities for its products, but its system does not trace variances to these products. Nevertheless, there is a reasonable expectation that variances are proportional to the standard quantities and thus that the actual material quantities are proportional to the standard quantities.

   b. A manufacturing firm uses standard purchase prices for its materials. Although standard purchase prices are not necessarily the same as actual purchase prices, the firm is able to associate major deviations from standard purchase prices with specific products or product lines.

c. Inward freight costs are added to direct material cost by a rate that approximates the actual cost, such as a percentage of price paid to the vendor or a percentage of the weight per unit of cost.

Material-Related Costs

32. Certain costs are closely related to the quantity of material acquired or used, but they cannot be specifically identified with a cost object in an economically feasible manner. These indirect costs are material-related costs. Material-related costs should be allocated to cost objects on the basis of some measure of direct material quantity or cost rather than on direct labor hours or cost. Costs for the following functions usually are considered material-related costs:
    - Purchasing,
    - Receiving,
    - Receiving inspection,
    - Material storage costs prior to purchased material entering production, and
    - Issuing costs for material initially entering the production process.

33. Certain cost items may be closely related to material quantities and may be allocated to cost objects based on direct material quantities or costs. They are, however, more closely related to the production process than to the acquisition of material and are not typically considered material-related costs. Furthermore, they may be applicable to different time periods than the period in which the direct material cost was incurred. Examples of those cost items are:
    - Material storage costs subsequent to entering the production process,
    - Issuing costs for material subsequent to entering the production process,
    - Production planning and control costs, and
    - Internal transportation costs.

Cost Systems

34. This Statement does not discuss standard cost systems in detail and does not address how standards should be deter-

mined. In most cases, cost analysis and control are improved if the standard material quantity includes normal scrap and waste as defined in this Statement but excludes all lost or defective units. Differentiating between good units and normally anticipated lost units helps focus management's attention on lost units. Additionally, including in direct material the standard material quantity of both good units and normally anticipated lost units helps focus management's attention on total material cost.

35. The cost accounting systems of some firms, particularly retail firms, include many material-related costs as direct material cost. In such systems, direct material is defined more broadly than in this Statement. Nevertheless, if the relevant material-related costs are allocated on the basis of direct material, the resulting product costs may be substantially the same under this Statement as under a broader definition of direct material cost. The broader definition is useful for certain management accounting purposes. However, it should be recognized that direct material cost as measured in such systems — and for other purposes — may be different from direct material cost as measured according to the concepts of this Statement.

36. The cost accounting systems of many firms allocate material-related costs on some measure of direct labor, as contrasted with a measure of direct material, as recommended by this Statement. Allocation based on direct labor is, in many cases, easier to compute. It is likely, however, that allocation on some measure of direct material yields a more accurate measure of both direct and total cost of a cost object.

SUBCOMMITTEE ON MAP STATEMENT PROMULGATION

*Allen H. Seed, III, *Chairman*

*Raymond H. Alleman

*Robert N. Anthony

Richard A. Curry
Senior Vice President — Finance
The Coleman Company
Wichita, Kan.

Robert A. Howell
*Clinical Professor of
Management and Accounting*
Graduate School of Business
New York University
New York, N.Y.

*Arthur D. Lyons

Daniel McBride
*Director of Financial
Accounting Policy*
Honeywell, Inc.
Minneapolis, Minn.

J. Charles Stracuzzi
Controller
Blount AgriProducts Group
Grand Island, Neb.

Donald J. Trawicki
Partner
Touche Ross & Company
New York, N.Y.

*Also a member of MAP Committee

NATIONAL ASSOCIATION OF ACCOUNTANTS
MANAGEMENT ACCOUNTING PRACTICES COMMITTEE
1985-86

Statements on Management Accounting

Statement Number 4F
December 15, 1986

PRACTICES AND TECHNIQUES

Allocation of Information Systems Costs

In accordance with the charge to the Management Accounting Practices (MAP) Committee to issue statements on management accounting principles and practices, Statements on Management Accounting are promulgated to reflect official positions of the National Association of Accountants (NAA). The work of the MAP Committee is based on a framework for management accounting, whose principal categories are:

1. Objectives
2. Terminology
3. Concepts
4. Practices and Techniques
5. Management of Accounting Activities

Statements on Management Accounting

Statement Number 4F
December 15, 1986

Practices and Techniques: Allocation of Information Systems Costs

National Association of Accountants

Acknowledgments

The National Association of Accountants appreciates the contributions made by those whose efforts have led to publication of Statement 4F, "Allocation of Information Systems Costs." Thanks are due to the members of the Management Accounting Practices Committee and its Subcommittee on Statement Promulgation. For their research and writing associated with the project, appreciation is extended to Allen H. Seed, III, Arthur D. Little, Inc., and past chairman of the Subcommittee on Statement Promulgation; Robert W. McGee, Seton Hall University and Prentice-Hall, Inc.; and Jonathan B. Schiff, NAA staff and Pace University.

Introduction

1. The allocation of information systems costs is of concern to operating executives as well as to management accountants. This concern stems from the substantial and growing nature of the costs that are often involved and their impact on segment profitability, product cost determination, and cost-type contract pricing.

2. This Statement is intended to help management accountants deal with specific issues associated with the allocation of these costs to internal users. It expands upon Statement on Management Accounting (SMA) No. 4B, "Allocation of Service and Administrative Costs." It discusses the elements of information systems costs, conceptual considerations, advantages and disadvantages of allocation, reasons for allocation, allocation methods, and pricing alternatives. A bibliography also is included.

3. There are three general types of cost construction: full costs, responsibility costs, and differential costs (see SMA 4B for a description of these concepts). Costs should be allocated for full costing and may be allocated for responsibility accounting purposes, but for differential costing the only relevant costs are those future costs that relate to the specific alternatives being considered. The term *allocation* in this Statement refers primarily to allocations for responsibility accounting purposes.

4. For purposes of responsibility accounting:
    a. Allocation should be applied where appropriate, generally by employing predetermined or standard rates or amounts, because business unit managers should not be held responsible for variances in certain shared service and administrative costs not traceable to their actions.
    b. Allocated expenses should be separated from nonallocated expenses in order to focus the cost object manager's attention on the costs that he or she can control directly.

5. Information systems cost control is enhanced if controllable information systems costs are charged to users on a predetermined or standard cost basis for responsibility account-

ing purposes. There are several appropriate methods for accounting for such allocations. A summary of recommendations may be found in paragraphs 25-28.

Elements of Information Systems Costs

6. There are three types of information systems costs: systems development costs, operating costs, and software maintenance costs. Systems development includes feasibility analysis, conceptual and detail design, coding, testing, training, and maintenance, all of which are involved when a new system or application is developed. Operating costs are the payroll and expenses incurred in the day-to-day operation of the data processing facility. They include the use of hardware, software, and telecommunications resources. Software maintenance includes monitoring of the updating cycle to assure that all valid transactions are processed properly, that corrections to invalid transactions are expedited, and that new procedures are designed, tested, and used.

7. Hardware consists of the physical equipment that can be located in an information systems department or in a user's area. If the hardware is used by one user exclusively, all costs of the hardware, including depreciation and operating costs, are assigned to that user. If the hardware is shared by more than one user, these costs should be allocated to those users on an appropriate basis.

8. Systems software makes the hardware usable. It usually is provided by the equipment manufacturer in the case of mainframes and minicomputers. It sometimes is provided by the manufacturer of a microcomputer. Where systems software is included with the equipment, it is said to be bundled with the hardware. When it is a separate cost item, it is said to be unbundled. The cost of systems software should be assigned or allocated to the users in the same manner as hardware costs.

9. Applications software usually is either purchased from outside vendors or written by or for a particular user. Whether costs of software for use internally are capitalized or expensed, the costs or amortization should be assigned to a user if the software was written specifically for that user.

10. Telecommunications hardware includes terminals, modems, multiplexers, and other similar equipment. Operating costs

depend upon the location of various pieces of hardware and the type of communication link used. The communication link is the transmission medium over which the message is sent.

11. In a centralized information systems facility, all data must pass from the user directly to the information systems department. If the user sends input forms directly to the information systems department for entry into the system, the communications cost will consist totally of the transportation costs of the input forms. However, if input is performed by the user, then the communications cost will include the connect time and cost of the communications link in addition to the cost of the hardware and software.

Responsibility Accounting Considerations

12. The decision to allocate information systems costs to users is a management accounting decision and depends on the concepts employed and the facts and circumstances of each case. Some advantages of allocation to users are:

   a. It increases user involvement. Allocation to users for information systems services causes managers to monitor their usage of information systems services and to discuss alternative solutions with the information systems department manager.

   b. It encourages efficient operation and allocation of resources. Allocating information systems services encourages users to decide which services are worthwhile to use and how extensively they should be used. It also motivates information systems managers to monitor costs more closely because costs will be scrutinized by users as well as by the accounting and internal audit departments.

13 Although allocating information systems costs is an effective responsibility accounting tool and generally is recommended, there may be circumstances in which problems arising from such allocations seem to outweigh the benefits. Some arguments that have been advanced for not charging users for information systems services are:

   a. Charging discourages development of new computer applications and may create conflict between the information systems department and users. If a new application cannot be utilized by several users, its cost must be borne by one or a few users. Charging full cost in such situations may seem unfair to users and may discourage them from using a new application.

b. The cost of determining the amount to charge may be greater than the benefits to be derived from charging.

c. Charging involves systems resources that could be used for other purposes.

d. The amount to be charged is not easy to determine, and the procedure used to arrive at the charge may be difficult to explain to users.

e. Charging for information systems services adds another layer of administrative detail to an already complex accounting system.

The following section discusses several methods associated with the allocation of information systems costs.

Allocation Methods

14. The allocation to users for information systems services may be based on a full cost construction or something less than a full cost construction. The allocation also may be based on cost plus an allowance or market price for an appropriate return on investment (mark-up).

15. Full costing allocates all information systems costs to the users. However, this method may discourage use of information systems services if rates are high as a result of underutilized facilities.

16. Use of less than full costing encourages the full utilization of information systems facilities. This method is especially appropriate in the early phases of computerization. However, it may lead to the overutilization of facilities, thus creating bottlenecks and delays.

17. Cost plus profit allocation reflects the concept that the information systems organization should seek to earn an adequate return on the entity's tangible and intangible investments in its facilities.

18. Market price charging seeks to provide an arm's-length price that would be paid for information systems services if they were provided by outside services. However, this price may be difficult to determine or may not exist.

19. The method selected should be appropriate and workable. Thus, the choice will depend on the organization, goals, and stage of computerization of each entity.

Allocation Bases

20. Allocations may be made using different bases, depending on the costs involved and particular circumstances:

    a. A labor-based charge (labor hours, labor cost) may be appropriate in those situations in which labor is a reasonable surrogate for total information system costs. Examples of such situations include high levels of systems development or systems maintenance.

    b. A machine-based charge, or central processing unit (CPU) time, may be appropriate in those situations in which machine usage is a reasonable surrogate for total information system costs. Examples of such situations would include environments in which operations predominate and systems development and maintenance are less significant.

    c. A multiple-based charge, such as labor and machine time, or additional factors, also may be deemed appropriate. Such multiple factors are, however, more difficult to develop and support and, thus, should be considered carefully.

    d. Allocated charges for recurring services such as payroll, billing, general ledger accounting, and so on may be fixed at the beginning of a period and reviewed at specific intervals. This permits the user to know the allocated charges and gives the provider the incentive to meet the budgeted charges.

21. The amount allocated to users may be based upon a single rate for all services or multiple prices based upon the services actually received by the users. The single-factor approach is the easiest to implement and explain to users. It is not always the most appropriate method to use.

22. A single-factor-based allocation is most appropriate when the information system is unsophisticated and/or is used primarily to process similar types of data. In this instance, the allocation can be based upon the amount of time utilized by the user as shown in the following algorithm:

    Amount allocated to user = (Unit Rate) x (Time Used)

23. Multiple-factor allocation methods usually are more satisfactory than single-factor methods in environments built around mainframes or large minicomputers because users are charged for the specific resources they consume. All applications do not utilize the same amount of computer

time or computer resources. For example, an application may require the availability of more input/output devices than another application that takes approximately the same amount of time to run. In this situation, the user of the first application is utilizing more resources and therefore should pay more for them. It should be noted that this method usually requires a sophisticated computer operations and control system and is therefore more expensive than a single-factor method. In addition, multiple-factor methods often are difficult to explain to users.

24. A multiple-factor system is more appropriate in information system environments that involve a significant amount of communications. The following algorithm, for example, may be used to allocate communications costs:

Amount allocated to user = (Communications Price x Usage)
+ (Systems Price x Usage)

This is a simple example because it combines only two factors, but the algorithm may be expanded to include many more. The following section contains summary recommendations reflective of the content of this Statement.

Summary of Recommendations

25. For responsibility accounting purposes, allocations should be made to users for information systems services that they receive. In most cases, a predetermined or standard rate should be used for this allocation.

26. When management wants to encourage the use of a new system and when the benefits of allocating information systems costs are outweighed by the costs of this allocation, not allocating information systems costs may be desirable.

27. Full costing, less than full costing, cost plus profit, or market pricing methods may be used, depending on the entity's organization, goals, and stage of computerization.

28. The amount allocated should be determined by using the single- or multi-factor algorithm appropriate for the circumstances.

Bibliography

Articles

a. Chan, K. H. and Shui F. Lam, "Transfer Pricing for Computer Services in Public Utilities," *Journal of Systems Management,* July 1986, pp. 23-29.
b. Finney, John E., "Controlling EDP Costs," *Journal of Accountancy,* April 1981, pp. 63-68.
c. Gauntt, James E. and Grover L. Porter, "Allocating MIS Costs," *Management Accounting,* April 1985, pp. 12, 74.
d. Grindley, K., "Internal Charging for Computer Services," *Accountancy,* March 1973, pp. 32-35.
e. Hansen, Gloria J., "Charge-Back Data: How It Can Help Manage Word Processing," *Office,* August 1981, pp. 73-74.
f. Nolan, Richard L., "Controlling the Cost of Data Services," *Harvard Business Review,* July/August 1977, pp. 114-124.

Statements

a. Institute of Cost and Management Accountants, *Management Accounting Guideline No. 4: Charging for Computer Services,* (London: ICMA, 1982).
b. National Association of Accountants, *Statement on Management Accounting No. 4B: Allocation of Service and Administrative Costs,* NAA, 1985.

Textbooks

a. Ahituv, Niv and Seev Neumann, *Principles of Information Systems for Management,* second edition (Dubuque, Iowa: Wm. C. Brown Company Publishers, 1986).
b. Cash, James I., Jr., F. Warren McFarlan and James L. McKenney, *Corporate Information Systems Management: Text and Cases* (Homewood, Ill.: Richard D. Irwin, Inc., 1983).
c. Cooke, John E. and Donald M. Drury, *Management Planning and Control of Information Systems* (Hamilton, Ontario: Society of Management Accountants of Canada, 1980).
d. Cortada, James W., *EDP Costs and Charges: Finance, Budgets, and Cost Control in Data Processing* (Englewood Cliffs, N.J.: Prentice-Hall, Inc., 1980).
e. Davis, Gordon B. and Margrethe H. Olson, *Management Information Systems: Conceptual Foundations, Structure, and Development,* second edition (New York: McGraw-Hill Book Company, 1985).

f. Drury, Donald H. and John E. Bates, *Data Processing Chargeback Systems: Theory and Practice* (Hamilton, Ontario: Society of Management Accountants of Canada, 1979).

g. Nolan, Richard L., *Management Accounting and Control of Data Processing* (New York: National Association of Accountants, 1977).

h. Reynolds, George W., *Introduction to Business Telecommunications* (Columbus, Ohio: Charles E. Merrill Publishing Company, 1984).

NATIONAL ASSOCIATION OF ACCOUNTANTS
MANAGEMENT ACCOUNTING PRACTICES COMMITTEE
1986-87

Chairman
William J. Ihlanfeldt
Assistant Controller
Shell Oil Company
Houston, Tex.

Raymond H. Alleman
Senior Vice President
& Comptroller
ITT Corporation
New York, N.Y.

Robert N. Anthony
Professor Emeritus
Harvard Business School
Boston, Mass.

James P. Colford
Director of Accounting Practices
IBM Corporation
Tarrytown, N.Y.

Patricia P. Douglas
Professor of Accounting and Finance
University of Montana
Missoula, Mont.

Bernard R. Doyle
Manager-Corporate
Accounting Services
General Electric Company
Fairfield, Conn.

Eugene H. Irminger
Senior Vice President of Finance
Centel Corporation
Chicago, Ill.

James J. Latchford
Vice President & Controller
W. R. Grace & Company
New York, N.Y.

Arthur D. Lyons
Vice President-Controller
FMC Corporation
Chicago, Ill.

Frank C. Minter
Vice President and CFO
AT&T International
Basking Ridge, N.J.

John J. Perrell, III
Vice President, Corporate
Accounting & Reporting
American Express Company
New York, N.Y.

J. Charles Stracuzzi
Controller
Blount AgriProducts Group
Blount Agri Industrial Corporation
Grand Island, Neb.

Norman N. Strauss
Partner
Ernst & Whinney
New York, N.Y.

Edward W. Trott
Partner
Peat, Marwick, Mitchell & Compan
Tampa, Fla.

Robert G. Weiss
Vice President & Controller
Schering-Plough Corporation
Madison, N.J.

NAA STAFF

Louis Bisgay, *Director*, Management Accounting Practices
Jonathan B. Schiff, *Manager*, Management Accounting Practices

SUBCOMMITTEE ON STATEMENT PROMULGATION

*Robert G. Weiss, *Chairman*

*Raymond H. Alleman

F. Gordon Bitter
*Senior Vice President
and CFO*
The Singer Company
Stamford, Conn.

Robert A. Howell
*Clinical Professor of
Management and Accounting*
Graduate School of Business
New York University
New York, N.Y.

*Arthur D. Lyons

Daniel McBride
*Director of Financial
Accounting Policy*
Honeywell, Inc.
Minneapolis, Minn.

*Frank C. Minter

Raymond H. Peterson
*Division Manager of
Accounting Standards*
Bell Communications
Piscataway, N.J.

L. Hal Rogero, Jr.
Assistant Controller
Mead Corporation
Dayton, Ohio

*J. Charles Stracuzzi

Donald J. Trawicki
Partner
Touche Ross & Company
New York, N.Y.

*Also a member of MAP Committee

Statements on Management Accounting

Statement Number 4G
June 1, 1987

PRACTICES AND TECHNIQUES

Accounting for Indirect Production Costs

In accordance with the charge to the Management Accounting Practices (MAP) Committee to issue statements on management accounting principles and practices, Statements on Management Accounting are promulgated to reflect official positions of the National Association of Accountants (NAA). The work of the MAP Committee is based on a framework for management accounting, whose principal categories are:

1. Objectives
2. Terminology
3. Concepts
4. Practices and Techniques
5. Management of Accounting Activities

Statements on Management Accounting

Statement Number 4G
June 1, 1987

Practices and Techniques:
Accounting for Indirect Production Costs

National Association of Accountants

Acknowledgments

The National Association of Accountants is grateful to the many individuals who contributed to the publication of Statement 4G, *Accounting for Indirect Production Costs*. Appreciation is extended to members of the Management Accounting Practices Committee and its Subcommittee on Statement Promulgation. Special thanks are extended to Subcommittee member Donald J. Trawicki for his research and writing associated with this project.

Introduction

1. For many purposes management accountants find it necessary, or desirable, to allocate indirect production costs to goods, projects, services, contracts, or other cost objects. These purposes include inventory valuation and related profit measurement, contract pricing and other pricing, measurement of product or segment profitability, control of costs, and other long- and short-term management decisions. A number of different techniques may be used to allocate indirect production costs to cost objects. Some techniques are preferable to others. The purpose of this Statement is to provide guidance to management accountants in the allocation of indirect production costs to cost objects.

2. The objective of allocating indirect production costs to cost objects is to assign an appropriate share of the total costs incurred during a specified period of time to each cost object. If feasible, costs should be allocated in proportion to the amount of cost that each cost object caused. If a causal connection is not feasible, some other criterion, such as benefits received, should be used.

Statement Scope

3. Production costs incurred for a cost object are either direct costs or indirect costs of that cost object. A cost item is a direct cost if it can be identified specifically with a single cost object in an economically feasible manner. Direct production costs include direct materials, direct labor, and other directly assignable costs. A cost item is an indirect cost if it is common to two or more cost objects and cannot be identified specifically with a single cost object in an economically feasible manner. Indirect production costs may include costs such as indirect labor, repairs and maintenance, indirect materials and supplies, depreciation, insurance, and property taxes. Indirect production costs also may be referred to as production overhead.

Indirect production costs may be divided further into categories for particular cost or profitability constructions. Examples of these categories are short-run controllable vs. long-run controllable costs and variable (with volume of production) vs. fixed costs. This Statement is concerned with the allocation of all categories of indirect production costs.

4. This Statement describes the allocation of indirect production costs to products. Products may be either tangible goods or intangible services, such as those provided by hospitals, schools, professional firms, and hotels.

5. a. There are two types of cost allocations: (a) the allocation of costs to time periods (e.g., the allocation of the cost of depreciable assets to the time periods that represent their useful lives, via the depreciation mechanism) and (b) the allocation of all the costs of a time period to cost objects for which costs were incurred during that time period. This Statement deals only with the latter type of allocation.

   b. There are three general types of production cost construction: responsibility costs, full costs, and differential costs. Each is intended to serve a specific set of purposes, but responsibility costs, full costs, and some information useful in estimating differential costs typically are outputs of a single cost accounting system. These three types of cost construction are discussed separately because the cost allocation problem for each is somewhat different.

   c. Indirect production costs may be viewed in either a historical perspective or an estimated future perspective. This Statement is concerned with both historical costs and estimated future costs.

6. This Statement applies only to allocations of indirect production costs that are material in amount, that is, to practices that might make a significant difference in the amount of cost measured.

7. This Statement is concerned with the allocation of service and administrative costs that are associated with the production function. Other service and administrative costs are covered in Statement on Management Accounting 4B.

Definitions

8. a. *Production Costs* - Costs incurred in the production

process to bring goods to the point at which they are ready for sale or costs incurred to produce services.

b. *Direct Cost* - A cost item that can be identified specifically with a single cost object in an economically feasible manner.

c. *Indirect Cost* - A cost item that is common to two or more cost objects and cannot be identified specifically with any one of these cost objects in an economically feasible manner; also called overhead cost.

d. *Full Cost* - The sum of the direct costs and applicable indirect costs assigned to a cost object.

e. *Cost Assignment* - The distribution of cost items to cost objects. A direct cost is assigned directly to a cost object. An indirect cost is allocated to cost objects.

f. *Cost Allocation* - The distribution of indirect production costs to individual cost objects.

g. *Cost Object* - A function, organizational subdivision, or product whose costs are measured.

h. *Final Cost Object* - In a cost accounting system, the product whose cost is measured.

i. *Intermediate Cost Object* - In a cost accounting system, a focal point for the grouping of costs prior to their assignment to final cost objects; a cost center. Intermediate cost objects may be cost responsibility centers, service cost centers, production cost centers, or production cost pools.

j. *Cost Responsibility Center* - An identifiable organization subdivision headed by a manager who is held accountable for the accomplishment of specific functions and for control of the costs of those functions.

k. *Service Cost Center* - A cost responsibility center whose functions are to provide support or service to other cost centers. Examples could be maintenance, general factory, and occupancy.

l. *Production Cost Center* - A cost responsibility center whose functions contribute directly to the production of a product.

m. *Production Cost Pool* - A grouping of indirect production costs that have a similar causal relationship to the cost objects to which they will be assigned. A production cost pool also may be a cost responsibility center. Alternatively, the cost items in several cost responsibility centers may be grouped in a single production cost pool, or the cost items in a single responsibility center may be disaggregated into several production cost pools. (See Figure 1.)

n. *Overhead Rate* - The ratio of indirect costs for a period of time to the volume of some measurable associated causal or beneficial factor in the same period of time.

o. *Variable Cost* - A cost that is expected to increase as the volume of production, sales, or some other cost-causing factor in a period increases and that is ·expected to decrease as the volume in a period decreases.

p. *Fixed Cost* - A cost that is expected to be at a constant amount in a given time period regardless of changes in volume in that time period.

q. *Discretionary Cost* - A cost whose amount within a time period is governed by a management decision to incur the cost. The amount is not related to the volume of production or sales or to the capacity of the organization. Most discretionary costs are fixed, but some may be variable.

r. *Contribution Margin* - The difference between revenues and total variable costs.

s. *Segment Contribution* - The difference between revenues and the total of the variable costs and the direct fixed costs assigned to a segment of the organization.

t. *Operating Income* - The difference between revenues and the total of the variable costs, the direct fixed costs, and the indirect fixed costs assigned to a segment of the organization.

u. *Cost Accounting System* - The system within an organization that provides for the collection and assignment of costs to intermediate and final cost objects.

v. *Standard Cost System* - A product costing system in which the costs assigned to individual products are the costs that should have been incurred rather than the costs that actually were incurred.

w. *Equivalent Units of Product* - A common denominator of the cost causation impact of different products produced in a product cost center.

Cost Accounting System

9. A cost accounting system collects direct and indirect costs and assigns these costs to cost objects. The cost accounting

FIGURE 1
Flow of Indirect Production Costs
From Incurrence to Final Cost Object

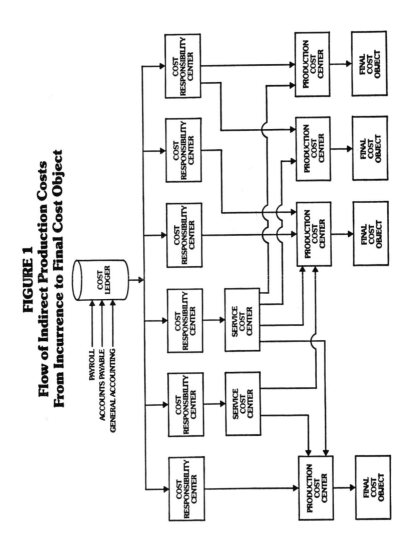

system for an organization should be designed to provide cost information that is useful to managers and cost information that is required for financial accounting purposes (inventory cost, contract cost). Such a system should identify costs initially by responsibility center (responsibility costs) and ultimately with final cost objects (full costs). See Figure 1. Production costs should be separated into *variable* and *fixed* components prior to assignment to final cost objects and thus provide an indication of those *differential costs* that vary with the volume of production. The data flowing through the cost accounting system should be internally consistent; that is, for each period, the total production costs incurred should be equal to the total of costs assigned to final cost objects.

Responsibility Costs

10. Responsibility costs are cost items classified in a way that aids in the *control* of costs. Usually implementation of this concept requires that each item be identified with the manager who is responsible for the control of that item.
11. Indirect production costs are difficult to control because they include a variety of different cost items with different behavioral characteristics. Some costs, such as occupancy costs and certain salaries, are expected to be the same amount per period regardless of changes in volume of production. Other items usually vary with changes in volume. Some cost items are discretionary; that is, they vary only in response to decisions of managers about the level of spending. Examples of discretionary costs are those related to research and development and management development and training.
12. *Flexible budgets* usually are the most effective tool for measuring management performance in controlling indirect production costs. A flexible budget is a plan that specifies the amount of cost for each item that should be incurred for any volume of production that might reasonably be expected to occur during a specified period of time. Differences between planned costs and actual costs are spending variances and, at least in part, are the responsibility of the manager of the responsibility center that incurs the costs. The identification of costs by responsibility should be the

first step in accounting for costs because once the process of assignment of costs to intermediate and final cost objects is begun, the opportunity to measure effectiveness in controlling costs is lost.

13. The cost accounting system should identify *service cost centers* and *production cost centers* separately. A dual responsibility exists for the costs of a service cost center. The service cost center manager is responsible for the costs incurred by the service cost center in providing units of service. Managers of the cost centers served are, at least in part, responsible for the amount of the service consumed by their cost centers.

Usually this dual responsibility for costs should be recognized by charging the production cost center and crediting the service cost center for actual services consumed at a predetermined rate per unit of service and by incorporating provisions for these charges and credits into the flexible budgets of the respective cost centers.

14. Responsibility cost items are identifiable directly with a responsibility center. Even though a cost item may not be controllable in the short run, such as depreciation expense on plant and equipment used by a department, the cost item nevertheless may be a responsibility cost.

Full Production Cost

15. The *full production cost* of a cost object is the sum of its direct production costs plus an appropriate share of applicable indirect production costs.

Full production cost is the cost at which completed products should be carried in inventory or in unbilled services. It also is the cost that should be recorded as cost of sales when products are sold. In addition to these uses, the measurement of full production cost is a necessary step in the accumulation of full costs of the organization, including direct and indirect selling, general and administrative expenses. (See Statement on Management Accounting 4B for the usefulness of full cost constructions.) Figure 2 is an illustration of a profitability model that incorporates full production costs.

16 The allocation of indirect production costs to final cost objects is accomplished in a series of steps:

a. Each indirect production cost item is assigned to a pro-

FIGURE 2
Profitability Model
Full Costs

	Total Company	Business Segments (Cost Objects)		
		A	B	C
REVENUES	$ 706	$423	$134	$149
COST OF SALES				
Direct production costs:				
Direct materials	$ 185	$107	$ 17	$ 61
Direct labor	85	57	7	21
Indirect production costs:	153	58	39	56
TOTAL COST OF SALES	$ 423	$232	$ 63	$138
GROSS PROFIT	$ 283	$201	$ 71	$ 11
SELLING AND ADMINISTRATION COSTS	143	85	29	29
OPERATING INCOME BEFORE INCOME TAXES	$ 140	$116	$ 42	$(18)

Accounting for Indirect Production Costs

duction cost center or a service cost center.

b. The total costs of each service cost center are reassigned to production cost centers.

c. The total indirect costs accumulated in each production cost center are allocated to products produced in the respective production cost centers.

17. Service cost centers incur costs to provide service to other cost centers or to the entire organization. The costs in service cost centers should be assigned to other cost centers in two ways:

a. Those costs that can be identified directly with the services rendered to another cost center should be assigned directly to that cost center at predetermined rates per unit of service, as described in paragraph 13.

b. The other costs in a service cost center should be allocated to other cost centers based on the causal relationship between the service costs and the cost center receiving the allocation.

18. Some service cost centers may receive services from other service centers. In such situations, the cost accounting system should provide for a step-down sequence of allocation of service center costs in which either the service center that provides the most service to other service centers or receives the least service from other service centers is allocated first, then the other service centers are allocated in order according to the criteria selected. Once the costs of a service center have been allocated, no additional costs are assigned to that service center. Alternatively, service center costs may be allocated to other service centers by a system of reciprocal distribution utilizing the techniques of matrix algebra.

19. Many cost items that are indirect costs with respect to a final cost object may be direct costs with respect to an intermediate cost object and are therefore assigned directly to that cost object. Those cost items that cannot be assigned directly to a cost center and those service center costs that cannot be assigned directly to other cost centers should be allocated to cost centers based upon the causal relationship between the costs and the cost center receiving the allocation.

The base for the allocation of indirect costs to cost centers should be the one that best expresses the causal relationship between the costs and the cost centers. Most of the possible allocation bases are included in the following principal categories:

a. *People-oriented costs.* Costs that are caused primarily by the number of employees should be allocated based on the number of employees or the number of labor hours in the respective cost centers.

b. *Payroll-oriented costs.* Costs that are related primarily to the amount that employees are paid should be allocated based on some measure of the labor costs in the respective cost centers.

c. *Equipment-oriented costs.* Costs that are related primarily to the usage of equipment should be allocated based on a measure of equipment utilization, such as machine hours.

d. *Materials-oriented costs.* Costs that are caused primarily by acquisition, storage, or movement of materials should be allocated based on either a physical measure or cost of direct materials used in the respective cost centers. See SMA 4E.

e. *Space-oriented costs.* Costs that are caused primarily by the need to provide and maintain work or storage space should be allocated based on a physical measure of the space required by the respective cost centers.

f. *Transaction-oriented costs.* Costs that are caused primarily by production transactions, such as production orders issued, engineering change orders, and scheduling and expediting activities, should be allocated according to the number of transactions generated by the respective cost centers.

g. *Total activity-oriented costs.* Those costs that are presumed to be caused by the overall activity of an organization should be allocated according to some measure of overall activity, such as total direct costs or total full costs in the respective cost centers.

20. The basic technique for the allocation of indirect production costs of a production cost center to final cost objects involves the use of *overhead rates.* An overhead rate applies a constant amount of cost to each equivalent unit of production.

To develop an overhead rate for a production cost center, the total indirect cost for a period is divided by the total units of production passing through the cost center in that period. The result is an overhead rate stated in cost per unit of production. The cost accounting system allocates this cost to each unit passing through the production cost center. Each product is assigned the appropriate cost for each production cost center it passes through.

The selection of the unit of volume used to develop the overhead rate for a production cost center and, subsequently, to allocate costs to products is a matter of judgment. The unit selected should:

a. Be common to and measureable for all products worked on in the production cost center.

b. Have a high correlation — i.e., a high causal relationship — between the volume measure and the amount of costs in the cost center.

The volume measures used most frequently and appropriately include direct labor hours, direct labor dollars, machine hours, production orders, engineering change orders, or some product-related physical measure such as tons, gallons, or equivalent units produced.

21. The procedures described above imply that the overhead rate is determined after the period has ended. In fact, in most situations it is desirable to estimate annually the incurrence and allocation of indirect costs and predetermine the overhead rate to be used in each production cost center for the coming year. The reasons for using predetermined overhead rates are:

a. Seasonal cost factors and monthly changes in volume of production may produce fluctuations in overhead rates that are calculated monthly. These fluctuations serve no useful purpose and often are misleading. They can be avoided by using predetermined overhead rates.

b. The use of predetermined overhead rates permits end-of-period accounting to be accomplished much more quickly.

c. Predetermining overhead rates annually requires less effort than going through the allocation process each period. An annual period is appropriate for the predetermination of overhead rates unless the production/marketing cycle of the entity is such that the use of a longer or shorter period would clearly provide more useful information.

22. Predetermined overhead rates require an estimate of the level of activity in each responsibility center and an estimate of the average production volume in each production cost center. The estimate of the average production volume for production cost centers is particularly sensitive because

many items of indirect cost are fixed or discretionary and do not vary with volume changes. If the estimate of average production volume is too high, too little cost will be assigned to final cost objects. If the estimate of average production volume is too low, too much cost will be assigned to final cost objects. The flexible budgets for indirect costs are used to simulate the amount of cost to be incurred for each cost item at the anticipated level of activity. Then the allocation methodology decided upon is used to simulate the amount of cost for each production cost center. The final step is to divide the estimated amount of indirect cost in each production cost center by the estimated equivalent units of volume anticipated to pass through the product cost center to obtain the predetermined overhead rate. Predetermined overhead rates should be revised during the year if there are significant changes in cost levels, anticipated production volumes, or the production process.

23. Actual indirect costs incurred in each period usually are greater or less than the estimated costs, and actual production volume usually differs from the estimated production volume used to calculate the predetermined overhead rate. Consequently, actual indirect costs incurred will differ from the amount of indirect costs allocated to final cost objects. When actual costs are greater than allocated costs, overhead is underabsorbed. When actual costs are less than allocated costs, overhead is overabsorbed. For management accounting purposes, overabsorbed or underabsorbed overhead should be credited or charged to earnings in the current period. For financial reporting, however, if the amounts involved are material, they should be assigned to cost of sales and inventory in the proportions in which the costs of production during the period have been assigned to cost of sales and inventory.

24. The procedures described for full costing are applicable when the primary objective of the cost accounting system is the assignment of actual costs to final cost objects. In many situations, however, management is concerned with what costs *should be incurred* for a final cost object and where in the organization and in what amount the actual costs incurred differ from the costs that should have been incurred. This kind of information is provided by a *standard cost system*. Standard costs are statements of what costs should be. Standard direct material costs and

standard direct labor costs are described in Statements 4E and 4D, respectively.

A standard cost system uses predetermined overhead rates to allocate indirect production costs to final cost objects following the procedures described in the preceding paragraphs, with two exceptions:

a. Both in the simulation described in paragraph 22 and in the actual allocation of costs to final cost objects, only the costs that should have been incurred are included. Any differences between planned costs and the actual costs incurred are identified as spending variances by the flexible budgeting system. Spending variances are identified by responsibility center and are signals to management that indirect costs are not being incurred as planned in those segments of the organization. For management accounting purposes, spending variances are charged or credited to earnings in the period in which they are incurred.

b. In the production cost center, the units of volume that are the basis for the allocation of production center costs to final cost objects are stated at standard rather than actual.

Because spending variances have been identified and dealt with separately, any remaining overabsorbed or underabsorbed overhead is attributable primarily to differences between the actual volume in a period and the estimated volume that was used to calculate the predetermined overhead rate. The differences are called volume variances and for management accounting purposes are charged or credited to earnings in the current period. For financial reporting purposes, if the amounts of spending and volume variances are material, they should be assigned to cost of sales and inventory in the proportions in which the costs of production during the period have been assigned to cost of sales and inventory.

Differential Production Costs

25. Differential costs are costs that are different under one set of conditions than they would be under another set of conditions. Differential costs always relate to the future and can be defined only in the context of a specific situation.

FIGURE 3
Profitability Model
Differential Costs

		Total Company	Business Segments (Cost Objects)		
			A	B	C
1	REVENUES	$ 706	$423	$134	$149
2	VARIABLE COSTS				
3	Direct production costs:				
4	Direct materials	$ 185	$107	$ 17	$ 61
5	Direct labor	85	57	7	21
6	Indirect production costs	61	20	24	17
7	Selling and administration costs	21	12	4	5
8	TOTAL VARIABLE COST	$ 352	$196	$ 52	$104
9	CONTRIBUTION MARGIN	354	227	82	45
10	% of Revenues	50.1%	53.7%	61.2%	30.2%
11	DIRECT FIXED COSTS				
12	Production costs	51	24	9	18
13	Selling and administration costs	28	19	7	2
14	TOTAL SEGMENT DIRECT COSTS	$ 79	$ 43	$ 16	$ 20
15	SEGMENT CONTRIBUTION	$ 275	$184	$ 66	$ 25
16	ALLOCATED SHARE OF INDIRECT FIXED COSTS				
17	Production costs	41	14	6	21
18	Selling and administration costs	94	54	18	22
19	TOTAL SEGMENT INDIRECT COSTS	$ 135	$ 68	$ 24	$ 43
20	OPERATING INCOME BEFORE INCOME TAXES	$ 140	$116	$ 42	$(18)

Accounting for Indirect Production Costs

Many management decisions require estimates of differences in some or all of the following:

a. Revenues
b. Direct production costs
c. Indirect production costs
d. Direct selling and administration costs
e. Indirect selling and administration costs

Many management decisions also require the estimation of these data for individual segments of the entity rather than for the entity as a whole. The cost accounting system should be designed to provide data that will be useful in estimating the differential costs for a wide variety of management decisions.

Profitability Model

26. This Statement is concerned primarily with indirect production costs. It is useful, however, to consider all elements of cost in the profitability model shown in Figure 3, which is the framework for this section of the Statement.

In this model, direct fixed costs are those costs that will exist if that business segment (cost object) continues to exist but should disappear if the business segment is discontinued. Indirect fixed costs are those overall costs of the entity that would continue if the segment were discontinued. These costs would have to be reallocated among the remaining segments. In this model, profitability is measured at three levels for each segment of the business:

a. Contribution margin
b. Segment contribution
c. Operating income

The measure of operating income in this profitability model is consistent with the same measure in the full cost profitability model illustrated in Figure 2. The classification of costs into their variable and fixed components, and the further classification of fixed costs into those that are direct to a segment of the business and those that are not, provide the necessary data from which to determine the differential costs relevant to a wide variety of management decisions. For example, if the alternatives in a decision involve operating at different volume levels, the differential costs may be equal to the variable costs. If the alternatives involve adding or dropping a segment of the business, the differential costs may include the direct fixed costs of the segment in addition to the variable costs.

27. The segregation of the fixed and variable components of indirect production costs can be accomplished by an extension of the simulation technique described in paragraphs 22-24 for the annual predetermination of overhead rates. In addition to using the flexible budgets to determine the total amount of cost for each indirect cost item each month at the anticipated level of activity, the flexible budget rates can be extended to a cost intercept at zero volume of activity. The cost at the point of intercept is deemed the *fixed component* of the cost. The fixed component is subtracted from the total cost at the anticipated level of activity, and the difference is deemed the *variable component*. The simulation then uses the allocation methodology decided upon to determine the amount of variable indirect costs for each product cost center. The final step of dividing the amount of variable indirect costs in each production cost center by the equivalent units of production anticipated to pass through the production cost center will produce a predetermined *variable overhead rate*. The fixed component of an indirect production cost item is stated as an amount per period rather than as a rate per unit of volume. Discretionary indirect production costs also are stated as an amount per period.

28. The subsequent classification of fixed and discretionary indirect production costs into those that are direct to a segment of the business and those that are not is done by examining and classifying each cost item.

29. Many entities have more than one dimension of segmentation that they find useful for management purposes. For example, one dimension of segmentation might be by product line, another might be by channel of distribution, and still another might be by geographical region. Variable costs follow the product or service and usually require no further analysis for a different dimension of segmentation. For each dimension of segmentation, however, fixed indirect production costs and other fixed costs should be examined separately and classified as either direct to a segment or not direct.

SUBCOMMITTEE ON STATEMENT PROMULGATION

*Robert G. Weiss, *Chairman*

*Raymond H. Alleman

F. Gordon Bitter
*Senior Vice President
and CFO*
The Singer Company
Stamford, Conn.

Robert A. Howell
*Clinical Professor of
Management and Accounting*
Graduate School of Business
New York University
New York, N.Y.

*Arthur D. Lyons

Daniel McBride
*Director of Financial
Accounting Policy*
Honeywell, Inc.
Minneapolis, Minn.

*Frank C. Minter

Raymond H. Peterson
*Director - Financial
Accounting Methods*
Pacific Bell
San Francisco, Calif.

L. Hal Rogero, Jr.
Assistant Controller
Mead Corporation
Dayton, Ohio

*J. Charles Stracuzzi

Donald J. Trawicki
Partner
Touche Ross & Company
New York, N.Y.

*Also a member of MAP
Committee

NATIONAL ASSOCIATION OF ACCOUNTANTS
MANAGEMENT ACCOUNTING PRACTICES COMMITTEE
1986-87

Chairman
William J. Ihlanfeldt
Assistant Controller
Shell Oil Company
Houston, Tex.

Raymond H. Alleman
Senior Vice President
& Comptroller
ITT Corporation
New York, N.Y.

Robert N. Anthony
Professor Emeritus
Harvard Business School
Boston, Mass.

James P. Colford
Director of Accounting Practices
IBM Corporation
Tarrytown, N.Y.

Patricia P. Douglas
Professor of Accounting and Finance
University of Montana
Missoula, Mont.

Bernard R. Doyle
Manager-Corporate
Accounting Services
General Electric Company
Fairfield, Conn.

Eugene H. Irminger
Senior Vice President of Finance
Centel Corporation
Chicago, Ill.

James J. Latchford
Controller
Chemical Bank
New York, N.Y.

Arthur D. Lyons
Vice President-Controller
FMC Corporation
Chicago, Ill.

Frank C. Minter
Vice President and CFO
AT&T International
Basking Ridge, N.J.

John J. Perrell, III
Vice President, Corporate
Accounting & Reporting
American Express Company
New York, N.Y.

J. Charles Stracuzzi
Controller
Blount AgriProducts Group
Blount Agri Industrial Corporation
Grand Island, Neb.

Norman N. Strauss
Partner
Ernst & Whinney
New York, N.Y.

Edward W. Trott
Partner
Peat Marwick
Tampa, Fla.

Robert G. Weiss
Vice President & Controller
Schering-Plough Corporation
Madison, N.J.

NAA STAFF

Louis Bisgay, *Director*, Management Accounting Practices
Jonathan B. Schiff, *Consulting Director*

Statements on Management Accounting

Statement Number 4H
January 1, 1988

PRACTICES AND TECHNIQUES

Uses of the Cost of Capital

In accordance with the charge to the Management Accounting Practices (MAP) Committee to issue statements on management accounting principles and practices, Statements on Management Accounting are promulgated to reflect official positions of the National Association of Accountants (NAA). The work of the MAP Committee is based on a framework for management accounting, whose principal categories are:

1. Objectives
2. Terminology
3. Concepts
4. Practices and Techniques
5. Management of Accounting Activities

Statements on Management Accounting

Statement Number 4H
January 1, 1988

Practices and Techniques:
Uses of the Cost of Capital

National Association of Accountants

Acknowledgments

The National Association of Accountants is grateful to the many individuals who contributed to the publication of Statement 4H, *Uses of the Cost of Capital*. Appreciation is extended to members of the Management Accounting Practices Committee and its Subcommittee on SMA Promulgation. Special thanks are extended to Jonathan B. Schiff, consulting director, NAA and Fairleigh Dickinson University, for his research and writing associated with this project.

Introduction

1. The cost of capital is a concern to operating executives, as well as to management accountants, because this cost is pervasive and often substantial. It can have a significant impact on the measurement of business unit profitability and product and service cost determination on cost-type contract pricing, on the financial implications of acquisitions and divestitures, and on other objectives of corporate finance.

2. This Statement is intended to help management accountants deal with the issues associated with the uses of the cost of capital. It also is intended to inform operating management about the cost of capital and sensitize them to its ramifications. The cost of capital should be related to the reported financial status and operations of an entity in either of two ways: (a) by using a measure such as return on investment (ROI) or return on capital employed, or (b) by using a measure such as residual income. Guidance on the computation of the cost of capital is provided by Statement on Management Accounting 4A, "Cost of Capital."

3. This Statement suggests the circumstances under which the cost of capital should be used or otherwise considered in the financial decision-making process. The Statement does not suggest inclusion of the cost of capital in the accounting routines that result in general purpose financial statements. In that regard, it should be recognized that the treatment of the cost of capital in this Statement — as a cost of doing business — is not in conformity with generally accepted accounting principles.

4. Inherent in this Statement is an underlying framework that makes use of historical cost. The Statement recognizes that utilization of historical cost as a basis for decision making may be dysfunctional sometimes and that other measures of economic value may be more appropriate.

Statement Scope

5. A business entity receives capital primarily from two sources: lenders and shareholders. Because there is a cost associated with all elements of capital employed by an entity, the cost

of capital resulting from shareholder investment, as well as that resulting from debt, should be considered in the financial decision-making process.

6. There are three general types of cost construction to which cost of capital is relevant: full costs, responsibility costs, and differential costs. Because each has a different objective, each will be discussed separately in this Statement. This Statement deals with the use of the cost-of-capital concept and not its determination. Moreover, this Statement pertains to the preparation of internal reports and the consideration of the cost of capital in financial analysis.

7. The cost of capital is relevant to the measurement of full cost, responsibility cost, and differential cost. The cost of capital should reflect economic reality tempered by the difficulties in measuring the uncertain future events that will influence the business unit.

Definitions

8. The *cost of capital* is a composite of the costs of various sources of funds that constitute the firm's capital structure. It is the minimum rate of return that must be earned on new investments so that shareholders' interests will not be diluted. (See SMA 4A, "Cost of Capital," Paragraph 3.)

Debt capital is that portion of total capital derived from the issuance of interest-bearing debt instruments.

Equity capital is that portion of total capital derived from permanent investments by shareholders, either as paid-in capital or as retained earnings.

A *cost object* is a product, contract, project, organizational subdivision, or other element for which costs are measured or estimated.

Return on investment (ROI) relates the net income an entity has earned to the assets that it has employed.

Residual income is net income of an entity less the cost of financing the entity's net assets employed.

The following section provides a summary of uses of the cost of capital reflective of the pervasive nature of this cost.

Uses of the Cost of Capital[1]

9. The cost of capital is important in making investment decisions, managing working capital, evaluating performance, and determining the costs of products, product lines, and services that include the use of capital resources.
10. For investment decisions, the cost of capital can be applied as a discount rate to evaluate the present value of project cash flows. It also may be the basis for a "hurdle" or "threshold" with which to compare a project's internal rate of return. To reflect the relative risk attributed to a proposal, the hurdle rate used may differ from the calculated cost of capital. The cost of capital also should be used in acquisition analyses, in divestment and liquidation studies, in research and development planning, and in source-of-financing decisions.
11. An entity should use the cost of capital to help manage its working capital. The cost of capital should be included in analyzing the cost of the firm's receivables, inventories, and payables, and it should be used to evaluate alternative policies and practices for these assets.
12. The cost of capital may be used as a benchmark for the measurement and evaluation of performance. The actual or expected return on capital or net assets may be compared with the cost of capital for this purpose.
13. The cost of capital should be used for product planning and as one of the factors in pricing decisions. In regulated industries, for example, the cost of capital is included in setting rates that will generate the allowable profit for the firm and resultant returns for its shareholders.
14. The following sections discuss the association of the cost of capital with the three cost constructs: full, responsibility, and differential.

Full Costs

15. The full cost of a cost object is the sum of its direct costs and indirect costs. Therefore, to measure full costs, an appropriate share of the cost of debt and equity capital should be associated with those cost objects to which they are applicable.

---

[1]This section is derived from SMA 4A, "Cost of Capital."

16. Conceptually, the cost of capital should be included in the measurement of full cost. In fact, at present it is included in full cost measurements in certain business environments, such as in the utilities industry. A common basis for relating the cost of capital is net assets employed. The measurement of net assets employed can be accomplished with the use of historical cost data. Alternatively, current or replacement cost or discounted future cash flows may be more relevant for this purpose.[2]

17. The cost of capital should be considered in product profitability analysis in order to derive a full cost measurement for product cost determination, to establish a baseline for pricing decisions, and to analyze entity performance.[3]

Responsibility Costs

18. For responsibility measurement, behavioral considerations determine appropriate approaches to assigning the cost of capital. The responsibility measurement system should motivate managers to make decisions that are in harmony with general corporate objectives. When the assignment of debt and equity capital contributes to the attainment of general corporate objectives, the assignment should be made. For example, when management desires to encourage market penetration, it may elect initially not to "fully load" the performance of this effort with a cost of capital. Alternatively, management may desire to sensitize business unit managers to the cost of capital by charging a cost for it, even though these managers do not control financing policy.

19. Residual income may be used to measure business unit performance. This approach involves a charge to the unit's earnings to reflect the cost of capital associated with the operations of the unit.

20. The cost of capital may be included as an element of central corporate costs by charging the cost object with an amount derived from a generalized activity base. This approach uses a uniform companywide cost of capital, which may serve

---

[2]It may be useful to consider intangible economic assets and other assets not captured in the traditional balance sheet.

[3]See Statement on Management Accounting 4D, "Measuring Entity Performance," for guidance on this issue.

as a suitable surrogate under some circumstances. Alternatively, companies may impute capital structures for business units with the intent to compute divisional costs of capital. In a multinational setting, different costs of capital may be associated with different geographical regions and regional effects on the debt and equity elements of cost of capital.

21. Business units should be charged for the cost of capital related to financing current asset growth. For example, with respect to accounts receivable, charging the cost of capital may cause costs to be associated with specific customer accounts and help in measuring customer profitability and assignment of responsibility to management. With respect to inventory, dysfunctional inventory growth may be discouraged if the cost of capital is charged. By charging the cost of capital, the business unit may avoid the acquisition or production of inventory that, by absorbing related overhead costs, may enhance short-term operating results but not contribute to shareholder value.

Differential Costs

22. Differential costs are elements of cost expected to vary if one course of action is adopted instead of another. Differential costs generally are used as one element of decision making. The decisions range in magnitude from a proposal to accept a lower-than-normal price on an individual order to a proposal to enter a new type of business involving the construction of new plants and the development of production and marketing organizations.

23. Differential costs relating to short-term decisions always involve specific alternatives. The cost of capital should be associated with the alternatives in the measurement of differential cash inflows and outflows and profits that result from the proposal. The technique for determining differential costs and the appropriate rate of cost of capital must be considered carefully to ensure that they reflect the nature of the decision precisely. It is important that differential costs isolate costs and revenue associated with the decision at hand and specifically that the cash-flow determination isolate the cash consequences of the decision on an after-tax basis. This approach is appropriate for short-

term decisions, which may include make or buy, purchase order quantity, and adding or dropping a product line.

24. A frequent and important use of differential costs is in investment decisions. Differential cash flows should be the primary financial criterion for investment decisions. Because cash flows differ in magnitude and timing, the cost of capital is critical to the evaluation of cash flows. The net differential cash flows are discounted by the capital cost in a net-present-value calculation, or the cost of capital is used as a "hurdle" rate for an internal rate-of-return calculation. The cash flow differences to be valued should not include interest costs or interest income because applying a cost of capital to interest causes a double counting of the time value of cash. The appropriate discount rate is the cost of capital adjusted for risks under certain circumstances.

25. When considering business alternatives, entities should be careful when relating the "financing" decision to the "investment" decision. Among the factors considered in the investment decision, the decision maker takes into account a "hurdle" rate that is based upon the cost of capital. If the potential investment appears attractive, the firm then would consider the financing decision. There are several sources of investment funds to be considered in the financing decision, and the decision maker decides which source or combination of sources is best under the circumstances. In determining the most effective financing approach, the decision maker should ensure that the cost of financing selected is consistent with the cost-of-capital assumption used in the investment decision. This criterion for the investment decision is influenced by the relative costs of financing. Other criteria would include the effect of the financing alternatives on the firm's financial statements and agreements with third parties, such as loan covenants.

Summary of NAA Recommendations

26. In the measurement of full costs, an appropriate share of both debt and equity capital should be assigned to cost objects to analyze entity performance, determine product costs, and establish a basis for pricing decisions.

27. In the measurement of responsibility costs, the cost of capital may be assigned to cost objects. This will contribute

to efficient asset utilization and reduce the possibility of dysfunctional asset growth. The assignment should be made when it contributes to the attainment of general corporate objectives.

28. When differential costs are used in the decision-making process, the cost of capital should be associated with the alternatives to determine cost differences for short-term decisions and incorporated into the discounted-cash-flow model for longer-term decisions.

29. The investment decision should be made separately from the financing decision. The analysis supporting the investment decision (whether or not to invest in a project) should include the allocation of the firm's cost of capital. This is in contrast to the financing decision, which involves the firm's most cost-effective approach to funding a project.

Bibliography

Articles

Anthony, Robert N., "Cost Allocation," *The Journal of Cost Analysis,* Spring 1984, pp. 5-15.

Anthony, Robert N., "Equity Interest – Its Time Has Come," *Journal of Accountancy,* December 1982, pp. 76-93.

Bartley, Jon W. and Lewis F. Davidson, "The Entity Concept and Accounting for Interest Costs," *Journal of Accounting & Business Research,* Summer 1982, pp. 175-182.

Bisgay, Louis, "CASB on Cost of Money," *Management Accounting,* October 1980, p.8.

Blanchard, Garth A. and Chee W. Chow, "Allocating Indirect Costs for Improved Management Performance," *Management Accounting,* March 1983, pp. 38-41.

Chatterjee, B.K., "Treatment of Interest as an Element of Product Cost," *The Chartered Accountant,* August 1983, pp. 85-91.

Ezzamel, Mahmoud A., "Estimating the Cost of Capital for a Division of a Firm and the Allocation Problem in Accounting: a Comment," *Journal of Business Finance & Accounting,* 1980, Vol. 7, #1, pp. 65-73.

Fuller, Russel J. and Halbert S. Kerr, "Estimating the Divisional Cost of Capital: an Analysis of the Pure-Play Technique," *The Journal of Finance,* December 1981, pp. 997-1009.

Hill, Alan, "Facts and Theory in Measuring Divisional Performance," *Accountancy,* April 1982, pp. 135-137.

Mackey, J.T., "Allocating Opportunity Costs," *Management Accounting,* March 1983, pp. 33-37.

McTague, Edward, "Capitalizing Interest Cost: How to Make the Computations," *The Practical Accountant*, November 1985, pp. 59-63.

Morais, Richard, "None for Me, Thanks," *Forbes*, October 22, 1984, pp. 134.

Weiner, Irving J., "A Simplified Approach to Allocating and Measuring Use of Capital," *Retail Control*, August 1981, pp. 12-18.

Welch, Jonathan B. and Timm L. Kainen, "Risk-Adjusted Multiple Hurdle Rates: Better Capital Budgeting," *Financial Executive*, May 1983, pp. 32-38.

Pronouncements and Research Papers

Allocating Corporate Expenses, Business Policy Study No. 108, The National Industrial Conference Board, New York, 1963.

Defliese, Philip L., "Accounting for the Cost of Capital," Presented to the Convention of the American Accounting Association, August 1974.

National Association of Accountants, *Statement on Management Accounting No. 4A: Cost of Capital*, NAA, 1984.

National Association of Accountants, *Statement on Management Accounting No. 4B: Allocation of Service and Administrative Costs*, NAA, 1985.

National Association of Accountants, *Statement on Management Accounting No. 4D: Measuring Entity Performance*, NAA, 1986.

The Allocation of Corporate Indirect Costs, National Association of Accountants, New York, 1981.

Toward Common Concepts of Cost Allocations in Cost Accounting, The Boeing Company, Seattle, Wash., 1978.

Textbooks

Anthony, R.N., *Accounting for the Cost of Interest*, Lexington, Mass., Lexington Books, 1975.

Anthony, R.N., J. Dearden and N. Bedford, *Management Control Systems: Text and Cases*, fifth edition, Homewood, Ill., Richard D. Irwin, Inc., 1984.

Horngren, Charles T., *Cost Accounting: A Managerial Emphasis*, sixth edition, Englewood Cliffs, N.J., Prentice-Hall, Inc., 1987.

Shillinglaw, Gordon, *Managerial Cost Accounting*, fifth edition, Homewood, Ill., Richard D. Irwin, Inc., 1982.

NATIONAL ASSOCIATION OF ACCOUNTANTS
MANAGEMENT ACCOUNTING PRACTICES COMMITTEE
1987-88

Statements on Management Accounting

Statement Number 41
June 1, 1989

PRACTICES AND TECHNIQUES

Cost Management For Freight Transportation

In accordance with the charge to the Management Accounting Practices (MAP) Committee to issue statements on management accounting principles and practices, Statements on Management Accounting are promulgated to reflect official positions of the National Association of Accountants (NAA). The work of the MAP Committee is based on a framework for management accounting, whose principal categories are:

1. Objectives
2. Terminology
3. Concepts
4. Practices and Techniques
5. Management of Accounting Activities

Statements on Management Accounting

Statement Number 4I
June 1, 1989

Practices and Techniques: Cost Management for Freight Transportation

National Association of Accountants, Inc.

Acknowledgments

The National Association of Accountants, Inc., is grateful to all who have contributed toward the publication of Statement 4I, *Cost Management for Freight Transportation*. Appreciation is extended to members of NAA's Management Accounting Practices Committee and its Subcommittee on SMA Promulgation. The NAA is especially thankful to Gene R. Tyndall, partner in charge of Transportation & Logistics Management Consulting at Ernst & Young, for his research and writing associated with this project.

Statement Outline

Introduction

1. This Statement is intended to provide guidance to management accountants and others in improving the manner in which the costs associated with the transportation of freight are identified, measured, and controlled. It does so by addressing the needs for transportation information, identifying the factors that contribute to costs, and suggesting a planning and flexible budgeting method for cost management.
2. In addressing the need for comprehensive information on the transportation of freight, this Statement provides a framework for the design of a transportation database. Companies may use such a framework to design and develop their own transportation information system, or obtain commercial software, in order to meet their unique circumstances and user requirements. The best available software packages include key support functions such as transportation analysis, traffic routing and scheduling, freight rate maintenance and audit, carrier cost comparisons, least-cost freight consolidation, freight cost allocations, budgeting, transporting performance, and management reporting.
3. This Statement focuses on costs as financial measures of performance in transportation. Nonfinancial performance and productivity measures are treated to the degree that they bear on managing the costs of transportation rather than on managing the transportation function itself.
4. The identification, measurement, and control of the costs of transporting goods, materials, and finished products is of increasing concern to operating executives and management accountants. This concern responds to: (a) the increasing level of these costs as markets are expanded, including international sources and customers; (b) rapidly diversifying channels of distribution in most industries; and (c) the expanding opportunities under transportation deregulation for reducing and/or controlling these costs by exercising available alternatives. These opportunities create more potential for profit contribution and value-added services through transportation management than was previously possible.

Statement Scope

5. This Statement applies to the total costs of freight transportation—whether these are for inbound freight, interfacility company shipments, or outbound transportation to customers. It encompasses the total costs of company-operated transportation as well as costs incurred for purchasing outside transportation services. It does not include: (a) material flow costs within production facilities or warehouses or (b) passenger transportation.

6. Transportation costs may exist for several modes of transport: trucking, rail, ocean, pipeline, barge, air freight, and intermodal services. In addition, transportation support costs, such as those associated with people and data, are included in transportation cost management.

7. This Statement applies to transportation costs incorporated into the cost of inbound materials or the price of goods sold as well as to freight charges or transportation costs incurred directly as transportation expenses.

8. This Statement addresses the direct assignment and allocation of transportation costs. Because of the complexities involved in transportation measurement, only when the actual causes of cost incurrence are understood can costs be assigned directly or allocated properly for effective decisions. Moreover, because tansportation costs often are incurred in meeting more than one cost object (e.g., two or more products), the capability to separate and allocate common costs will vary by cost accounting practice.

9. The Statement applies only to cost issues that are material in amount; that is, to practices that might make a difference in the actions of the person(s) who might use the cost information.

Information for Transportation Cost Management

10. Managing and controlling the costs of transportation is only as effective as the completeness and timeliness of the data and information available. Transportation operations are quite

transaction-intensive (e.g., freight bills); thus the control of expenditures for transportation activities requires current information on shipments.

11. Effective transportation information must be comprehensive enough to include all relevant costs and assets associated with transportation activities. The information should include all costs of inbound, interfacility, and outbound shipments. Both for-hire and private fleet costs should be included.

12. Information should be consistent across divisions and subsidiaries to facilitate company-wide decisions. The database should include all capital assets employed (trucks, rail cars, etc.), and their related costs of depreciation. It should incorporate all transportation-related expenses, and asset and expense support costs related to transportation management and administration.

13. The information should be categorized by cost element to identify corrective actions to control transportation costs. This should be reflected in cost behavior patterns, and cost variability must be identified (e.g., fixed and variable costs isolated). The traditional natural expense categories (e.g., labor, materials, fuel, etc.) and organizational classifications of cost for responsibility accounting should be provided. Exhibit I illustrates the data elements required for comprehensive and flexible management control of transportation costs.

14. Transportation information should be readily accessible to all departments involved in decisions about materials sourcing and product distribution. It should be in a form that facilitates analysis and decision support, not mere processing and summarization of transactions, such as the administration of freight bills.

15. Information should provide for financial measures of transportation activity, performance measurement and evaluation, and productivity improvement.

16. With these information requirements in mind, and with today's information technology capabilities, more companies are designing/implementing information systems for transportation management. These systems increasingly take advantage of Electronic Data Interchange (EDI) with outside suppliers and customers.

EXHIBIT I

SAMPLE WORKSHEET OF DATA ELEMENTS NEEDED FOR TRANSPORTATION CONTROL MANAGEMENT TECHNIQUES

Data Elements Needed*

Transportation Control Management Techniques	Shipment Cost	Movement Type	Mode	Carrier	Origin	Destination	Route	Product	Number of Units
Cost Reporting									
Responsibility Accounting									
Freight Bill Auditing									
Standard Costing									
Variance Analysis									
Carrier Performance Analysis									
Productivity Management									
Cost Allocation									
Transfer Pricing									

* In each cell, indicate whether the data is needed to apply the technique

Data Elements Needed*

Commodity Class	Weight	Cubic Volume	Customer Number	Vendor Number	Shipment Terms	Shipment Time	Number of Stops	Tariff Reference	BL #	FB #	Pro #	District or Region

17. A properly designed transportation management system will provide for simultaneous capture (single-point data entry) of important operations and financial data. These data include: origin and destination of shipments; cube (volume) and weight indicators; service indicators (times and miles); and equipment capacity utilization.

18. It is necessary, for integration purposes, to design/implement the transportation information system with interfaces to other logistics, distribution, purchasing, manufacturing, and accounting systems. Exhibit II illustrates the integrated system database. Exhibit III illustrates the data sources for key data elements in a comprehensive transportation database system.

19. There are distinct phases to transportation information system development, ranging from personal computer-based data to the fully integrated transportation system. Each company should formulate its own information strategy for transportation cost management.

Factors Contributing to Transportation Costs

20. Transportation costs are driven by the overall logistics strategy and operations of the company. Logistics encompasses all material flow functions across the company's product supply chain from vendors to customers—transportation, warehousing and distribution, customer services, inventory management, procurement, and materials handling. Transportation costs are determined by the role of the transportation function in this overall logistics environment. The key drivers of overall logistics costs of a company include:

- Materials supply network
- Materials inventory
- Production volumes
- Finished goods distribution network
- Finished goods inventory
- Customer demand levels and patterns
- Customer services and service levels

EXHIBIT II

TRANSPORTATION DATABASE IN THE
INTEGRATED INFORMATION SYSTEM

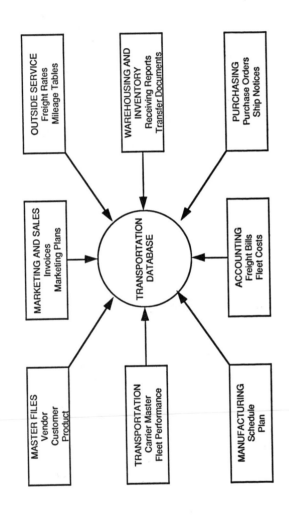

SAMPLE WORKSHEET TO SUMMARIZE DATA SOURCES FOR EACH DATA ELEMENT

DATA SOURCES

Data Elements Needed	Freight Bills	Bills of Lading	Fleet Log	Orders	Invoices	Transfer Documents	Vendor File	Customer File	Product File	Marketing File	Production Forecast
Mode	X		X								
Carrier	X	X	X								
Bill of Lading No.	X										
Pro Number	X						X				
Movement Type	X	X	X	X	X	X	X	X			
Origin	X	X	X	X	X	X		X			
Destination	X	X	X	X	X	X		X			
District/Region	X		X	X	X	X		X			
Customer Number	X	X	X	X	X	X	X	X			
Vendor Number	X	X	X	X	X	X	X	X			
Route	X		X					X	X	X	
Order Number	X		X	X	X	X	X	X	X	X	X
Product		X	X	X	X	X			X		
Units	X	X							X		
Weight	X	X	X						X		
Cubic Volume			X								
Tariff		X							X		
Commodity Class	X										
Shipment Cost	X		X			X					
Shipment Terms							X	X			
Shipment Dates	X	X									
Shipment Time			X								
Number of Stops	X		X								
Mileage			X								

X – Denotes that the source document contains the indicated data element

- Transportation (inbound/outbound)
- Warehousing (storage and handling)

Exhibit IV illustrates how leading companies manage core logistics processes—both strategically and operationally—from an understanding of overall logistics costs.

21. There are numerous specific factors contributing to the determination of transportation costs. These include, but are not limited to, the following:

- Shipment origin and destination
- Product shipped
  — Value
  — Specific shipping characteristics (e.g., special handling, weight, packaging, etc.)
- Mode of shipment (truck, rail, air, ocean, barge, or pipeline)
- Outside carrier used
- Volume shipped
- Shipment size—e.g., full truckload (TL) or carload (CL) or less-than-truckload (LTL)
- Shipment weight
- Frequency of shipments
- Packaging type and unit (e.g., pallet load or air container)
- Shipment routing and total distance travelled
- Shipment tracking
- Rehandling of product (e.g., consolidation or break-bulk operations)
- Origin and destination handling
- Payment terms
- Desired speed or transit time (one-day service, cheapest route, etc.)
- Special services
- Claims (loss and damage)
- Transportation of hazardous materials (routing implications, special handling charges, insurance costs)

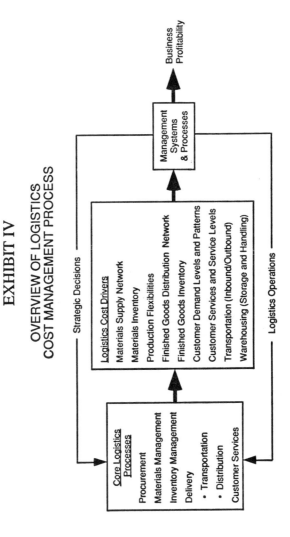

EXHIBIT IV

OVERVIEW OF LOGISTICS
COST MANAGEMENT PROCESS

Strategic Decisions

Core Logistics Processes

Procurement
Materials Management
Inventory Management
Delivery
• Transportation
• Distribution
Customer Services

Logistics Cost Drivers

Materials Supply Network
Materials Inventory
Production Flexibilities
Finished Goods Distribution Network
Finished Goods Inventory
Customer Demand Levels and Patterns
Customer Services and Service Levels
Transportation (Inbound/Outbound)
Warehousing (Storage and Handling)

Logistics Operations

Management
Systems
& Processes

Business
Profitability

22. In determining for-hire carrier costs, several types of special charges should be identified and measured. These include: linehaul charges; occasional charges for extra services (e.g., diversions, reconsignment, demurrage, and transit privileges); claims administration and loss and damage reimbursement; and terminal overhead.

23. Companies using for-hire carriers normally audit freight bills to ensure that all charges are correct and that correct amounts are paid to carriers. Freight bill audits and payments can be done internally or through third-party service organizations. In either case, the systems used for auditing and paying freight bills not only should ensure correct charges and accurate payments but also should provide the data required for comprehensive transportation cost management.

24. If company-owned service (private fleet) is being used, all associated costs should be identified and measured. These include: maintenance, terminal, and operating costs, including driver wages and fringes; fuel and oil; interest; equipment depreciation; and insurance. The dynamics of the deregulated transportation industry today continually change the relative economics of private vs. for-hire transportation. Companies with private fleets periodically should study the possible cost and ROI relationships of the for-hire option.

25. For costing *inbound* transportation movements, the following circumstances or factors should be considered:

    • Inbound transportation costs often are incorporated into the materials purchase cost. The freight expenses need to be separated in order to manage and control their incurrence.

    • Inbound transportation movements typically consist of low-value, commodity-type materials. Companies often "forward buy" to take advantage of lower prices; thus shipments are typically made in large volumes, requiring minimal packaging and special handling. These factors will affect decisions concerning carrier selection, receiving practices (quality control and storage), and other factors affecting transportation costs.

- With the current emphasis on Just-in-Time (JIT) deliveries, many companies may be paying premium transportation rates for more frequent and smaller inbound shipments.

26. For *outbound* movements, products are typically of higher value and represent lower volumes. In addition, more emphasis is placed on customer service requirements, such as loss and damage, on-time deliveries, packaging, and so on. These factors affect decisions including mode selection, shipment sizes, carrier selection, and use of private fleet, which contribute to total transportation costs.

27. Because the company's policies for customer services are a significant factor in the incurrence of transportation costs, it is essential that transportation decisions and resulting costs be consistent with and support the overall customer service strategy.

Transportation Planning and Budgeting

28. Logistics planning represents a process whereby the company strives for ongoing, continuous improvements in all aspects of logistics operations. Effective logistics plans derive from and support overall company plans and objectives. The transportation planning and budgeting process should link transportation strategy and operations to the logistics and business strategies of the company.

29. A transportation budget should be a primary tool in planning, monitoring, and controlling the activities and costs of transporting materials, supplies, and products. Because budgeting integrates the transportation function into the complete range of corporate or business unit activities through the profit plan, its use by management accountants for monitoring and control purposes can ensure that transportation activities and costs remain consistent with the business plan.

30. Exhibit V illustrates an effective budgeting process. It requires transportation managers to link service with sales forecasts and production or purchasing forecasts.

EXHIBIT V

TRANSPORTATION BUDGETING PROCESS

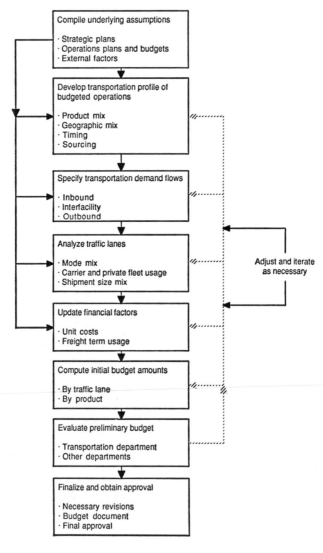

31. The key step in budgeting is to estimate, in a precise manner, expected transportation costs given the planned level of operations. This requires a detailed specification of the expected demand for transportation service, with the primary parameters being miles, weight, and cubic volume.

32. Identifying and costing out planned shipment volumes by traffic lane and mode is an effective approach to specifying service demand in terms of budgeted sales and production. Exhibits VI through X illustrate the budgeting process for a typical manufacturer using this approach.

33. Budgeting is affected directly by the freight terms used by the company for inbound and outbound shipments. Most companies budget only for transportation costs paid directly, i.e., carrier freight bills, freight charges on vendor invoices, private fleet expenses, and traffic and administrative expenses. Thus the extent to which the company pays freight charges for each product group and traffic lane must be specified.

34. Profitability analysis, or service costing, requires that fixed overhead costs be allocated to specific shipments, products, or traffic lanes. Thus, while overhead rates reflect changes in activity, it is often necessary to adopt fixed overhead rates (e.g., depreciation) in order to allocate them properly.

35. Standard costs may be established for many transportation activities, whether for product or commodity, traffic lane, sales and shipping unit, or mode and shipment size. Once standard costs are developed for key activities, flexible budgeting methods can be used to control and plan transportation costs.

36. Transportation costs can be measured and controlled effectively by comparing actual costs against budget standards. Variance analysis based on flexible transportation budgets (flexed for volume levels and shifts) can point to the key factors affecting transportation costs. Exhibit XI illustrates how overall variance in costs can be segmented to volume, rate, mode use, and freight absorption by product. Exhibit XII shows the computation of the variable cost budget variances for Product C.

EXHIBIT VI

BUDGET DEVELOPMENT EXAMPLE:
PRODUCTION/DISTRIBUTION MATRIX (In Units)

PRODUCT	PLANT	SALES REGION						
		1	2	3	4	5	6	TOTAL
A	I	20,000	20,000	20,000	20,000	-0-	-0-	80,000
	II	-0-	-0-	-0-	-0-	20,000	20,000	40,000
B	I	15,000	7,500	7,500	15,000	-0-	-0-	45,000
	II	-0-	-0-	-0-	-0-	7,500	7,500	15,000
C	I	-0-	-0-	-0-	-0-	-0-	-0-	-0-
	II	30,000	10,000	10,000	20,000	10,000	10,000	90,000
		65,000	37,500	37,500	55,000	37,500	37,500	270,000

Note: This matrix matches the budgeted sales (in units) of each product by sales region, with the plant supplying the products.

SALES REGION/DISTRIBUTION CENTER
ASSIGNMENTS MATRIX

Sales Region	Product	Plant	From Dist Center
1	A	1	1
	B	1	1
	C	11	1
2	A	1	1
	B	1	1
	C	11	1
3	A	1, 11	2
	B	1, 11	2
	C	11	2
4	A	1, 11	2
	B	1, 11	2
	C	11	2
5	A	11	3
	B	11	3
	C	11	3
6	A	11	3
	B	11	3
	C	11	3

EXHIBIT VII

BUDGET DEVELOPMENT EXAMPLE:
MODE MIX BY TRAFFIC LANE AND PRODUCT

Traffic Lane		Product	Percentage of Traffic by Mode			
Origin	Destination		Private Fleet	Car Load	Truck Load	LTL
Plant I	Dist Ctr 1	A	100%			
Plant I	Dist Ctr 1	B	100%			
Plant I	Dist Ctr 2	A	100%			
Plant I	Dist Ctr 2	B			75%	25%
Plant II	Dist Ctr 1	C		100%		
Plant II	Dist Ctr 2	C		100%		
Plant II	Dist Ctr 3	A			100%	
Plant II	Dist Ctr 3	B			75%	25%
Plant II	Dist Ctr 3	C		100%		
Dist Ctr 1	Sis Reg 1	A	50%		50%	
Dist Ctr 1	Sis Reg 1	B	50%		50%	
Dist Ctr 1	Sis Reg 1	C	50%		50%	
Dist Ctr 1	Sis Reg 2	A	50%		50%	
Dist Ctr 1	Sis Reg 2	B			25%	75%
Dist Ctr 1	Sis Reg 2	C	50%		50%	
Dist Ctr 2	Sis Reg 3	A	75%		25%	
Dist Ctr 2	Sis Reg 3	B			25%	75%
Dist Ctr 2	Sis Reg 3	C	75%		25%	
Dist Ctr 2	Sis Reg 4	A			75%	25%
Dist Ctr 2	Sis Reg 4	B			75%	25%
Dist Ctr 2	Sis Reg 4	C			75%	25%
Dist Ctr 3	Sis Reg 5	A			50%	50%
Dist Ctr 3	Sis Reg 5	B			25%	75%
Dist Ctr 3	Sis Reg 5	C			50%	50%
Dist Ctr 3	Sis Reg 6	A	75%		25%	
Dist Ctr 3	Sis Reg 6	B			25%	75%
Dist Ctr 3	Sis Reg 6	C	75%		25%	

EXHIBIT VIII

BUDGET DEVELOPMENT EXAMPLE:
SUMMARY OF TRANSPORTATION COST PER UNIT

| TRAFFIC LANE | | | TRANSPORTATION COST PER UNIT | | | |
Origin	Destination	Product	Private Fleet	Car Load	Truck Load	LTL
Plant I	Dist Ctr 1	A	$5			
Plant I	Dist Ctr 1	B	$7			$20
Plant I	Dist Ctr 2	A	$5			
Plant I	Dist Ctr 2	B			$8	
Plant II	Dist Ctr 1	C		$16		
Plant II	Dist Ctr 2	C		$8		
Plant II	Dist Ctr 3	A			$6	
Plant II	Dist Ctr 3	B		$8	$8	$18
Plant II	Dist Ctr 3	C				
Dist Ctr 1	Sis Reg 1	A	$6		$7	$25
Dist Ctr 1	Sis Reg 1	B	$9		$10	
Dist Ctr 1	Sis Reg 2	C	$12		$14	$22
Dist Ctr 1	Sis Reg 1	A	$6		$7	
Dist Ctr 1	Sis Reg 2	B			$10	$12
Dist Ctr 1	Sis Reg 2	C	$12		$14	$24
Dist Ctr 2	Sis Reg 3	A	$5		$6	$30
Dist Ctr 2	Sis Reg 3	B			$10	
Dist Ctr 2	Sis Reg 3	C	$13		$14	$12
Dist Ctr 2	Sis Reg 4	A			$6	$23
Dist Ctr 2	Sis Reg 4	B			$10	
Dist Ctr 2	Sis Reg 4	C			$14	$30
Dist Ctr 3	Sis Reg 5	A			$6	$25
Dist Ctr 3	Sis Reg 5	B			$10	
Dist Ctr 3	Sis Reg 5	C			$14	
Dist Ctr 3	Sis Reg 6	A	$6		$7	
Dist Ctr 3	Sis Reg 6	B			$10	
Dist Ctr 3	Sis Reg 6	C	$13		$15	

Cost Management for Freight Transportation

EXHIBIT IX

BUDGET DEVELOPMENT EXAMPLE:
PERCENTAGE OF TRANSPORTATION COST ABSORBED

Traffic Lane			Percentage of Transportation Cost Absorbed		
Origin	Destination	Product	Private Fleet	Truck Load	LTL
Dist Ctr 1	Sis Reg 1	A	100%	65%	NA
Dist Ctr 1	Sis Reg 1	B	85%	80%	NA
Dist Ctr 1	Sis Reg 1	C	90%	80%	NA
Dist Ctr 1	Sis Reg 2	A	100%	75%	NA
Dist Ctr 1	Sis Reg 2	B	NA	70%	65%
Dist Ctr 1	Sis Reg 2	C	90%	80%	NA
Dist Ctr 2	Sis Reg 3	A	90%	80%	NA
Dist Ctr 2	Sis Reg 3	B	NA	75%	70%
Dist Ctr 2	Sis Reg 3	C	80%	75%	NA
Dist Ctr 2	Sis Reg 4	A	NA	90%	85%
Dist Ctr 2	Sis Reg 4	B	NA	85%	75%
Dist Ctr 2	Sis Reg 4	C	NA	90%	75%
Dist Ctr 3	Sis Reg 5	A	NA	90%	70%
Dist Ctr 3	Sis Reg 5	B	NA	80%	80%
Dist Ctr 3	Sis Reg 5	C	NA	80%	80%
Dist Ctr 3	Sis Reg 6	A	90%	70%	NA
Dist Ctr 3	Sis Reg 6	B	NA	85%	70%
Dist Ctr 3	Sis Reg 6	C	90%	75%	NA

Note: This exhibit illustrates a summary of the percentage of transportation cost absorbed for each product over each traffic lane. This type of summary can be developed by analyzing the freight term usage for each shipment type.

EXHIBIT X

BUDGET DEVELOPMENT EXAMPLE:
BUDGETED TRANSPORTATION COST BY
TRAFFIC LANE AND PRODUCT

Traffic Lane			Total Budgeted Transportation Cost				
Origin	Destination	Product	Private Fleet	Car Load	Truck Load	LTL	Total
Plant I	Dist Ctr 1	A	$200,000				$200,000
Plant I	Dist Ctr 1	B	157,500				157,500
Plant I	Dist Ctr 2	A	200,000				200,000
Plant I	Dist Ctr 2	B			$135,000	$112,500	247,500
Plant II	Dist Ctr 1	C		$640,000			640,000
Plant II	Dist Ctr 2	C		240,000			240,000
Plant II	Dist Ctr 3	A			240,000		240,000
Plant II	Dist Ctr 3	B			90,000	67,500	157,500
Plant II	Dist Ctr 3	C		160,000			160,000
Dist Ctr 1	Sis Reg 1	A	60,000		45,500		105,000
Dist Ctr 1	Sis Reg 1	B	57,375		60,000		117,375
Dist Ctr 1	Sis Reg 1	C	162,000		168,000		330,000
Dist Ctr 1	Sis Reg 2	A	60,000		52,500		112,500
Dist Ctr 1	Sis Reg 2	B			13,125	91,400	104,525
Dist Ctr 1	Sis Reg 2	C	54,000		56,000		110,000
Dist Ctr 2	Sis Reg 3	A	67,500		24,000		91,500
Dist Ctr 2	Sis Reg 3	B			14,100	86,625	100,725
Dist Ctr 2	Sis Reg 3	C	78,000		26,250		104,250
Dist Ctr 2	Sis Reg 4	A			81,000	51,000	132,000
Dist Ctr 2	Sis Reg 4	B			95,625	67,500	163,125
Dist Ctr 2	Sis Reg 4	C			189,000	112,500	301,500*
Dist Ctr 3	Sis Reg 5	A			54,000	84,000	138,000
Dist Ctr 3	Sis Reg 5	B			15,000	103,500	118,500
Dist Ctr 3	Sis Reg 5	C			56,000	120,000	176,000
Dist Ctr 3	Sis Reg 6	A	81,000		24,500		105,500
Dist Ctr 3	Sis Reg 6	B			15,950	98,450	114,400
Dist Ctr 3	Sis Reg 6	C	87,750		28,125		115,875
TOTAL			$1,265,125	$1,040,000	$1,483,675	$994,975	$4,783,775

* This amount – the total cost of transporting Product Group C from Dist Ctr 2 to Sis Reg 4 –
is computed, as an example, as follows:

   1. 20,000 units x 75% truckload x $14 per unit = $210,000
   2. $210,000 x 90% cost absorbed = $189,000
   3. 20,000 units x 25% LTL x $30 per unit = $150,000
   4. $150,000 x 75% cost absorbed = $112,500
   5. Budget Total = $301,500

Similar computations are used to compute preliminary budget amounts for the other
combinations of traffic lanes, products, modes, etc.

EXHIBIT XI

SAMPLE FLEXIBLE BUDGET REPORT:
VARIANCE ANALYSIS BY TRAFFIC LANE

| Cost Type | Product | Budget | Actual | Variances* | | | | | |
				Volume	Parts	Mode Mix	Freight Absorption	Fixed Budget	Total
Variable	A	$114,250	$102,825	$5,710	$4,420	$(12,560)	$13,855		$11,425
	B	150,750	135,675	7,540	5,830	(16,580)	18,285		15,075
	C	267,000	240,540	13,350	10,260	(29,070)	31,920		26,460
		532,000	479,040	26,600	20,510	(58,210)	64,060		52,960
Fixed	A	17,750	15,875					$1,875	1,875
	B	12,375	11,750					625	625
	C	34,500	35,250					(750)	(750)
		64,625	62,875					1,750	1,750
Total	A	132,000	118,700	5,710	4,420	(12,560)	13,855	1,875	13,300
	B	163,125	147,425	7,540	5,830	(16,580)	18,285	625	15,700
	C	301,500	275,790	13,350	10,260	(29,070)	31,920	(750)	25,710
		$596,625	$541,915	$26,600	$20,510	$(58,210)	$64,060	$1,750	$54,710

* See Exhibit XII for the computation of these variances for Product C, as an example.

EXHIBIT XII

FLEXIBLE BUDGET EXAMPLE: COMPUTATION OF VARIANCES

	DESCRIPTION OF COMPUTATION	VALUES		VARIANCE AMOUNT
VARIANCE VOLUME:	Budgeted Units (Actual Units)	Truck Load 20,000	LTL 20,000	
	Variance in Units	(19,000)	(19,000)	
X	Budgeted Mode/Size Max %	1,000	1,000	
		x 75% 750	x 25% 250	
X	Budgeted Unit Cost			
X	Budgeted % of Cost Absorbed	x $12 $9,000	x $28 $7,000	
		x 90%	x 75%	
	VOLUME VARIANCE	$8,100	$5,250	$13,350
RATE	Actual Units by Load Size	11,400	7,800	
	Budgeted Unit Cost (Actual Unit Cost)	$12 $(11)	$28 $(28)	
X	Unit Rate Variance		x —0— / —0—	
X	Budgeted % of Cost Absorbed	x $1 11,400		
		x 90%		
	RATE VARIANCE	$10,260	—0—	$10,260
MODE MIX:	Budgeted Mode/Size Mix %	75 %	25 %	
	Actual Units by Mode Size Actual Total Units (Actual Mode Size Mix %)	11,400 ÷ 19,000 (60 %)	7,600 ÷ 19,000 (40%)	
	Variance in %	15%	(15%)	
X	Actual Total Units	x 19,000 2,850	x 19,000 (2,850)	
X	Budgeted Variable Cost per Unit			
X	Budgeted % of Cost Absorbed	x $12 34,200	x $28 (79,800)	
		x 90%	x 75%	
	MODE MIX VARIANCE	$30,780	$(59,850)	$(29,070)
FREIGHT ABSORPTION:	Actual Units by Load Size	11,400	7,600	
X	Budgeted Unit Cost	X $12 $136,800	X $28 $212,850	
	Budgeted % of Cost Absorbed (Actual % of Cost Absorbed)	90 % (90 %)	75 % (60%)	
X	Variance in %	x —0— / —0—	x 15%	
	FREIGHT ABSORPTION VARIANCE	—0—	$31,920	$31,920
	TOTAL BUDGET VARIANCE — FAVORABLE			$26,460

Direct Assignments and Allocations

37. A key objective of management cost accounting for any function is the direct assignment and allocation of costs to the business elements that consume the resources incurring the cost (the "cost objects," such as products or destination). The direct assignment and/or allocation of transportation costs should be made on causal factors (activities) in order to determine the amount of cost incurred.

    Direct assignment and/or allocation of costs should occur at the transaction level of detail or otherwise at the lowest level of detail practical, such as activity. For example, freight costs associated with individual shipments should be assigned to the products and destinations on those shipments and then aggregated, or rolled up, as required for management cost reporting purposes. Good judgment must be exercised regarding which costs should be specifically assigned and which should be allocated as miscellaneous, or "overhead" costs, based on their relative amounts and impact for management decision making (materiality).

38. Transportation costs often are incurred in providing service to more than one cost object, for example, the cost of a shipment containing two different products. The allocation base normally applied is weight or volume, although number of loads or number of shipments may be used. The choice of an allocation base should reflect, to the degree practical, the resources actually consumed by the elements to which costs are being charged.

39. The transportation function varies substantially among companies in its organization, objectives, and cost structure; thus different costing methodologies may be applied. A typical costing system uses detailed financial information as well as numerous operational statistics regarding weights, volumes, and miles.

40. The objective in transportation costing is to have data available on all transportation-related costs, preferably organized

by functional cost categories. For example, with a private fleet, categories of cost would include:

- Driver wages and fringes
- Fuel and oil
- Equipment depreciation and leases
- General and administrative
- Tractor and trailer maintenance
- Facility expense
- Tires/tubes
- Dispatching
- Other operating expenses
- Insurance and accidents

These costs then may be assigned or allocated to loads (shipments), hours, and/or miles.

41. Functional costs may be assigned directly to cost behavior classifications, e.g., short-run variable, long-run variable, and fixed costs. This method permits effective marginal cost pricing, cost-volume-profit analysis, flexible budgeting, and variance analysis.

42. Time-related costs, such as depreciation, frequently are allocated based on hours of use. The total hours computation for these time-related costs includes the total hours the equipment is normally in use (including the empty and loaded portion of the trip) and hours the vehicle is in service but not being operated over the highway (e.g., loading and unloading time). Average hours is generally used for costing purposes. It requires the development of average driving speed by zone, or geographic region, based on mileage brackets. It can be determined based on continuous analysis of the actual performance of each load or by use of statistical sampling techniques.

43. For costs that are a function of miles operated, both loaded and empty miles should be included, and the per-mile charge is determined using system averages or averages for each major traffic lane. This approach may be used to allocate other

functional costs (e.g., fuel and oil, tractor maintenance, tires/tubes, and accidents and insurance), depending on how they are incurred. The total load cost is calculated by accumulating the functional cost allocations using the hours, loads, and mile bases.

44. When allocating load costs to shipments, select a descriptive allocation base that considers important factors such as weight and distance. The most commonly used allocation base for this purpose is hundredweight (cwt) miles. Exhibit XIII illustrates how the costs of a truckload with six shipments (or stops) can be allocated based on shipment cwt-miles.

EXHIBIT XIII

SHIPMENT COST ALLOCATION EXAMPLE

(1) Shipment Number	(2) Miles: Origin to Destination	(3) Weight Per Shipment	(4) Shipment Cwt-Miles	(5) Percent of Total Cwt- Miles	(6) Allocated Shipment Cost
1	50	9,000	4,500	7 %	$ 80.50
2	100	8,000	8,000	12 %	$ 138.00
3	150	7,000	10,500	16 %	$ 184.00
4	200	1,000	2,000	3 %	$ 34.50
5	350	7,000	24,500	38 %	$ 437.00
6	500	3,000	15,000	24 %	$ 276.00
Total		35,000	64,500	100 %	$1,150.00

45. Allocating costs to a product is similar to the approach used in allocating costs to a shipment. Again, cwt-miles is commonly used as the allocation base. The primary difference is that total cwt-miles by product or product grouping, rather

EXHIBIT XIV

DISTRIBUTION OF WEIGHT AND MILES BY PRODUCT LINE

Shipment Number	Product Code	Product Line Weight by Shipment	Miles	Cwt-miles
1	1	2,000	50	1,000
	3	3,000	50	1,500
	5	4,000	50	2,000
2	1	2,000	100	2,000
	6	1,000	100	1,000
	9	3,000	100	3,000
	8	2,000	100	2,000
3	2	3,000	150	4,500
	4	1,000	150	1,500
	6	3,000	150	4,500
4	10	1,000	200	2,000
5	5	1,000	350	3,500
	6	1,000	350	3,500
	2	2,000	350	7,000
	10	3,000	350	10,500
6	4	1,000	500	5,000
	6	1,000	500	5,000
	7	1,000	500	5,000
Total		35,000		64,500

EXHIBIT XV

PRODUCT COST ALLOCATION METHODOLOGY

(1) Product Code	(2) Product Line Weight	(3) Cwt-miles	(4) Percentage of Total Cwt-miles	(5) Cost Allocated to Product Line
1	4,000	3,000	5%	$57.50
2	5,000	11,500	18%	207.00
3	3,000	1,500	2%	23.00
4	2,000	6,500	10%	115.00
5	5,000	5,500	9%	103.50
6	6,000	14,000	22%	253.00
7	1,000	5,000	8%	92.00
8	2,000	2,000	3%	34.50
9	3,000	3,000	5%	57.50
10	4,000	12,500	18%	207.00
Total	35,000	64,500	100%	$1,150.00

than shipment, must be determined. This method of allocating transportation costs to shipments and products can be used for both inbound and outbound traffic. Exhibits XIV and XV illustrate this approach to allocating costs to products for the shipments in Exhibit XII.

46. The allocation of empty miles is normally applied on a post-deadhead basis—i.e., all empty miles incurred after the load has been delivered are assigned to the original loaded trip.

47. The accuracy of transportation costing can be enhanced through the use of cube/density factors, which are used jointly with the cwt-miles allocation base. This enables the costing system to account for the weight, distance, and cube/density factors of the products being shipped when a combination of light and bulky products and dense products are being shipped together.

48. The first step in accounting for cube/density is to develop an optimum density factor as the base index. The optimum density is the weight per cubic foot needed to fill each vehicle type to both its space and weight capacity. It is computed by dividing the cubic-foot capacity of the vehicle by the lower of the actual weight capacity or the lowest weight limitation for any state through which the traffic is moving. A cost adjustment is then made for all products that fall above or below the optimum base density factor.

49. Corporations that operate private fleets to provide transport services for their departments, divisions, or subsidiaries commonly develop internal charge-backs for those services. Cost-based transfer pricing requires standard (full) costing or variable costing approaches, depending on the company's charge-back strategy. Another method, market-based charge-back, charges units what the private fleet department would charge external customers. Some companies today prefer to let the parties in question negotiate the charges for the service, based on factors such as prevailing market rates for transportation and overall corporate asset utilization objectives. The negotiation method works well as long as the user department has the option to purchase alternate (for-hire) services.

Definitions

50. **Total transportation costs** are those transportation expenses, either for company-operated or company-owned assets or for purchased transportation service, that are associated with the making, moving, or selling of products.

51. **Inbound transportation** is the movement of raw materials, supplies, or products from outside suppliers to company facilities. Costs associated with inbound receipts should be included in inventory cost but should be controlled as separate elements.

52. **Interfacility transportation** is the movement of materials, supplies, or products between company facilities, whether these are plants, distribution centers, or outside storage facilities.

53. **Outbound transportation** refers to the movement of finished (or semifinished) products from company facilities to customers or to third parties that store or deliver to customers.

54. **For-hire carriage (or purchased transportation)** refers to the movement of materials, supplies, or products by an outside service—whether a common carrier, contract carrier, freight forwarder, customs broker, or other form of transportation or distribution company.

55. **Traffic lane** is the combination of two geographic locations between which commodities are transported. A traffic lane is identified by its "origin/destination pairs."

References

A. Ernst & Whinney, *Transportation Accounting and Control: Guidelines for Distribution and Financial Management.* National Association of Accountants and National Council of Physical Distribution Management, 1983.

B. Stock, James R. and Douglas M. Lambert, *Strategic Logistics Management,* Second Ed. Homewood, IL: Richard D. Irwin, 1987.

C. Tyworth, John E., Joseph L. Cavinato, and John C. Langley, Jr., *Traffic Management: Planning, Operations, and Control.* Addison-Wesley Publishing Company, 1987.

D. Robeson, James F. and Robert G. House, eds., *The Distribution Handbook.* New York: Free Press, 1985.

E. Ernst & Whinney, *Corporate Profitability & Logistics: Innovative Guidelines for Executives.* National Association of Accountants and Council of Logistics Management, 1987.

F. Morse, Leon William, *Industrial Traffic Management,* Sixth Ed. Washington, DC: The Traffic Service Corporation, 1980.

G. Cavinato, Joseph L., *Finance for Transportation and Logistics Managers: Evaluating Capital Investments in Transportation and Distribution.* Washington, DC: The Traffic Service Corporation, 1977.

Statements on Management Accounting

Statement Number 4 J
July 1, 1989

PRACTICES AND TECHNIQUES

Accounting for Property, Plant, and Equipment

In accordance with the charge to the Management Accounting Practices (MAP) Committee to issue statements on management accounting principles and practices, Statements on Management Accounting are promulgated to reflect official positions of the National Association of Accountants (NAA). The work of the MAP Committee is based on a framework for management accounting, whose principal categories are:

1. Objectives
2. Terminology
3. Concepts
4. Practices and Techniques
5. Management of Accounting Activities

Statements on Management Accounting

Statement Number 4J
July 1, 1989

Practices and Techniques: Accounting for Property, Plant, and Equipment

National Association of Accountants

Acknowledgments

The National Association of Accountants extends appreciation to members of the Management Accounting Practices Committee and its Subcommittee on SMA Promulgation for their contribution toward publication of SMA 4J *Accounting for Property, Plant, and Equipment*. The NAA is especially grateful to Michael J. Sandretto for his research and writing associated with this project.

Introduction

1. This document is a comprehensive accounting recommendation for property, plant, and equipment. It combines and updates two NAA Statements on Management Accounting Practices: Statement Number 4: *Fixed Asset Accounting: The Capitalization of Costs*, and Statement Number 7: *Fixed Asset Accounting: The Allocation of Costs.*
    Readers should recognize that this SMA is intended as guidance for management accountants. Since the Statement deals with issues covered to a greater or lesser extent in the authoritative financial accounting literature, readers are urged to review the applicable literature (including FASB pronouncements, Emerging Issues Task Force abstracts, and relevant special industry accounting or auditing guides) for complete treatment of any subject.

Statement of Scope

2. Part I recommends current practice on capitalizing the costs of property, plant, and equipment.
3. Part II recommends current practice on allocating the costs of property, plant, and equipment to future periods (depreciation and depletion).

PART I: CAPITALIZATION OF COSTS

4. Property, plant, and equipment is recorded and maintained at historical cost. At the time of acquisition the cost is the market price, or cash-equivalent price, of putting the asset into service. Subsequent costs related to an asset's use must be capitalized if they increase the asset's estimated life or if they improve its productive capacity (except that minor costs usually are treated as period expenses even though they have the characteristics of capital expenditures). Both the initial outlay and subsequent expenditures are recorded at historical cost and are not adjusted for subsequent price changes.

Land (Property)

5. The acquisition cost of land includes all costs necessary to prepare it for its intended use, including:

   a. Contract price.
   b. Cost of an exercised option.
   c. Cost of real estate surveys.
   d. Closing costs, such as title search, title insurance, legal costs, and recording fees.
   e. Costs necessary to physically prepare land for its intended use, such as clearing, grading, and filling. If the property includes structures that must be removed, removal costs, reduced by any salvage value of the structures, are added to the acquisition cost.
   f. Cost of cancelling an unexpired lease to vacate the building.
   g. Payment of noncurrent accrued property taxes if payable by purchaser.
   h. Commissions, permits, or fees paid by the buyer.
   i. Interest costs capitalized per SFAS No. 34.

6. Special assessments for relatively permanent improvements, such as pavements or drainage and sewage systems, are usually added to the cost of land. Improvements with a limited life, such as parking lots and decorative landscape, should be charged to a land improvement account and depreciated over their useful lives. As a practical matter, distinguishing between the two often is very subjective and should be thoroughly reviewed with the company's external auditor.

Land (Sales Inventory and Investments)

7. Land held for resale by an organization in the real estate business should be classified as inventory. If land is held as an investment, it is proper to capitalize direct costs of holding that

land and to classify it as an investment. These costs may not exceed net realizable value.

Buildings

8. Acquisition cost of a building includes all expenditures directly related to the acquisition or construction of that building. Once land has been prepared for use as a construction site, all subsequent costs, beginning with excavation, are included in the cost of the building. These include:

   a. The contract or invoice price of construction.
   b. Costs incurred in self-construction or in remodeling or altering a purchased building to prepare it for its intended use.
   c. Cost of construction trailers or temporary buildings used for the construction project.
   d. Professional fees, such as architectural and engineering services and legal costs.
   e. Construction permits.
   f. Interest costs capitalized per SFAS No. 34.

9. As in the case of real estate, buildings held for resale should be classified as inventory and those held for investment should be classified as investments.

Machinery and Equipment

10. Machinery and equipment includes office furniture and equipment, production machinery and equipment, vehicles, inventory handling equipment, and similar physical assets. These assets may either be purchased or self-constructed. Acquisition cost includes all costs necessary to acquire and prepare the asset for its intended use, including:

    a. Purchase price.
    b. Freight, import duties, and insurance.

c.   Installation costs, including special foundations or plant modifications.
d.   Special training or test runs.
e.   Sales, use, or other taxes related to the acquisition of new equipment.
f.   Costs associated with reconditioning purchased used equipment or with self-constructed equipment. (See subsequent section on self-constructed assets.)
g.   Spare parts. (Initial inventory of spare parts necessary to keep equipment in operating condition. Replacements of spare parts inventory should be charged to expense.)
h.   Operating system software necessary to operate equipment for any system. (See the NAA issues paper, "Accounting for Software Used Internally," and SFAS No. 86, "Accounting for the Costs of Computer Software to be Sold, Leased, or Otherwise Marketed.")
i.   Capitalized interest, if material.

11. In some cases equipment may be classified as stores and supplies prior to being placed in service. For example, expensive circuit boards that will be used to repair a firm's electronics equipment may be classified as supplies prior to being placed in service. If the economic life of spare equipment depends on the life of assets being serviced, it may be preferable to treat new replacement units as equipment, and depreciate them.

Preliminary Engineering and Feasibility Study Costs

12. Often in connection with a proposed large project, management of an organization will commission a detailed study of the project's operational feasibility. Such a study usually is directed by an organization's senior engineering personnel but often is conducted primarily by one or more outside engineering-oriented consulting firms. Generally, management has itself conducted some very preliminary market and engineering studies sufficient to provide a reasonable expectation of the project's

ultimate approval. However, to assist in fine-tuning cost estimates, identifying building and machinery configurations, gaining insight into the most up-to-date technologies, and providing the Board of Directors and senior corporate management (in the case of divisions or subsidiaries or larger organizations) with a higher level of certainty, more formal and systematic preliminary engineering and feasibility study work often is undertaken.

13. In such a situation, the costs of the engineering and feasibility work should be capitalized initially as a part of the construction-in-process and apportioned among building and equipment categories as appropriate once the project is complete.

14. If the project appears doubtful during or at the end of the study, costs capitalized to date should be written off.

15. It is important to distinguish between charges for preliminary engineering and feasibility of a specific project, and more general, ongoing strategic planning and related studies. These more general charges should be expensed as incurred.

Determining Base Unit

16. The choice of a base unit partially determines when capitalized costs will be charged as depreciation expense. Building systems typically have shorter lives than the structure itself, so the average life of the comprehensive base unit would be a dollar-weighted-average life of the building systems and the longer-lived structure. In some cases, the choice of a base unit determines whether an expenditure is capitalized or expensed. Inexpensive items that are not base units are expensed.

17. The choice of a base unit also is influenced by IRS rules and regulations, since the IRS may reject overly large base units. Because of the importance of the base unit, firms should establish a formal policy for choosing a base unit for various capital asset groups. Among the factors that should be considered are recordkeeping costs, the value of having detailed information for analytic purposes, and the value of detailed information for control and tax purposes.

Lump Sum or Basket Purchases

18. At times, organizations acquire groups of assets and the price of individual assets is not specified. This may be the purchase of land to be subdivided into lots, the purchase of many units of used machinery or equipment, or the purchase of an entire organization.

19. The total acquisition price must be allocated to individual assets in some equitable and, to the extent possible, objective manner. In the case of equipment, estimates may be based on published prices of similar equipment, on independent estimates by engineering appraisal firms, or on estimates by a firm's own personnel. In the case of real property, acquisition cost might be allocated based on tax assessments or on insurance appraisals. In no case should allocated costs exceed the acquisition cost (so that a gain is recorded on the purchase of a group of assets).

20. Where an entire business has been acquired, it is common for the acquisition cost (including assumed liabilities), to exceed the cost allocated to tangible and identifiable intangible assets. As opposed to the purchase of equipment or real estate, the value of a going concern is determined by more than the sum of the value of individual assets. Customer and supplier relationships, proprietary production processes, skilled employees and other factors determine the earnings stream of a firm and, hence, its worth. Where the acquisition cost exceeds the value of an acquired firm's tangible and identifiable intangible assets, the difference is recorded as goodwill. If less than fair value of total assets is paid, property, plant, and equipment must be reviewed and revalued.

Self-Constructed Assets

21. Many organizations construct some of their own production equipment and some construct their entire production facilities (particularly in the case of large utilities). Construction

may be accomplished by the firm's employees or by contractors. The cost of a self-constructed asset includes the following:

a. Cost of direct materials used in construction.
b. Cost of direct labor used in construction.
c. Direct overhead costs related to construction.
d. Indirect overhead costs related to construction. (However, as a practical matter, many firms do not include indirect overhead costs in the cost of self-constructed assets, for reasons discussed in paragraphs 25 and 26.)
e. Interest costs (see subsequent section).

22. There are few problems in tracing direct material and direct labor costs to self-constructed assets. Minor cost elements are sometimes ignored as immaterial, while others are estimated. However, these are normal materiality decisions.

23. Direct overhead costs should be charged to the cost object that caused them to be incurred. For example, the direct overhead cost of self-constructed production machinery includes the direct costs of design engineers or equipment engineers. The direct overhead costs of those engineers should be allocated to the self-constructed asset. In the case of an accountant assigned part time to control the cost of a self-constructed building, the direct overhead costs of the accountant should be allocated to the building. Direct overhead cost includes fringe benefit costs as well as salaries.

24. The primary problem in allocating direct overhead costs is determining how detailed those allocations should be. Manufacturing or office supplies used in self-construction may be great enough to be charged to the project as direct overhead, may be allocated as indirect overhead, or may be ignored, depending on the circumstances. The same is true for heat, light, and power.

25. While most firms that construct their own assets capitalize direct overhead costs, most do not capitalize indirect overhead costs. One reason is the administrative cost of doing so. Sup-

port costs associated with employees, such as the rent-equivalent cost of their office space and a pro-rata share of secretarial, computer, and copying costs, can be allocated to self-constructed assets. However, the expense of allocating these costs may exceed any resulting benefit.

26. Another reason that indirect overhead costs seldom are capitalized is that self-construction often is an infrequent but major activity. A firm's managers and executives may spend considerable time on a major facilities project. When the project is complete, however, they will return to work full time on normal operations. If their salaries and related support costs of services were capitalized, there could be a significant decrease in administrative expenses and a distorting increase in operating income during the period of construction.

27. Any firm which regularly constructs assets for internal use should have a detailed written policy stating which costs should be allocated to self-constructed assets. Such firms also should have a formal system to record the cost of self-constructed assets.

Capitalized Interest Costs

28. SFAS No. 34, as amended by Statements No. 42 and No. 62, stipulates that the historical cost of acquiring certain qualifying assets should include the interest cost incurred during the period such assets are undergoing activities to get them ready for their intended use. Cost Accounting Standard No. 417 also stipulates rules for the capitalization of interest cost incurred during a period of construction.

29. For an asset to "qualify" for interest capitalization, all three conditions must be present:

   a. Expenditures for the asset have been made. Expenditures include cash payments, asset transfers, and the assumption of liabilities on which interest is incurred (as opposed to normal trade payables).

b. Activities that are necessary to prepare the asset for its intended use are in progress.

c. Interest cost is being incurred by the company (it is not necessary that there be a specific borrowing associated with acquiring the asset).

30. The capitalization period commences with the first expenditure, and should cease when the qualifying asset is ready for its intended use. The amount of interest cost to be capitalized is that portion of the interest cost incurred by the company during the acquisition period that theoretically could have been avoided if expenditures for the assets had not been made (e.g., by avoiding additional borrowings or by using the funds expended to acquire assets instead of repaying existing borrowings).

31. If borrowings can be associated with a qualifying asset, the capitalization rate (interest rate to be capitalized) is the interest rate on those borrowings. In the absence of specific new borrowings, the capitalization rate used should be the weighted average of the interest rates applicable to other borrowings of the enterprise. This weighted average rate may be the average rate for the subsidiary or division acquiring the asset, the average rate for all operations in a certain country or region, or the average rate for the parent company, depending on the circumstances.

32. If a project will be capitalized as more than one asset, the interest cost should be allocated to each asset, or group of assets, in a systematic and rational manner, usually on the basis of cost.

33. The total capitalized interest cost may not exceed the total amount of interest cost incurred by the enterprise in that period. For consolidated operations, the total capitalized interest may not exceed the total interest incurred by the parent and consolidated subsidiaries on a consolidated basis.

34. Except in the case of assets funded with tax-exempt borrowings (such as industrial revenue bonds or pollution control bonds), total interest expense incurred and the capitalization rate shall be determined without regard to an enterprise's

interest income. In the case of tax-exempt borrowings where proceeds may be invested prior to use for purchase of a specified asset, interest expense should be offset by interest income in determining both total interest expense and the effective capitalization rate.

Discounts

35. Cash discounts are commonly offered for machinery and equipment. If the discount is taken, it should be considered a reduction in the acquisition cost of the asset. If the discount is not taken, the lost discount can be ignored or the acquisition cost can be reduced by the amount of the discount lost, with the cost of the lost discount charged to expense.
36. Both methods are employed in practice. Reducing the asset cost by the discount lost is generally preferable for two reasons. First, it reflects the cash equivalent price of the asset, so it is preferable theoretically. Second, it records discounts lost in a separate account. Discounts are often large enough that they should be taken in all but cases of extreme financial distress. A separate account highlights for management action either an ineffective payables system or financing problems.

Acquisition of Assets for Securities

37. Where assets are acquired for actively traded securities, the cost of the property acquired is equal to the market value of the securities exchanged at the time the exchange takes place. Where the securities are not actively traded, or where trading volume is low relative to the value of the assets acquired, the estimated market value of the assets acquired is likely to be the more objective estimate of the cash-equivalent price of the transaction.
38. In some cases, securities given up are not actively traded and the asset received has no readily determinable market value. In such cases the cost should be based on the item that has the most readily determinable market value.

Acquisition of Assets for Nonmonetary Consideration

39. When assets are acquired for nonmonetary consideration, two problems may arise. First, the cash-equivalent acquisition price (or fair value) may be uncertain. Second, the exchange may be for dissimilar assets, in which case the transaction may involve a gain on the retirement of the assets given up. Whether the exchange is for similar or dissimilar nonmonetary assets, if a loss occurs on the exchange, the loss is recorded immediately. That is, if the asset exchanged has a fair value of less than its net book value, the loss is recorded when an exchange occurs.

40. *Acquisition for similar nonmonetary assets.* If an asset is acquired in an even exchange for a similar asset used in the same line of business, then no gain is recorded on the exchange. The cost of the new asset is equal to the book value of the asset or assets given up. This rule avoids manipulation. For example, in a real estate swap, two firms may exchange similar parcels of land, or similar buildings, without cash being exchanged. If gains were permitted on such exchanges, both firms could record their acquired property at an inflated estimate of fair value and could recognize profits although neither made a sale to a customer.

41. There is also no gain on an exchange if a nonmonetary asset is acquired in an exchange for a similar asset used in the same line of business plus a cash payment (boot) of less than 25 percent. The cost of the new asset to the payer of boot is the book value of the asset or assets given up, plus the cash payment. However, if the exchange involves a significant cash payment (of at least 25 percent) then the exchange is considered a monetary transaction and both parties must record the exchange at fair value and, hence, record any gain or loss on the transaction. (On real estate transactions, only the receiver of boot must recognize a pro-rata gain on the cash portion of the exchange.) See Emerging Issues Task Force (EITF) Abstracts of Issues Nos. 86-29 and 87-29.

42. If an asset is acquired in an exchange for a similar asset used in the same line of business, and if a cash payment of less than 25 percent is received because the asset given up is more valuable than the asset received, then a partial sale of the asset given up has occurred. If the transaction involves a loss, the entire loss must be recorded. If the transaction involves a gain, then the transaction is treated as a partial sale and a partial gain must be recorded by the receiver of boot (but not by the payer of boot). The total gain is the difference between the fair value of the asset given up and its net book value. The portion of the gain that must be recognized is the fraction that cash received bears to the fair value of the asset given up.

43. *Acquisition for dissimilar nonmonetary assets.* When dissimilar assets (or similar assets used in different lines of business) are exchanged, the parties are considered to be in a new economic position, so gains and losses are recognized when the exchange occurs. The cost of the asset acquired is determined by the fair value of the asset given up, or the fair value of the asset received, whichever is most readily determinable.

Minimum Capitalization Policy

44. As a practical matter, not all long-lived assets are capitalized. To maintain a reasonable balance between record-keeping costs and proper accounting, most firms have minimum capitalization rules for determining which costs should be capitalized and which should be expensed. Many firms have a formal policy of not capitalizing any item with a cost of less than $1000. Most firms use the same minimum for tax and book purposes. Although neither generally accepted accounting principles (GAAP) nor IRS rules and regulations formally recognize minimum capitalization rules, their use is widespread. A minimum capitalization rule specifying a significant dollar limit is highly desirable as a method of reducing recordkeeping costs and for maintaining consistency.

45. Firms may modify their minimum capitalization policy for group purchases. For example, a firm with a minimum capi-

talization rule of $1000 might purchase 10 office chairs for $200 apiece. With a group purchase rule, each chair would be capitalized since the group purchase of $2000 exceeds the minimum capitalization amount. Some firms establish higher minimum capitalization limits for group purchases than for individual assets. It is not necessary to capitalize a large order for minor cost objects, such as wastebaskets, staplers, or similar items.

Tooling

46. Firms often have major expenditures for production items such as dies, tooling, and minor pieces of production equipment. In many cases firms spend significant amounts to maintain, modify, and repair such items. For example, a firm may have a piece of equipment costing several thousand dollars that is used to produce items in their initial production stage. As soon as volume increases, production is moved to a different manufacturing area, and the equipment is modified for use in producing another new product. As another example, a firm purchases dies for several thousand dollars apiece. These dies can last for many years, but require frequent maintenance. In both cases it can be reasonably argued that these are not long-lived assets. Where this is the case, expensing the costs of these minor pieces of production equipment (tools, dies, etc.) may be reasonable.

Costs Incurred Subsequent to Acquisition

47. After buildings and equipment are acquired and placed in service, additional expenditures are incurred during the period of ownership. Most cost outlays related to a capital asset, including repairs and maintenance, benefit future periods to some extent. However, under GAAP, repair and maintenance expenses must be expensed. A useful criterion in differentiating between capital and expense charges is that costs should

be capitalized if they increase the productive capacity of an asset. Any one of at least four conditions satisfy this requirement:

a. The rate of production must increase. For example, a modification to the loading mechanism of a press may increase the output from 50 units per minute to 75 units per minute.

b. The quality of the output must improve. For example, a modification to a die may reduce the rejection rate from 1 percent to .1 percent.

c. The production cost must decrease by a material amount. For example, a modification to a press may maintain the same rate of production, but may significantly decrease the direct labor needed to produce a unit.

d. The life of the asset must increase by a material amount. This is the most subjective of the four requirements, since it can be argued either that major repairs extend the useful life of an asset or that they simply maintain the original estimated life.

48. When deciding whether a cost qualifies for capitalization under one of the above four rules, it is helpful to group costs in the following categories:

a. Repairs and maintenance.
b. Improvements and additions.
c. Replacements and renewals.
d. Rearrangements and relocations.

Repairs and Maintenance

49. The terms *repair* and *maintenance* are often used interchangeably. A distinction is sometimes made, with repair meaning putting assets back in working order and maintenance meaning keeping them in working order. Maintenance work, such as cleaning, lubricating, painting, calibrating, and adjusting, is a normal activity required to keep plant and equipment in a

productive state. Such expenditures are expenses of the current period, since they are recurring and have short-term benefit. Minor repair work also is recurring and has short-term benefit. It is necessary to the ordinary operation of a business and is a period expense. Examples include replacing minor parts, such as inexpensive circuit boards or electric motors.

50. Under GAAP, major repair work is also expensed. However, a distinction must be made between major repair work, which is expensed, and replacements and renewals, which are capitalized. The general rule is that if the work extends the life of the asset beyond its normal expected life, the cost is capitalized. For example, a piece of equipment used to draw steel bars may have a normal useful life of 20 years. Major overhauls, however, can extend the life almost indefinitely, to the point where no part of the machine is original equipment. At this extreme, where none of the original equipment exists, expenditures should be capitalized as replacements and renewals, since they benefit future periods. A minimum capitalization rule may, however, be used to determine whether an expenditure is a repair expense or whether it should be capitalized.

Improvements and Additions

51. Improvements and additions are major expenditures which improve the productive capacity of an existing asset; they are capital expenditures. Examples of improvements and additions include adding space to a factory, upgrading a computer by replacing major circuit boards, and modifying production equipment to simplify the change of dies or tooling. Improvement and addition costs should be added to the cost of the asset if they have the same useful life as the affected asset. If their lives differ, improvement and addition costs should be recorded in a separate account and depreciated over their useful lives.

Replacements and Renewals

52. A replacement is the substitution of one asset for another. For example, old carpet may be replaced with new carpet. If the old carpet was capitalized as a separate asset, the proper treatment would be to remove the remaining book value of the old carpet (and record the book value as a loss), and capitalize the cost of the new carpet. If the cost of the old carpet was capitalized as a part of the building, the cost of the new carpet could be added to the cost of the building and depreciated over the remaining life of the building, or recorded in a separate account and depreciated over its estimated useful life. As a practical matter, minor replacements and renewals are usually expensed, sometimes applying a minimum capitalization policy as a cutoff rule.

Rearrangements and Relocations

53. Rearrangements and relocations are major costs that are expected to benefit future periods. They include relocating an office and rearranging production or office facilities. There are no definitive accounting guidelines on whether such costs should be expensed or capitalized. To qualify for capitalization these costs must increase the productive capacity of the asset being rearranged or relocated (see Paragraph 47). In most cases the cost of moving corporate headquarters should be considered a period expense (see Emerging Issues Task Force Abstract of Issue 88-10). A major rearrangement of production facilities might be capitalized as an improvement in productive capacity or could be expensed as a restructuring cost. In practice, firms treat such costs both ways. If the amounts are material it is important to disclose the costs incurred and whether those costs were expensed or capitalized.

Leases

54. If a lease transfers to the lessee most of the characteristics of ownership the lease is considered a capital lease by the lessee.

The present value of the lease must be capitalized as an asset and must also be recorded as a liability (lease obligation). If the lessee does not assume most of the characteristics of ownership, the lease is considered an operating lease. Assuming equal lease payments on a regular basis, no transaction is recorded, other than to charge each lease payment to an expense account.

55. SFAS No. 13 requires that a lease be classified as a capital lease if it is noncancelable and if, at its inception, it satisfies any one of the following four criteria:

   a. Ownership of the leased property is transferred to the lessee at the end of the lease term.
   b. The lease contains a bargain purchase option.
   c. The lease term is equal to at least 75 percent of the estimated economic life of the leased property.
   d. The present value of the minimum lease payments is at least 90 percent of the fair market value of the leased property.

   If the inception of the lease occurs during the remaining 25 percent of the economic life of the leased property, neither condition c. nor d. applies.

56. *Transfer of ownership.* If ownership is transferred to the lessee, the transaction is equivalent to an installment sale. Such a transaction has the characteristics of ownership, and the lease must be capitalized.

57. *Bargain purchase option.* If ownership will almost certainly transfer to the lessee at the end of the lease because of a bargain purchase option, the lease is similar to an installment sale and must be capitalized. In some cases the bargain purchase option condition is simple to apply. An option to purchase a building for one dollar at the end of the lease is obviously a bargain purchase option. In other cases the stipulated price may be high enough that it is unclear whether the option will be exercised. In such cases this may be a difficult condition to apply.

58. *Economic life.* If a lease covers at least 75 percent of the economic life of the leased property, the lessee is assuming most of the risks of ownership. This condition may be difficult to apply both because the economic life of the property must be estimated and because the lease may contain renewal clauses that must be included when determining the life of the lease. For example, if the lessee has an option to renew the lease at a bargain rate, the extension period must be added to the original term of the lease. The original term of the lease must also be extended if the lessee is required to renew the lease; if the lessee has guaranteed a loan for or made a loan to the lessor during the period covered by the renewal option; or, if there are substantial penalties for not renewing the lease.

59. *Minimum payment.* If the present value of the minimum payments is at least 90 percent of the fair market value of the leased property, the lessee is, in effect, engaging in an installment purchase. Minimum lease payments include:

   a. Minimum rental payments, including payments during any extensions to the term of the original lease.
   b. Any guarantee of a minimum residual value. However, a requirement that the lessee pay for damage or excessive wear or usage should not be added to the minimum rental period.
   c. Penalties for nonrenewal.

60. The minimum lease payment should be reduced by any operating costs that will be assumed by the lessor during the period of the lease, such as insurance, taxes, and repair and maintenance costs. Since the purpose of the minimum payment test is to determine whether the present value of those payments is reasonably close to the purchase price, the lease payments should be reduced by any operating expenses (executory costs) paid by the lessor.

61. The total minimum lease payment usually is discounted at the lessee's incremental borrowing rate to determine the present value of those payments. However, if the lessee knows the

implicit rate computed by the lessor, and that rate is less than the lessee's incremental borrowing rate, then the implicit rate must be used (the *implicit rate* is that rate which, when applied to the minimum lease payment, and the unguaranteed residual value, causes the aggregate present value to be equal to the fair market value of the leased property).

PART II. ALLOCATING PROPERTY, PLANT, AND EQUIPMENT COSTS

Measuring Depreciation

62. To develop a systematic and rational method of allocating capital costs, it is necessary to consider three variables:

    a. *Economic Life.* The economic life of an asset is determined by specifying the unit of service and by estimating the units of service that an asset will produce. For example, the unit of service may be years of estimated use, miles flown, units produced, or hours of operation.

    b. *Allocation base.* The allocation base is the historical cost of the asset being depreciated, reduced by its estimated salvage value.

    c. *Allocation method.* When choosing an allocation method, it is necessary to decide whether all service units should be allocated the same. That is, if the service unit is years, should costs be allocated evenly over the life of the asset, or should more cost be allocated to earlier years when the machine is more efficient and reliable?

Economic Life

63. The economic life of an asset may be determined by its expected physical life, its expected useful life, or the expected economic life of the product it will produce. For example, an airplane may have an economic life of 10 years to a major

carrier, after which time it will be replaced with a newer, more efficient model. For a regional airline, the economic life may be the physical life of the airplane. For many assets the economic life is determined by the expected life of the product they will produce. A semiconductor manufacturer may build a production line designed to produce a product line with an expected life of five years. Although the production line may have a physical life of 20 years, its economic life is five years. Computers are a current example of a product with a very short economic life.

64. The following factors should be considered when establishing the economic life of an asset:

a. *Operating considerations.* Some firms routinely operate machines for two or three shifts and on weekends while other firms rarely operate machines more than 40 hours per week.

b. *Investment considerations.* Some firms continually add improved equipment while others rarely replace their machines with improved models.

c. *Engineering consideratons.* Many firms have large production engineering departments whose primary function is to modify production equipment. In those firms, machines may have a far longer than normal economic life because they are less likely to become obsolete and because frequent modifications keep them in excellent condition.

d. *Maintenance consideration.* Some firms are far more careful than normal in maintaining equipment, so the expected economic life of their equipment is longer.

e. *Marketing concerns.* Where the economic life of equipment depends on the economic life of the product being produced, it is important to determine whether marketing expects the useful lives of their products to change.

f. *Industry studies.* Many industries publish physical life estimates for asset classes based on detailed studies of their members. These studies, modified by a firm's own experience, can be valuable guidelines.

g. *Asset groups.* As a practical matter, firms group their assets into a few categories when estimating economic life. A firm may depreciate mechanical production equipment over 15 years, office equipment over 10 years, electronic equipment over 7 years, and vehicles over 4 years. The choice of number of asset groups is normally based on industry practice, firm experience, IRS regulations, and the need to balance more accurate estimates with added administrative effort.

h. *Consistency.* As a practical matter, firms rarely change the estimated lives of their asset categories. For additional guidance, refer to APB Opinion No. 20, "Accounting Changes."

Allocation Base

65. The allocation base is the acquisition cost of an asset less its salvage value. Salvage value can be significant, as in the case of firms that regularly trade in large vehicle fleets with many years of useful life remaining. In other cases assets have significant salvage value because of their metal content or because their component parts are valuable. To ignore salvage value in these circumstances would be misleading. However, in most instances, salvage value is negligible, or negative, after considering removal costs. As a practical matter, except for vehicles and for a few other assets where resale is normal and significant, most firms assume a zero salvage value for their capital assets.

Allocation Methods

66. A wide variety of depreciation methods are available for financial reporting. Of the methods that will be described, all meet the GAAP requirement that a depreciation method be systematic and, depending on the circumstances, all meet the GAAP requirement that the method be rational. Most companies use straight-line depreciation for financial re-

porting and the appropriate accelerated depreciation method for federal income taxes.

67. In choosing a depreciation method, a firm typically must make two decisions. First, it must determine whether the allocation method will be based on years of estimated useful life or on some measure of output. Second, it must decide whether all service units should be charged the same allocation rate, or if earlier units should be charged a higher rate since most capital assets perform better when new. The following topics will be discussed in detail:

a. Straight-line depreciation.
b. Declining-charge (accelerated) depreciation. This includes sum-of-the-years-digits depreciation and declining-balance depreciation.
c. Combination of declining-balance and straight-line depreciation.
d. Units-of-production depreciation.
e. Composite or group depreciation.
f. Replacement or retirement depreciation.

Straight-line Depreciation

68. The straight-line depreciation charge is computed by dividing the allocation base by the estimated years of useful life. If an asset costing $100,000 has no salvage value, and has a useful life of 10 years, the annual depreciation charge is $10,000.

69. Straight-line depreciation is the most widely used method for financial reporting. It is also simple to compute and easy to understand. The primary criticism is that it results in depreciation charges that are constant through the economic life of an asset, while most assets are more valuable when new. Newer assets usually have lower repair costs and less down-time. Their output may also be higher or more valuable, since they require less adjustment and their output is rejected less often for quality problems.

Declining-Charge Depreciation (Accelerated Depreciation)

70. Declining-charge depreciation methods allocate costs to the early years of an asset's life, when it usually has higher productive value. The two most common declining-charge methods are sum-of-the-years-digits depreciation and declining-balance depreciation (usually double declining or 150 percent declining-balance depreciation). Although these methods adjust for the main deficiency of straight-line depreciation, they may charge too much depreciation expense in earlier years.

Sum-of-the-Years-Digits Depreciation

71. Sum-of-the-years-digits depreciation is based on computational simplicity. The annual depreciation charge is the product of an asset's depreciation base and a different fraction for each year. The numerator of the fraction is the years of remaining asset life and the denominator is the sum of the years from one to the years of estimated useful life $(1 + 2 + \ldots + n)$. For an asset with a cost of $60,000, and an expected life of five years, annual depreciation for each year is computed as follows:

Table 1

Year of Service	Fraction	Allocation Base	Depreciation Expense
1	5/15	$60,000	$20,000
2	4/15	60,000	16,000
3	3/15	60,000	12,000
4	2/15	60,000	8,000
5	1/15	60,000	4,000
Sum 15			$60,000

Declining-Balance Depreciation

72. Declining-balance depreciation is determined by multiplying the net book value (a declining balance) by a constant percentage. There is no reduction of cost for salvage value in declining-balance depreciation. The most commonly used method is double-declining-balance depreciation, where the percentage is twice the straight-line depreciation rate (200 percent). Common variations include 175 percent, 150 percent, and 125 percent-declining-balance depreciation rates.

73. An asset with an expected useful life of five years has a double-declining rate of 40 percent (twice the straight-line rate of 20 percent). For an asset with a cost of $100,000, the initial year depreciation is $40,000. Depreciation in the second year is the 40 percent annual rate multiplied by the new net book value of $60,000 ($100,000 — $40,000), or $24,000.

74. A mathematical method of declining-balance depreciation can be used to compute that depreciation rate which will reduce the net book value to the asset's salvage value at the end of an asset's estimated useful life. This method, which is rarely used in practice, computes the depreciation rate as follows:

$$rate = 1 - \sqrt{\frac{salvage\ value}{cost}}$$

where n = asset life in years.

Combination of Declining-Balance and Straight-Line Depreciation

75. At the end of an asset's depreciable life, declining-balance depreciation results in a positive net book value. To fully depreciate assets (i.e., to zero or to their salvage value), or to assure that assets are not depreciated below their salvage value, firms sometimes combine declining-balance depreciation with straight-line depreciation. The shift usually occurs when the straight-line depreciation charge exceeds the depreciation charge from the declining-balance method.

Footnote 3 of APB Opinion No. 20, "Accounting Changes," states that consistent application of such a policy does not constitute a change in accounting principle for purposes of applying this Opinion.

Units-of-Production Depreciation

76. Some capital assets have a useful life that is better measured by hours of operation or units of production than by years of service. For example, a furnace lining may have a useful life of 2000 hours of operation or a die may have a useful life of 50,000 units of output. With this method, the depreciation rate is simply the allocation base divided by the estimated units which the asset will produce during its life. If a furnace lining has a cost of $50,000 and no salvage value, with a 2000 hour estimated life the depreciation rate is $25.00 per hour of operation.

Composite or Group Depreciation

77. It is sometimes far easier to depreciate assets as a group than separately. If the assets are similar the method is referred to as group depreciation; if they are dissimilar it is termed composite depreciation.

78. If a firm using group depreciation purchases 150 pieces of office furniture for $50,000, the purchase is treated as if it were one asset. With an estimated life of 10 years and no salvage value, the depreciation rate is 10 percent and the first year depreciation expense is $5000. If assets with a cost of $5000 are sold in the second year for $4000 no gain or loss would be recorded. Asset cost would be reduced by $5000 and accumulated depreciation reduced by the difference between historical cost and the sale price of $4000, or $1000. The second-year depreciation would be 10 percent of the new historical cost of $45,000, or $4500.

79. If dissimilar assets are combined in a group, the method is similar, but the asset life is an average of the lives of individual

assets, weighted by their cost. If the following two assets with lives of 5 and 10 years, and with a 10 percent salvage value, were combined in a composite depreciation pool, depreciation would be computed as follows:

Table 2

Cost	Allocation Base	Useful Life	Annual Depreciation (straight-line)
$200,000	$180,000	5	$36,000
50,000	45,000	10	4,500
$250,000	$225,000		$40,500

Composite depreciation rate = $40,500/$225,000 = 18%
Composite useful life = $225,000/$40,500 = 5.55 years

80. If the average useful life and the average depreciation rate remain relatively constant for a pool of assets, the composite depreciation rate and composite useful life may be used for many years. The composite depreciation rate and the composite useful life may also be recomputed each year and applied to the assets acquired during that year.

Replacement or Retirement Depreciation

81. Replacement or retirement depreciation methods are no longer used. They were used primarily by railroads (prior to 1983) to simplify accounting for many similar units of relatively low value (e.g., poles and ties). No depreciation expense was recorded until the original asset was replaced, or retired. These methods were even more simple to apply than group depreciation. With replacement depreciation the original cost of the assets became their permanent cost. As the original equipment was replaced with new assets, the cost of the replacements was charged to depreciation expense. With retirement deprecia-

tion, the original cost was recorded as a capital cost. When old assets were replaced, the cost of the original asset was charged to depreciation expense and the cost of the new asset was recorded as a capital cost. These methods were formerly required by some regulatory authorities, but were not recognized as GAAP. FASB SFAS No. 73, "Reporting a Change in Accounting for Railroad Track Structures," was issued in 1983 to specify how a railroad should report the change from RRB (retirement-replacement-betterment) accounting to GAAP for general purpose financial statements.

Partial Year Depreciation

82. Most firms establish some simple rule for depreciating assets acquired during a year. A common method charges a full year of depreciation for assets acquired in the first half of a fiscal year and no depreciation for assets acquired in the second half of the fiscal year. Other conventions are also used, including one-half year of depreciation in the year of acquisition for all assets. IRS regulations on partial year depreciation vary by the type of asset.

83. If a partial year's depreciation is recorded, the sum-of-the-years-digits method requires additional record keeping. Using the example in Paragraph 71 for an asset that was depreciated for only one-half of a year in the year of acquisition, first year depreciation would be one-half of the first year charge of $20,000, or $10,000. Depreciation in the second year would be one-half of the year one charge ($10,000) plus one-half of the year two charge ($8000), or $18,000. Each company should have a policy on partial year depreciation since it is important to maintain a consistent policy.

Impairment in Value

84. Assets are generally maintained at historical cost unless there is evidence of permanent impairment. Assets should be written down to their net realizable value only if the impairment

in value is both material and permanent. A permanent impairment includes both assets that are no longer useful for productive purposes, and assets that are still productive, but will not recover their carrying value. The SEC position is that an asset should be written down in value if it is probable that the undiscounted future cash flows will be less than the net book value of an asset. The SEC will accept, but does not require, that an asset be recognized as impaired if discounted cash flows are less than its net book value. Determining if an impairment is permanent is subjective both because estimates are required and because the tests can be applied to either individual assets or to groups of assets (EITF 84-28). GAAP is not entirely clear on accounting for partial asset impairments.

85. A permanent impairment in value is recorded by charging the amount to a loss account and by crediting that amount to the asset account. If the asset has no productive use, it should be reclassified to an investment account until it is sold. Once an asset has been written down because of an impairment in value, it may not be subsequently written back up in value.

86. In November 1988, the Financial Accounting Standards Board established a major agenda project dealing with the broad subject of impairment, which could significantly impact GAAP on the subject. Readers should follow the progress made on that project and also take note of Emerging Issues Task Force Abstract of issue 84-28, which contains a discussion about impairment.

Depletion

87. Depletion is a method of allocating the cost of natural resources to the periods benefited by their cost. Timber, petroleum, and minerals are all natural resources that are depleted for accounting purposes. Unlike assets that are depreciated, natural resources are completely consumed in the production process. As in the case of depreciation, to compute depletion expense it is necessary to (1) determine the cost of the asset being depleted and (2) develop a method of allocating costs to future periods.

88. The cost of a natural resource can be separated into three categories: (1) acquisition cost, (2) exploration cost, and (3) development cost.
89. The acquisition cost of a natural resource is the cost paid to obtain the property rights to search for a natural resource or the property rights to a discovered resource.
90. There are two primary methods of recording the exploration cost of natural resources. With Successful Efforts accounting, only the exploration costs directly associated with successful exploration are recorded as depletable assets. The costs of unsuccessful exploration, such as the cost of a dry hole when drilling for oil, are written off as a period expense. With the alternative method, Full-Cost accounting, exploration costs are capitalized whether or not the exploration was successful.
91. The cost of a natural resource is normally allocated to accounting periods based on the number of units of the natural resource that were consumed each period. The cost of the natural resource is multiplied by the ratio of the units consumed to the total units of natural resource available.
   In the case of timber resources the estimate of the units available may be reasonably objective. In the case of other natural resources, such as petroleum, the estimate may be highly subjective. This method of cost allocation is similar to the units-of-production depreciation method discussed in Paragraph 76.
92. Estimates of available units sometimes change over time; e.g., estimates of proved oil reserves can increase or decrease. Unit-of-production amortization rates should be revised when such estimates change, which, as a general rule, is annually. Such revisions should be accounted for prospectively as changes in accounting estimates.

Fully Depreciated Assets

93. Assets that continue to be used beyond their expected lives will be completely depreciated [except for (a) group or composite depreciation, which are based on average asset lives and consequently result in no fully depreciated assets, and (b) declining-balance depreciation, which always results in

a residual balance]. Although no further depreciation will accrue, these items remain on the organization books, the asset at original cost with an offsetting accumulated depreciation allowance.

Definitions

94. *Cost object*: a function, organizational subdivision, contract or other work unit for which cost data are desired and for which provision is made to accumulate and measure the cost of processes, products, jobs, capitalized projects, and so on.

95. *Base unit*: the least expensive cost object to be capitalized. If a computer system is capitalized as a single asset, then a computer system is a base unit. If the central processor (CPU), the disk drives, and each work station are recorded as separate assets, then a CPU is a base unit as are the disk drives and work stations.

96. *Direct cost*: a cost that can be specifically identified with a cost object in an economically feasible manner.

97. *Depreciation*: the process of allocating the cost of tangible assets to operations over periods benefited (expected life of the asset). This represents the expected gradual exhaustion through periodic charges to operations of the service capacity of fixed assets. It is the consequence of such factors as use, obsolescence, inadequacy, and wear.

98. *Indirect cost*: a cost that cannot be specifically identified with a particular cost object, either because the cost is associated with more than one cost object, or because it is economically infeasible to identify that cost with a particular cost object.

99. *Property, plant, and equipment*: assets that are used in operations, which have an economic life of more than one year, and which have physical substance.

100. *Operating system software*: software supplied with computers (or other equipment) without which the computer will not function. It is generally capitalized as part of computer equipment.

References

FINANCIAL ACCOUNTING STANDARDS BOARD

Financial Accounting Standards Board, *Statement of Financial Accounting Standards No. 13: Accounting for Leases,* as amended and interpreted through May 1980. Norwalk, CT: Financial Accounting Standards Board, 1980.

_____, *Statement of Financial Accounting Standards No. 19: Financial Accounting and Reporting by Oil and Gas Producing Companies.* Norwalk, CT: Financial Accounting Standards Board, 1977.

_____, *Statement of Financial Accounting Standards No. 25: Suspension of Certain Accounting Requirements for Oil and Gas Producing Companies.* Norwalk, CT: Financial Accounting Standards Board, 1979.

_____, *Statement of Financial Accounting Standards No. 34: Capitalization of Interest Cost.* Norwalk, CT: Financial Accounting Standards Board, 1979.

_____, *Statement of Financial Accounting Standards No. 42: Determining Materiality for Capitalization of Interest Cost.* Norwalk, CT: Financial Accounting Standards Board, 1980.

_____, *Statement of Financial Accounting Standards No. 58: Capitalization of Interest Cost in Financial Statements That Include Investments Accounted for by the Equity Method.* Norwalk, CT: Financial Accounting Standards Board, 1982.

_____, *Statement of Financial Accounting Standards No. 61: Accounting for Title Plant.* Norwalk, CT: Financial Accounting Standards Board, 1982.

_____, *Statement of Financial Accounting Standards No. 62: Capitalization of Interest Costs in Situations Involving Certain Tax Exempt Borrowing and Certain Gifts and Grants.* Norwalk, CT: Financial Accounting Standards Board, 1982.

_____, *Statement of Financial Accounting Standards No. 67: Accounting for Costs and Initial Rental Operations of Real Estate Projects.* Norwalk, CT: Financial Accounting Standards Board, 1982.

_____, *Statement of Financial Accounting Standards No. 71: Accounting for the Effects of Certain Types of Regulation.* Norwalk, CT: Financial Accounting Standards Board, 1982.

_____, *Statement of Financial Accounting Standards No. 73: Reporting a Change in Accounting for Railroad Track Structures.* Norwalk, CT: Financial Accounting Standards Board, 1983.

_____, *Statement of Financial Accounting Standards No. 86: Accounting for the Costs of Computer Software to be Sold, Leased, or Otherwise Marketed.* Norwalk, CT: Financial Accounting Standards Board, 1985.

_____, *Statement of Financial Accounting Standards No.90: Regulated Enterprises—Accounting for Abandonments and Disallowances of Plant Cost.* Norwalk, CT: Financial Accounting Standards Board, 1986.

_____, *Statement of Financial Accounting Standards No. 92: Regulated Enterprises—Accounting for Phase-in Plans.* Norwalk, CT: Financial Accounting Standards Board, 1987.

Emerging Issues Task Force Abstract of Issue No. 84-28, *Impairment of Long-Lived Assets.*

Emerging Issues Task Force Abstract of Issue No. 86-29, *Nonmonetary Transactions: Magnitude of Boot and the Exceptions to the Use of Fair Value.*

Emerging Issues Task Force Abstract of Issue No. 87-29, *Exchange of Real Estate Involving Boot.*

Emerging Issues Task Force Abstract of Issue No. 88-10, *Costs Associated with Lease Modification or Termination.*

Cost Accounting Standards Board

Cost Accounting Standards Board, "Part 404, Capitalization of Tangible Assets." Code of Federal Regulations, Chapter III, General Accounting Office (CASB), Washington, DC, July 1, 1973.

_____, "Part 409, Cost Accounting Standard—Depreciation of Tangible Capital Assets." Code of Federal Regulations, Chapter III, General Accounting Office (CASB), Washington, DC, October 1, 1976.

_____, "Part 414, The Cost of Money As an Element of the Cost of Facilities Capital." Code of Federal Regulations, Chapter III, General Accounting Office (CASB), Washington, DC, 1976.

_____, "Part 417, Cost of Money As an Element of the Cost of Capital Assets Under Construction." Code of Federal Regulations, Chapter III, General Accounting Office (CASB), Washington, DC, December 15, 1980.

Other References

Accounting Principles Board Opinion No. 20, *Accounting Changes,* American Institute of Certified Public Accountants, New York, 1971.

Accounting Principles Board Opinion No. 29, *Accounting for Nonmonetary Transactions,* American Institute of Certified Public Accountants, New York, 1973.

Carslaw, Charles and Roger Skillen, "Revaluation of Fixed Assets—an Examination of the Valuation Policies." *The Accountant's Journal* (June 1985), pp. 59-61.

Danos, Paul and Eugene A. Imhoff, Jr., *Intermediate Accounting,* Second Ed., Englewood Cliffs, NJ: Prentice-Hall, 1986.

Defliese, Philip L., Henry R. Jaenicke, Jerry D. Sullivan, and Richard A. Gnospelius, *Montgomery's Auditing,* Tenth Ed., New York: John Wiley & Sons, 1984.

Fremgen, James M. and Shu S. Liao, "The Allocation of Corporate Indirect Costs." New York: National Association of Accountants, 1981.

Haggis, Florence L., "Property, Plant and Equipment." In John C. Burton, Russell E. Palmer, and Robert S. Kay, eds., *Handbook of Accounting,* Boston: Warren, Gorham & Lamont, 1981, pp. 20-1 to 20-32.

Hendricksen, Eldon S., *Accounting Theory,* Homewood, IL: Richard D. Irwin, 1977.

International Accounting Standards Committee, "Accounting for Property, Plant and Equipment. International Accounting Standard 16." *The Accountant's Journal* (2nd Semester 1982): pp. 28-31.

Kay, Robert S. and D. Gerald Searfoss, eds., *Handbook of Accounting and Auditing, Second Ed.* Boston: Warren, Gorham & Lamont, 1989.

Kieso, Donald E. and Jerry J. Weygandt, *Intermediate Accounting, Fifth Ed.* New York: John Wiley & Sons, 1986.

Livingstone, John Leslie, "Buildings and Equipment." In Sidney Davidson and Roman L. Weil, eds., *Handbook of Modern Accounting.* New York: McGraw-Hill, 1983, pp. 19-1 to 19-50.

Mosich, A. N. and E. John Larsen, *Intermediate Accounting.* New York: McGraw-Hill, 1986.

National Association of Accountants, Issues Paper, *Accounting for Software Used Internally.* Montvale, NJ, 1985.

Ordway, Nicholas and Jacqualyn A. Fouse, "New Rules for Allocating the Purchase Price of a Business." *Management Accounting* (May 1988): pp. 50-53.

Railroad Accounting Principles Board, *Railroad Accounting Principles, Final Report, Volume 2—Detailed Report.* September 1, 1987.

Shohet, Jack and Richard Rikert, eds., *Accounting Trends & Techniques.* American Institute of Certified Public Accountants, 1986, pp. 82-96 and 128-133.

Welsch, Glenn A., D. Paul Newman, and Charles T. Zlatkovich, *Intermediate Accounting,* Seventh Ed. Homewood, IL: Richard Irwin,1986.

Williams, Jan R., Keith G. Stanga, and William W. Holder, *Intermediate Accounting: Second Ed.* San Diego: Harcourt Brace Jovanovich, 1987.

NATIONAL ASSOCIATION OF ACCOUNTANTS
MANAGEMENT ACCOUNTING PRACTICES COMMITTEE
SUBCOMMITTEE ON SMA PROMULGATION
1988-89

Robert G. Weiss*, *Chairman*

Dennis C. Daly
Professor
University of Minnesota
Minneapolis, MN

Lee D. Dobbins
Director, Professional
Development Activities
ITT Corp.
New York, NY

James C. Hawley
Group Controller
Pharmaceutical and
Dental Products Group
3M Company
St. Paul, MN

Robert A. Howell*

Tom Huff
Wharton School and
Financial Consultant
New Canaan, CT

Frank C. Minter*

Raymond H. Peterson
Director of Financial
Accounting Methods (Ret.)
Pacific Bell
San Francisco, CA

L. Hal Rogero, Jr.
Vice President, Administration
Publishing Paper Division
Mead Corp.
Escanaba, MI

Donald J. Trawicki
Partner
Touche Ross & Co.
New York, NY

*Also a member of the MAP Committee.

Statements on Management Accounting

Statement Number 4 K
September 7, 1989

PRACTICES AND TECHNIQUES

Cost Management for Warehousing

In accordance with the charge to the Management Accounting Practices (MAP) Committee to issue statements on management accounting principles and practices, Statements on Management Accounting are promulgated to reflect official positions of the National Association of Accountants (NAA). The work of the MAP Committee is based on a framework for management accounting, whose principal categories are:

1. Objectives
2. Terminology
3. Concepts
4. Practices and Techniques
5. Management of Accounting Activities

Statements on Management Accounting

Statement Number 4K
October 1, 1989

Practices and Techniques:
Cost Management for Warehousing

National Association of Accountants, Inc.

Acknowledgments

The National Association of Accountants, Inc. is grateful to all who have contributed toward the publication of Statement 4K, *Cost Management for Warehousing*. Appreciation is extended to members of NAA's Management Accounting Practices Committee and its Subcommittee on SMA Promulgation. The NAA is especially thankful to Gene R. Tyndall, partner in charge of Transportation & Logistics Management Consulting at Ernst & Young, for his research and writing associated with this project.

Statement Outline

Introduction

1. This Statement is intended to provide guidance to management accountants and others in improving the manner in which the costs of warehousing goods and products are identified, measured, and managed. It does so by addressing the needs for warehousing information, identifying the factors that contribute to costs; and suggesting a planning and flexible budgeting method for cost management.

2. The Statement focuses on costs as financial measures of warehousing performance. Nonfinancial performance and productivity measures are treated to the degree that they bear on managing the costs of warehousing rather than on managing only the operations of warehousing.

3. The business and economic climate of recent years, characterized by increasing operations costs, high-interest rates, increasing competitive pressures, international sourcing and product marketing, and increasing customer demands for better service, has forced many companies to reevaluate their logistics and distribution policies. Transportation (addressed in a separate Statement) and warehousing costs are the largest cost components of these policies. Analyses sponsored by the Council of Logistics Management and others suggest that the costs of "storage and warehousing" range from 20 to 30 percent of logistics and distribution costs, or 2 to 10 percent of sales in most companies.

4. Another factor of increasing interest to modern businesses is the need to compress the time required to cycle orders, including production and distribution activities. The just-in-time philosophy applied to logistics, or distribution, involves minimizing the handling, storage, and transportation times for products and/or material. Warehousing activities (and their

associated costs) are fundamental components of order-cycle time reduction. Just-in-time requires smaller, more frequent orders and deliveries so that inventory is there when it is needed.

5. The basic processes of storage and handling of products and/or materials sometimes have been characterized as non-value-adding activities, thus making them cost-adding steps in the product supply chain. Indeed, in many companies this has been the business philosophy. The true value of warehousing, however, lies in having the right product in the right place at the right time. Where the value of warehousing is evaluated continuously, and the locations, types, and levels of inventories are determined scientifically, the costs of product flow (versus storage) can be identified as value added for the business.

6. The identification and management of these costs are fundamental to the effective management of the warehousing function because such costs often are a decisive factor in making logistics and distribution decisions. Moreover, warehousing costs also can have a significant impact on product or segment profitability, product cost, or pricing, and ultimately on corporate profitability.

Statement Scope

7. The Statement addresses the total costs of the warehousing of goods and finished products. It encompasses the costs of company-owned (private) warehousing as well as costs incurred for purchasing outside (public or contract) warehousing services. It does not include the handling costs of raw and/or work-in-process materials that are directly associated with the manufacturing process.

8. Warehousing costs may exist for goods or products at various stages of the company's supply chain including: (a) inbound materials, (b) semifinished products at different stages of assembly, and (c) finished goods to be shipped to customers. In

addition, warehousing support costs, such as those associated with people and information, are included in warehousing cost management.

9. This Statement assumes that a company has determined the justification for the warehousing activities that generate costs. As mentioned in the Introduction, warehousing activities can be value added if they support true business needs.

10. This Statement applies to warehousing costs that are part of the cost of inbound materials, or the cost of goods sold, as well as to warehousing costs incurred directly as warehousing expenses.

11. This Statement addresses the direct assignment and allocation of warehousing costs. Because of the complexities involved, only when the actual warehousing activity-based causes of cost incurrence are understood can costs be directly assigned or allocated properly for effective decisions. Moreover, since warehousing costs often are incurred in meeting more than one cost object (e.g., two or more products), the capability to identify, separate, and allocate common activity costs will vary by cost accounting practice.

12. The Statement applies only to cost issues that are material in amount, that is, to practices that might make a difference in the actions of the person(s) who might use the cost information.

Information for Warehousing Cost Management

13. Information for warehousing cost management may be classified according to two distinct, but related, categories: (a) information on levels of inventories needed and available, and (b) information on warehousing activities. The completeness and accuracy of inventory information can affect the volume of warehousing activities required, e.g., the better the information, the lower the amount of excess storage and handling activities. This principle supports just-in-time programs, for

example, by enabling warehousing managers to know what inventory is on hand, what has been selling, what is needed, and when. Most important, this information can be updated and available for on-line inquiry.

14. Managing and controlling the costs of warehousing is only as effective as the completeness and timeliness of the data and information available about activities. Warehousing operations are necessarily activity-intensive, yet most companies rely on averages and composite data for cost control, which often mask cost behavior patterns and cost variability.

15. Effective warehousing information must be comprehensive enough to include all relevant costs and assets associated with warehousing activities. The information should include all costs of labor, work activities, equipment, inventory carrying, and facilities. Both public and private warehousing activities and costs should be included. Exhibit I provides a summary of the primary warehouse activities for which information is needed.

16. To a large extent, the appropriate volume of warehousing space and services needed depends on the timeliness and accuracy of information. The better the information on demand and activity costs, the fewer storage and handling services are needed—all other factors being equal. Thus, the quality and timeliness of information is invaluable in terms of effective warehousing cost management.

17. Information should be consistent across divisions and subsidiaries to facilitate company-wide decisions. The database should include all capital assets employed (e.g., equipment for put-away, packing, and shipping) and their related costs of depreciation. The database also should incorporate all warehousing-related expenses and asset and support costs related to warehousing management and administration.

18. The cost information should be categorized by warehousing activity in order to identify corrective actions to control warehousing costs. For example, the information should assist in understanding key cost behavior patterns, such as the isolation

Exhibit I

SUMMARY OF WAREHOUSE ACTIVITIES

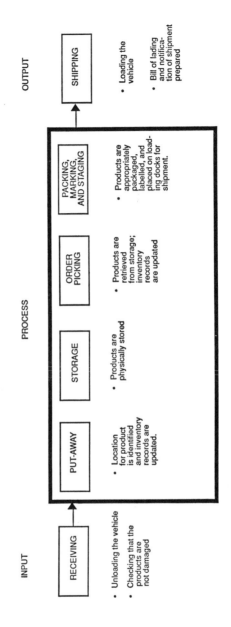

INPUT		**PROCESS**		**OUTPUT**
RECEIVING	PUT-AWAY, STORAGE, ORDER PICKING, PACKING, MARKING, AND STAGING			SHIPPING

INPUT

RECEIVING

- Unloading the vehicle
- Checking that the products are not damaged

PROCESS

PUT-AWAY

- Location for product is identified and inventory records are updated.

STORAGE

- Products are physically stored

ORDER PICKING

- Products are retrieved from storage; inventory records are updated

PACKING, MARKING, AND STAGING

- Products are appropriately packaged, labelled, and placed on loading docks for shipment.

OUTPUT

SHIPPING

- Loading the vehicle
- Bill of lading and notification of shipment prepared

of fixed and variable costs. Traditional expense categories (e.g., labor, equipment, storage, clerical support, etc.) and organizational classifications of cost for responsibility accounting also should be provided.

19. Warehousing information should be readily accessible to all departments involved in decisions about materials sourcing, space utilization, inventory planning and control, customer service, and product distribution. It should be in a form that facilitates analysis and decision support, not just the mere processing and summarization of expenses, such as labor or payroll costs.

20. Warehousing information should provide for measures of performance and its evaluation, and for productivity improvement. It also should support capital planning (building, leasing, or disposing of storage facilities) by providing for warehouse space requirements.

21. With these information requirements in mind, and with today's computer power and software capabilities, more companies are designing and implementing computer-based information systems for warehousing management.

22. Properly designed and applied, such systems will provide for simultaneous capture (single-point data entry) of important operations and financial data. These data include activities associated with receipts, storage, handling, shipping, and labor and equipment utilization.

23. It is necessary, for integration purposes, to design and implement the warehousing information system with interfaces to related logistics activities, e.g., distribution, purchasing, manufacturing, and accounting systems. Exhibit II illustrates certain of these interfaces.

24. There are distinct phases to warehousing-information system development, ranging from personal computer-based data to the fully integrated decision support system, such as that illustrated in Exhibit III. Each company should formulate its own information development strategy for warehousing cost management.

EXHIBIT II

SAMPLE DATA FLOW DIAGRAM: DISTRIBUTION CENTER AND RELATED ACCOUNTING ACTIVITY

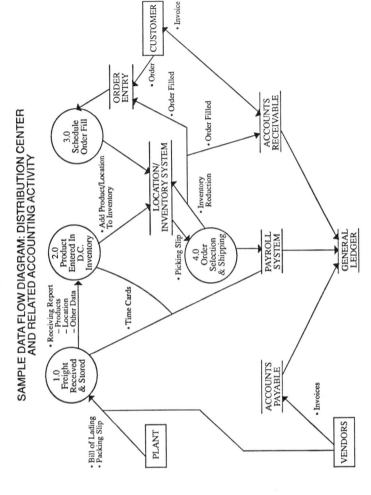

Exhibit III
Conceptual Model of Warehouse
Decision Support System

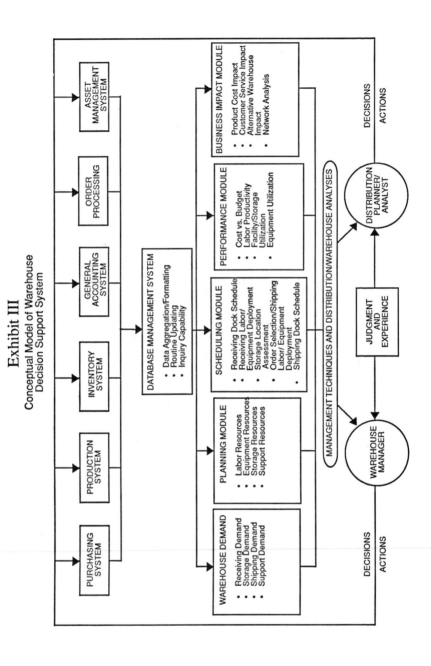

Cost Management for Warehousing

Factors Contributing to Warehousing Costs

25. Warehousing activities and their related costs are driven by the overall logistics strategy and operations of the company. Logistics encompasses all materials flow functions across the company's product supply chain from vendors to customers — transportation, warehousing, customer services, inventory management, procurement, and materials handling. The justification and levels of warehousing costs are determined by the role of the warehousing function in the overall logistics environment. The key drivers of overall logistics costs of a company include:

- Materials Supply Network
- Materials Inventory
- Production Flexibilities
- Finished Goods Distribution Network
- Finished Goods Inventory
- Customer Demand Levels and Patterns
- Customer Services and Service Levels
- Transportation (Inbound/Outbound)
- Warehousing (Storage and Handling)

Exhibit IV illustrates how leading companies manage core logistics processes — both strategically and operationally — from an understanding of overall logistics costs.

26. There are numerous activities and other factors that contribute to the determination of warehousing costs. These include, but are not limited to, the following:

- Receiving characteristics
  - Volumes by product group
  - Transportation mode (truck or rail)
  - Load characteristics
    - Full pallet
    - Partial pallet
    - Floor load

EXHIBIT IV

OVERVIEW OF LOGISTICS COST MANAGEMENT PROCESS

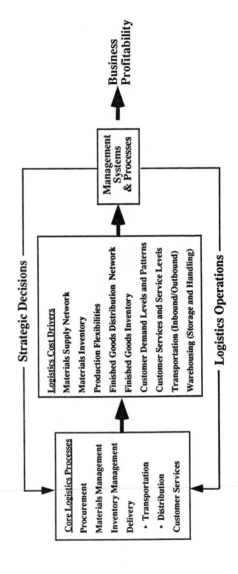

Business Profitability

Management Systems & Processes

Strategic Decisions

Logistics Cost Drivers
Materials Supply Network
Materials Inventory
Production Flexibilities
Finished Goods Distribution Network
Finished Goods Inventory
Customer Demand Levels and Patterns
Customer Services and Service Levels
Transportation (Inbound/Outbound)
Warehousing (Storage and Handling)

Logistics Operations

Core Logistics Processes
Procurement
Materials Management
Inventory Management
Delivery
  • Transportation
  • Distribution
Customer Services

- Storage characteristics
  - Cases per pallet
  - Pallet stacking
  - Temperature required
- Order selection and shipping characteristics
  - Volumes by product groups
  - Order pick quantity
  - Transportation mode
  - Order fill rate
  - Order fill (days or hours)
- Labeling requirements
- Repacking characteristics
  - Damaged goods
  - Repack specials
- Direct labor resource requirements
- Direct equipment resource requirements
- Direct storage resource requirements
- Indirect resource requirements
  - Supervision
  - Clerical support
  - Equipment maintenance
  - Facility maintenance
  - Supplies

27. Warehousing costs are sensitive to the different components that comprise the distribution or product supply chain. For example, the raw materials used in manufacturing products, along with the sources of those materials, help determine the capacity and size requirements of each warehouse. Also, the physical characteristics and seasonality of materials or finished goods can affect the volume and timing of storage requirements.

28. Transportation costs, a major factor in considering warehouse needs and locations, influence and interact closely with warehouse costs, depending on the need for, type, and mode of movements. Primary transportation movements, i.e., shipments from plants to warehouses, increase with additional

warehouses, thus increasing transportation costs. Conversely, additional warehouses usually reduce the cost of transporting products from warehouses to customers. Therefore, the proper balance between overall costs and needs should be determined.

29. The costs of warehousing, however, also increase with the number of warehouses. This includes inventory carrying costs as well as costs for labor, activities, facilities, equipment, order processing, support, and communications.

30. Since the company's policies for customer services are a significant factor in the incurrence of warehousing costs, a key challenge of warehousing cost management is to ensure that warehousing strategies and decisions are consistent with and support.the overall customer service strategy of the company. This includes programs such as Just-In-Time or Quick Response, high order fill rates, and customer pickups.

Planning and Budgeting for Warehousing

31. Logistics planning represents a process through which the company strives for ongoing, continuous improvements in all aspects of logistics operations. Effective logistics plans will reflect and support overall company plans and objectives. The warehousing planning and budgeting process should link the warehousing strategy and operations to the logistics and business strategies of the company. The process should support both short-term needs for operations and long-term objectives for customer service strategies; thus, the process supports inventory location.

32. A warehousing budget should be the primary tool in planning and monitoring the costs of warehousing materials, supplies, and products. Since budgeting integrates the warehousing function into the complete range of corporate or business unit activities through the profit plan, its use by management accountants for monitoring purposes can ensure that warehousing activities and costs remain consistent with the business plan.

33. Exhibit V illustrates an effective budgeting process. It requires warehousing managers to link activities with sales forecasts and production or purchasing forecasts.

34. The key step in budgeting is to estimate expected warehousing costs given the planned level of operations. This requires a detailed specification of the expected demand for warehousing activities, with primary parameters being product flows, volume and mix, and customer service goals.

35. Identifying and costing out planned warehouse activities by product group is the most effective approach to specifying service demand in terms of budgeted sales and production. Exhibits VI-XI illustrate the budgeting process for a typical manufacturer using this approach.

36. The fundamental step in warehouse budgeting involves the grouping of products to be handled and stored. This is because the level of warehousing activities and the resources required to reach that level depend on the characteristics of the products being warehoused. Thus, stockkeeping units (SKUs) should be grouped logically into product groups (PGs) according to organization, product volume and mix, handling requirements and storage, and order selection and shipping. This procedure is illustrated in Exhibit VI for four finished goods product groups.

37. The next key step in the process is to outline the demand for warehouse throughput, by PG and by Distribution Center (DC), for the budget period. This is illustrated in Exhibit VII.

38. An analysis of warehouse activity is necessary to translate the effects of warehouse demand to the amount of physical resources required to service that demand. Examples of the three types of resource requirements—direct labor, direct equipment, and direct storage—are provided in Exhibits VIII, IX and X. Indirect source requirements, such as supervision, equipment maintenance, supplies, etc., may be determined using factors that link direct and indirect relationships. An example Warehouse Resources Summary required for one DC is illustrated in Exhibit XI.

39. The budgeting of warehouse activity is affected directly by the

EXHIBIT V

WAREHOUSING BUDGETING PROCESS

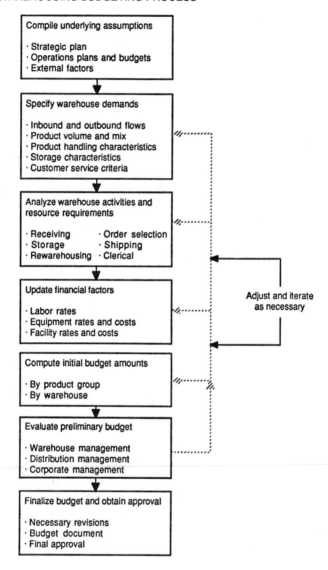

Compile underlying assumptions

· Strategic plan
· Operations plans and budgets
· External factors

Specify warehouse demands

· Inbound and outbound flows
· Product volume and mix
· Product handling characteristics
· Storage characteristics
· Customer service criteria

Analyze warehouse activities and resource requirements

· Receiving   · Order selection
· Storage   · Shipping
· Rewarehousing · Clerical

Update financial factors

· Labor rates
· Equipment rates and costs
· Facility rates and costs

Compute initial budget amounts

· By product group
· By warehouse

Evaluate preliminary budget

· Warehouse management
· Distribution management
· Corporate management

Finalize budget and obtain approval

· Necessary revisions
· Budget document
· Final approval

Adjust and iterate as necessary

EXHIBIT VI
BUDGET DEVELOPMENT EXAMPLE:
WORKSHEET FOR GROUPING PRODUCTS

	FINISHED GOODS PRODUCT GROUPINGS			
RECEIVING CHARACTERISTICS	FG 01	FG 02	FG 03	FG 04
Transportation Mode:				
Truck	50%	100%	100%	100%
Rail	50%	—	—	—
Load Characteristics:				
Full Pallet	100%	50%	90%	90%
Partial Pallet	—	—	10%	10%
Floor Load	—	50%	—	—
STORAGE CHARACTERISTICS				
Cases per Pallet:				
≤20	—	—	10%	—
>20≤50	80%	20%	90%	100%
>50	20%	80%	—	—
Pallet Stacking Height:				
1	—	—	—	—
2	—	70%	100%	—
3	—	30%	—	100%
4	100%	—	—	—
Temperature Required:				
Ambient	100%	100%	—	100%
Frozen	—	—	100%	—
ORDER SELECTION AND SHIPPING CHARACTERISTICS				
Order Pick Quantity:				
Pallet Load	20%	—	—	—
Case Pack	80%	80%	100%	80%
Item Pack	—	20%	—	20%
Transportation Mode:				
Truckload	50%	10%	10%	10%
LTL	50%	90%	90%	90%
Maximum Order Fill Days:				
>3≤8	90%	90%	100%	15%
>8	10%	10%	—	85%
REPACKING CHARACTERISTICS				
Damaged Goods:				
% Requiring	1%	1%	2%	1%
At Warehouse?	No	No	No	Yes
Special Repack:				
% Requiring	—	—	—	100%
At Warehouse?	—	—	—	Yes

EXHIBIT VII

BUDGET DEVELOPMENT EXAMPLE:
DISTRIBUTION CENTER RECEIPTS
DEMAND BY PRODUCT GROUP (IN 000s UNITS)

| PRODUCT GROUP | PLANT | DISTRIBUTION CENTERS | | | | | |
		1	2	(Contract) 3	4	5	TOTAL
FG 01	I	20,000	20,000	20,000	10,000	- 0 -	70,000
	II	- 0 -	- 0 -	- 0 -	10,000	20,000	30,000
FG 02	I	15,000	7,500	7,500	7,500	- 0 -	37,500
	II	- 0 -	- 0 -	- 0 -	7,500	15,000	22,500
FG 03	III	10,000	10,000	10,000	15,000	10,000	55,000
FG 04	I	5,000	5,000	5,000	5,000	- 0 -	20,000
	II	- 0 -	- 0 -	- 0 -	5,000	10,000	15,000
TOTAL		50,000	42,500	42,500	60,000	55,000	250,000

DISTRIBUTION CENTER SHIPMENTS
DEMAND BY PRODUCT GROUP (IN 000s UNITS)

| PRODUCT GROUP | DISTRIBUTION CENTERS | | | | | |
	1	2	3	4	5	TOTAL
FG 01	17,500	20,000	15,000	15,000	20,000	87,500
FG 02	15,000	7,000	7,500	12,500	13,000	55,000
FG 03	8,000	8,000	9,000	14,000	10,000	49,000
FG 04	4,500	5,000	4,000	8,000	9,000	30,500
TOTAL	45,000	40,000	35,500	49,500	52,000	222,000

EXHIBIT VIII

BUDGET DEVELOPMENT EXAMPLE:
DIRECT LABOR RESOURCE REQUIREMENTS

DISTRIBUTION CENTER #1

WAREHOUSE ACTIVITY	PRODUCT GROUP FG 01		
	Volume (000 Units)	Labor Hours Per 1,000 Units	Direct Labor Hours
RECEIVING SUBTOTAL	20,000	1.5	30,000
ORDER SELECTION/SHIPPING			
Order Picking	17,500	2.5	43,750
Packaging	17,500	.3	5,250
Staging	17,500	.1	1,750
Loading	17,500	.6	10,500
OS&S SUBTOTAL	17,500	3.5	61,250
OTHER DIRECT ACTIVITIES			
Rewarehousing	10,000	.5	5,000
Recase/Repack	—	—	—
Damage Repack	—	—	—
Labelling	—	—	—
OTHER DIRECT LABOR SUBTOTAL	10,000	.5	5,000
TOTAL DIRECT LABOR HOURS			96,250
+ Available Hours/Employee			1,900
EMPLOYEES REQUIRED	—	—	50.6

EXHIBIT IX

BUDGET DEVELOPMENT EXAMPLE:
DIRECT EQUIPMENT RESOURCE REQUIREMENTS

DISTRIBUTION CENTER #1

WAREHOUSE ACTIVITY	PRODUCT GROUP FG 01		
	Volume (000 Units)	Equipment Hours Per 1,000 Units	Direct Equipment Hours
RECEIVING SUBTOTAL	20,000	1.5	30,000
ORDER SELECTION/SHIPPING			
Order Picking	17,500	2.0	35,000
Packaging	—	—	—
Staging	17,500	.1	1,750
Loading	17,500	.6	10,500
OS&S SUBTOTAL	17,500	2.7	47,250
OTHER DIRECT ACTIVITIES			
Rewarehousing	10,000	.4	4,000
Recase/Repack	—	—	—
Damage Repack	—	—	—
Labelling	—	—	—
OTHER DIRECT EQUIPMENT SUBTOTAL	10,000	.4	4,000
TOTAL DIRECT EQUIPMENT HOURS			81,250
+ Available Hours/Equipment			4,000
EQUIPMENT UNITS REQUIRED	—	—	20.3

EXHIBIT X

BUDGET DEVELOPMENT EXAMPLE:
DIRECT STORAGE RESOURCES REQUIREMENTS

Distribution Center #1

WAREHOUSE ACTIVITY	PRODUCT GROUP FG 01	PRODUCT GROUP #	TOTAL
STORAGE Estimated Total Volume	18,750,000		
+ Annual Turnover Rate	18		
Average Inventory Level in Units	1,041,667		
+ Units Per Pallet	40 1/		
Average Inventory Level in Pallets	26,042		
+ Stacking Height	4		
Estimated Number of Pallet Positions	6,510		
x Square Feet Per Pallet Position	15		
x Honeycombing Factor	1.15		
Total Direct Storage Space Required	112.305		500,000
Indirect Storage (e.g., staging and receiving areas and office space) Factor: 20%			100,000
Total Storage Space Required			600,000

NOTES:

1/Exhibit VI-3 shows cases per pallet:
    80% — 20 to 50 cases
    20% — more than 50 cases

.80 x 35 cases avg. per pallet =   28 cases

.20 x 60 cases avg. per pallet =
case quantity for over 50-case range =   12 cases

TOTAL   40 cases per pallet

EXHIBIT XI
BUDGET DEVELOPMENT EXAMPLE:
WAREHOUSE RESOURCES SUMMARY
Distribution Center #1

RESOURCE CATEGORY	FG 01		TOTAL DIRECT	INDIRECT	TOTAL	CURRENT AVAILABLE
DIRECT LABOR						
Receiving Labor	15.8		46.7		46.7	48
Order Selection/Shipping Labor	32.2		74.3		74.3	70
Other Direct Labor	2.6		10.5		10.5	7
Total Direct Labor	50.6		131.5		131.5	125
INDIRECT LABOR						
Supervision				1.0	1.0	1
Clerical				4.0	4.0	4
Foreman				10.0	10.0	9
Equipment Maint.				4.0	4.0	4
Facility Maint.				3.0	3.0	2
Janitorial				5.0	5.0	4
Total Indirect Labor				27.0	27.0	24
DIRECT/INDIRECT EQUIPMENT						
Forklifts	20.3		45.0	—	45.0	40.0
Other Equipment	—		—	—	—	—
DIRECT/INDIRECT STORAGE	112,305		500,000	100,000	600,000	575,000

PROPOSED ACTIONS AND COMMENTS

Direct Labor _____
_____
_____
_____

Indirect Labor _____
_____
_____
_____
_____

Equipment (Direct _____
& Indirect) _____
_____
_____
_____

Storage _____
_____
_____

activities of other company functions, especially production and sales, which change during the budget period. Thus, it is useful to develop by division or product group a preliminary budget based on general profit plan guidelines, and a revised budget reflecting sales and production throughput targets.

40. Profitability analysis, or service costing, requires that detailed warehousing activity costs be identified in order to analyze profits by shipment, product, channel, or customer. Analysis may also be appropriate to determine what warehouse volume is required to cover fixed costs and to reach the break-even point (e.g., cases per period per warehouse).

41. Standard costs should be established for many warehousing activities by identifying the elements, or inputs, of the activity along with the standard unit cost for each input. Once standard costs are developed for the key activities, flexible budgeting methods can be used to control and plan warehousing costs (see Exhibit XII).

42. Warehousing costs can be measured and controlled effectively by benchmarking actual costs against budget standards. Variance analysis based on flexible warehousing budgets (flexed for volume levels or product groups) can point to the key factors affecting warehousing costs. Exhibit XIII illustrates the variance analysis computation for the warehouse receiving cost for a product group.

Direct Assignments and Allocations

43. A key objective of management cost accounting for any function is the direct assignment and allocation of costs to the business elements that consume the resources incurring the cost (the "cost objects," such as products or product groups). The direct assignment and allocation of warehousing costs should be based on activities performed and business functions served in order to determine the amounts of cost and the reasons such costs were incurred. As many costs as possible should be assigned to specific product or groups.

EXHIBIT XII

SAMPLE BUDGET REPORT FOR
PRODUCT GROUP FG 01 BUDGET VS. ACTUAL

Distribution Center #1

COST TYPE	COST CATEGORY	ACTUAL NO. OF UNITS (000s)	STANDARD COSTS/1000 UNITS	FLEXIBLE BUDGET	ACTUAL COSTS	VARIANCE FAV. (UNFAV.)
DIRECT	Labor					
	Receiving	17,000	$19.38	$329,460	$400,000	$(70,540)[3]
	Order Selection & Shipping	17,500	$45.22	$791,350	$750,000	$41,350
	Other Direct	10,000	$6.46	$64,600	$60,000	$4,600
	Equipment	17,250[1]	$17.62	$303,945	$320,000[2]	$(16,055)
	Storage	17,250[1]	$19.44	$335,340	$300,000[2]	$35,340
VARIABLE	Total Variable					
INDIRECT	Indirect	17,250[1]	$4.64	$80,040	$80,000[2]	$40
TOTAL				$1,904,735	$1,910,000	$(5,265)

Notes:
[1] Average throughput derived by actual (inbound + outbound)/2 for product group FG 01.
[2] Allocated by accounting department based on established percentage for budget period.
[3] See Exhibit XIII for variance analysis computation.

Exhibit XIII

VARIANCE ANALYSIS COMPUTATION
WAREHOUSE RECEIVING COST
FOR PRODUCT GROUP FG 01

DISTRIBUTION CENTER #1

	VARIANCE FACTOR				Variance
	Volume (in 000s)	Labor Hours	Labor Rate	Budget Total	Fav.(Unfav.)
Planned Units at Standard	20,000	1.5	$12.92	$387,600	
Actual Volume at Standard	17,000	1.5	$12.92	$329,460	
• Actual Labor Hours Labor Efficiency Variance	17,000	1.8	$12.92	$395,352	(65,892)
• Actual Labor Rate Labor Rate Variance	17,000	1.8	$13.072	$400,000	(4,648)
Flexible Budget Variance					$(70,540)[1]

Note:

[1] See receiving variance in Exhibit XII.

Direct assignment and allocation of costs should occur at the lowest level of detail, i.e., the warehousing activity. For example, warehousing costs for activities associated with individual products, or product groups, should be assigned to the products and/or product groups. Sound business judgment must be exercised regarding which costs should be specifically assigned and which should be allocated as miscellaneous, or "overhead," costs based on their relative amounts and analytical value for purposes of management decision making (materiality). In all cases, the allocations of costs (versus direct costing) should be minimized.

44. To the extent that it is practical and costs are material, activity-based cost information should be identified and measured and assigned to the products and/or groups. Products incur overhead costs by requiring resource-consuming activities, including warehousing. The costs of products, then, differ according to their different actual requirements for support activities, such as warehousing, as opposed to volume-based allocations.

45. To reflect the true cost difference in handling various types of inbound and outbound shipments (and thus products or groups), separate allocation bases are selected for the components of each activity, reflecting different cost relationships. For example:

Warehousing Activity	Common Allocation Bases
• Receiving and checking	• Shipments, orders, pallets, cases, units, weight
• Put-away	• Pallets, cases, units
• Replenishment	• Pallets, cases, units
• Order selection	• Orders, lines, pallets, cases, units
• Packing	• Pallets, cases, units
• Staging	• Orders, pallets, cases, units
• Loading and shipping	• Orders, pallets, cases, units

- Bulk storage
- Order pick storage

- Square feet, pallet positions, rack positions
- Square feet, pallet positions, rack positions

Categorizing costs by specific activities is essential in determining the cost of certain warehouse practices such as crossdock shipments, in which shipments are received and reshipped without being put in storage. It also permits the application of control methods, i.e., the managing of warehousing activities.

46. When there is more than one cost object involved, e.g., the cost of activities to receive or ship two different products, the allocation base normally applied is weight or volume, although number of loads or number of shipments may be used. The choice of an allocation basis should reflect, to the degree practical, the resources actually consumed by the activities to which costs are being charged.

47. Activity costs may be directly assigned to cost behavior classification, e.g., short-run variable, long-run variable, and fixed costs. This method permits effective marginal cost pricing, cost-volume-profit analysis, flexible budgeting, and variance analysis.

48. These activity costs may be aggregated into the three major categories or warehousing services, i.e., handling, storage, and administration, and then allocated to products or groups. As mentioned in Paragraph 36 and Exhibit VI, the categorization of products into a group, where necessary, is based on a detailed warehouse profile that defines each group. The specific factors often include the following:

- Mode of shipment
- Loading method, e.g., palletized, slip-sheeted, floor-loaded
- Order size
- Line items per order
- Allowable stacking height
- Temperature or odor control required
- Weight and dimensions per case or unit

- Cases per pallet
- Pallet size

Product grouping enables management accountants and warehouse managers to identify by product the "cost drivers" that are contributing to non-value-adding activities (waste).

49. The warehousing function varies substantially among companies in its organization, objectives, and cost structure; thus, different activity-based costing methodologies may be applied. An effective costing system uses detailed cost information as well as numerous operational statistics regarding warehouse activities. The system is then able to trace direct product costs by activities and to help identify delay, excess, and unevenness in the product supply chain.

50. Activity-based warehousing cost information also contributes to management decision making about product mix, product profitability, and customer profitability. The costs of warehousing activities — whether deemed value added or not — represent resources that can make the difference in the competitiveness of the business with respect to its products and margins.

Definitions

51. Total Warehousing Costs — Those warehouse expenses, either for company private, public, or contract warehousing services, that are associated with the storage and handling of materials or products within the warehouse facility.

52. Warehouse Activity — Refers to a specific function in the warehouse, e.g., receiving, put-away, storage, shipping, etc.

53. Private Warehouse — A facility owned and operated by a company for the purpose of storing its own goods.

54. Public Warehouse — Operated by a warehouser contracting with the public for the storage of goods. There are several types of public warehouses including commodity, bulk, household goods, field, refrigerated, and merchandise.

55. Contract Warehouse—A form of warehousing, combining elements of private and public warehousing, in which an outside party performs specific warehouse operations under a formal agreement using facilities which may be owned or leased by either party. Contract provisions often stipulate a longer-term commitment than does conventional public warehousing in exchange for more favorable rates.

56. Distribution Center—A facility that receives products and/or materials, stores them, and then distributes to customers, often in product mixes based on customer orders. The emphasis is on product flow as opposed to storage. Warehousing and distribution center often are used interchangeably, but there are technical differences in functions.

57. Customer Service—A general term used to describe several measures of the quality of client interaction, such as order lead time, consistency in filling orders, reliable delivery time, number of stockouts, and special provisions.

58. Logistics or Distribution—The planning, implementing, and controlling of all inbound, in-process, and outbound goods and inventory from the point of origin to the point of consumption. It consists of the integration of purchasing, transportation, and warehousing functions to provide the most efficient flow of materials and products in the most cost-effective manner to meet customer needs.

59. Plant Warehouse—A warehouse area located either in the same facility as a production plant or nearby.

60. Field Warehouse—A warehouse not located close to a plant, but instead placed in the "field" near customer locations. Also called "distribution centers" or "forward warehouses."

61. Inventory Carrying Costs—The imputed costs associated with holding inventory in storage, including capital costs, storage and handling costs, and product spoilage and obsolescence.

62. Order Cycle—The time spent and the processes performed from the time an order is made to the actual delivery of the order to a distribution center or customer. The handling and shipping activities in the warehouse are an integral part of this process.

63. Order Fill Rate—A measure of the number of orders processed without stockouts, or the need to back order, expressed as a percentage of all orders processed in the warehouse.
64. Warehouse-Related Taxes—Taxes, whether federal, state, or local, that are related to the warehousing function. These include taxes on inventory, real estate, and special taxes. Taxes are important economic factors in warehouse location, investment, and use.

References

A. Ernst & Whinney. *Warehouse Accounting and Control: Guidelines for Distribution and Financial Management.* Oak Brook, IL: National Association of Accountants and National Council of Physical Distribution Management, 1985.

B. Tompkins, James A. and Jerry D. Smith, editors in chief. *The Warehouse Management Handbook.* McGraw-Hill, 1988.

C. LaLonde, Bernard J., Cooper, Martha C. and Thomas G. Noordewier, The Ohio State University. *Customer Service: A Management Perspective.* The Council of Logistics Management, Oak Brook, IL, 1988.

D. Lambert, Douglas M. and James R. Stock. *Strategic Physical Distribution Management.* Homewood, IL: Richard D. Irwin, 1982.

E. Robeson, James F. and Robert G. House, eds. *The Distribution Handbook.* New York: Free Press, 1985.

F. Ernst & Whinney. *Corporate Profitability & Logistics: Innovative Guidelines for Executives.* National Association of Accountants, Montvale, NJ, and Council of Logistics Management, 1987.

L. Hal Rogero, Jr.
V.P., Administration
Publishing Paper Division
Mead Corporation
Escanaba, Michigan

John E. Stewart
Partner
Arthur Andersen & Co.
Chicago, Illinois

Norman N. Strauss
Partner
Ernst & Young
New York, New York

Edward W. Trott
Partner
Peat Marwick Main & Co.
New York, New York

NAA STAFF
Louis Bisgay, *Director,* Management Accounting Practices
Wagdy Abdallah, *Manager,* Management Accounting Practices

NATIONAL ASSOCIATION OF ACCOUNTANTS, INC.
MANAGEMENT ACCOUNTING PRACTICES COMMITTEE
SUBCOMMITTEE ON SMA PROMULGATION
1989-1990

Frank C. Minter,* *Chairman*

Robert W. Backes
*Manager of Accounting
  Implementation and Control*
Schering-Plough Corporation
Madison, New Jersey

Dennis C. Daly
Professor
University of Minnesota
Minneapolis, MN

Lee D. Dobbins
  irec' Professional Development

ιΓT Corp
New Yoιₙ, NY

James C. Hawlₑ ɟ
*Group Control er Pharmaceutical and
  Dental Products Group*
3M Company
St. Paul, MN

Neil E. Holmes*
Vice President
The Marley Company
Mission Woods, Kansas

Tom Huff
*Wharton School and Financial
  Consultant*
New Canaan, CT

Raymond H. Peterson
*Director of Financial Accounting
  Methods (Retired)*
Pacific Bell
San Francisco, CA

L. Hal Rogero, Jr.*
Vice President, Administration
Publishing Paper Division
Mead Corp.
Escanaba, MI

Donald J. Trawicki
Partner
Deloitte & Touche
Short Hills, NJ

Barrington C. Turner
Policy Liaison Division
Defense Contract Audit Agency
Alexandria, Virginia

Robert F. Wurzelbacher
Director, Product Supply — Finance
The Procter & Gamble Company
Cincinnati, Ohio

*Also a member of the MAP Committee.